SPIRAL to the STARS

MEANING IN HERE EVERYDAY
Metaphysics in the

Critical Issues in Indigenous Studies
Jeffrey P. Shepherd and Myla Vicenti Carpio
SERIES EDITORS

ADVISORY BOARD
Hōkūlani Aikau
Jennifer Nez Denetdale
Eva Marie Garroutte
John Maynard
Alejandra Navarro-Smith
Gladys Tzul Tzul
Keith Camacho
Margaret Elizabeth Kovach
Vicente Diaz

SPIRAL to the STARS

MVSKOKE TOOLS OF FUTURITY

LAURA HARJO

THE UNIVERSITY OF
ARIZONA PRESS

TUCSON

The University of Arizona Press
www.uapress.arizona.edu

ISBN-13: 978-0-8165-3801-0 (cloth)
ISBN-13: 978-0-8165-4110-2 (paper)

Cover design by Nicole Hayward
Cover art: *Chain of Being* by Daniel McCoy Jr.

Publication of this book is made possible in part by the proceeds of a permanent endowment created with the assistance of a Challenge Grant from the National Endowment for the Humanities, a federal agency.

Library of Congress Cataloging-in-Publication Data
Names: Harjo, Laura, author.
Title: Spiral to the stars : Mvskoke tools of futurity / Laura Harjo.
Other titles: Critical issues in indigenous studies.
Description: Tucson : The University of Arizona Press, 2019. | Series: Critical issues in indigenous studies
Identifiers: LCCN 2018043116 | ISBN 9780816538010 (cloth : alk. paper)
Subjects: LCSH: Creek Indians—Ethnic identity. | Creek Indians—Cultural assimilation. | Decolonization.
Classification: LCC E99.C9 H276 2019 | DDC 975.004/97385—dc23 LC record available at https://lccn.loc.gov/2018043116

Printed in the United States of America
♾ This paper meets the requirements of ANSI/NISO Z39.48-1992 (Permanence of Paper).

In loving memory of my father, Duke Monroe Harjo, my source of power, who loved Mvskokvlke and modeled an example of all the themes of this book: the sustaining power of self, kinship, community, and community knowledge.

Duke M. Harjo outside of Pawnee, Oklahoma. Photograph by Hotvlkuce Harjo.

CONTENTS

ILLUSTRATIONS

Figures

Maps

Table

ACKNOWLEDGMENTS

As I sorted through what futurity means for my community, I had support from individuals whom I wish to acknowledge, because without their energy and kinship this project would not have happened.

I would like to acknowledge the University of Arizona Press for championing my project. I appreciate Myla Carpio, the Critical Issues in Indigenous Studies series co-editor, for her willingness to work through readings and feedback, and for always welcoming me back like kin when I disappeared. I appreciate Jeffrey Shepherd, Critical Issues in Indigenous Studies co-editor, for his efforts and support. I would like to thank Kristen Buckles, University of Arizona Press editor, for believing in and championing this project, and for her enthusiastic support. Thank you to Amanda Krause, Stacey Wujcik, Leigh McDonald, Abby Mogollon, and Matthew Gleeson, who have helped in aptly pulling this book together. I appreciate Mvskoke poet Joy Harjo; her work has invigorated, consoled, guided, and encouraged me. Mvto to Mvskoke / Citizen Potawatomi artist Daniel McCoy for graciously sharing his vivid and elucidative artwork for the book cover. I would like to thank my academic mom, Ruthie Wilson Gilmore, for her warmth, love, and support, and for herding me when I was wandering around like a rez dog. She mentored me, provided financial support from her research funds to assist in my research, and let me bounce my ideas off her. Just as her mentor Neil Smith prodded her to think systematically about society and space, she also pushed me in the same ways. I am eternally grateful to Ruthie, and to other geographers and scholars whose training and work keep me imagining—Laura Pulido, Carolyn Cartier, Andrew Curtis, Francille Rusan Wilson, Macarena Gomez-Barris, John Carlos Rowe, Janelle Wong, and the late Clyde Woods. I appreciate the kinship I have had with the American Studies graduate students and faculty at the University of Southern California. The mentorship of Fred Moten has been important in shaping some of the key questions I think about as well: how to find emancipation in the everyday and interstices.

I would like to thank Muscogee (Creek) Nation for the graduate fellowship that I relied upon while in graduate school pursuing this research. I would like to thank Muscogee (Creek) Nation elected officials and staff for allowing me to embark on this research and providing me with insights, perspectives, and support. These folks include Claude Sumner and his staff, A. D. Ellis, Judge Patrick Moore, Mike Flud, Julie Moss, Thomas Yahola, Kristie Sewall, Alicia Stroble, Lizanne Holata, April Lindsey, Rita Williams, Joyce Bear, Mona "KoKo" Lowe, Bill Fife, Rhonda Beaver, all the staff of MCN Health Administration, Robert Bible, and the staff of the Muscogee (Creek) Nation National Council. Thank you to the tribal members I interviewed. I thank all of the Mvskoke people who participated in my community survey; without their input, a large chunk of this project would not have been possible. Thank you for sharing your hopes, wishes, and disappointments, and for giving suggestions on how we as Mvskoke people can do better. I would like to thank Andrea Smith for reading my draft and providing feedback, and for her mentorship through the years. Thank you to my reviewers for your insight, and for helping to make this book stronger. The Green Corn Collective has been a source of happiness, power, and intellectual dialogue; thank you to my sisters Kimberly Robertson and Jenell Navarro, who are members of the collective, for providing support and feedback. The faculty of Community and Regional Planning at the University of New Mexico (UNM) have been supportive and patient as I have marched through this colossal writing endeavor. Sincere appreciation to my faculty chair, Renia Ehrenfeucht, for reading many of my drafts—even the ones that were not ready for prime time, or even for a back-page ad! She is a fantastic mentor, and I surely couldn't have completed the last few laps of this project without her mentorship and support. When I think about my ancestors sending someone to look after me, I think of UNM's dean of the School of Architecture and Planning (SAP), Geraldine Forbes, for her help, levity, and ear to vent to, and for making me feel like I am at home by always asking me, "When are you going to be finished with your book?"

I am grateful for the funding support and resources I received from SAP that directly supported the writing of this book. Thanks to Virginia Sharff for helping me bounce titles around and nail one down, and to my UNM American Studies colleagues Jennifer Denetdale, Alyosha Goldstein, and Irene Vasquez for their support. The fellows at the School of Advanced Research provided support for my writing project, including Maylei Blackwell, Susan McKinnon, and Karen Hebert; our writing group had weekly meetings in Santa Fe where we shared food, laughter, and a compassionate scholarly community. Thanks to Sarah Ohmer for being my writing partner, accountability buddy, and kindred spirit; we texted and phoned each other to make sure we were writing and had a sounding board. Thanks to the Indigenous feminist planning group and allies who kept me up and standing, including Amanda Montoya, Michaela Shirley, Marissa Joe, Angelina Grey, Allison Johnson, Shynoke Ortiz, Thelma Antonio, Diana Chávez, and Saray Argumedo. My planning practices have been edified by the Indigenous peoples, and I am also grateful to the Indigenous Design and Planning Institute, Tribal Planners Roundtable for their meetings, and to the Indigenous communities in New Mexico, Minnesota, California, and Arizona who have graciously welcomed me into their territory, in particular Tohatchi Navajo Chapter, Taos Pueblo, Zuni Pueblo, Ysleta Del Sur Pueblo, Nageezi Navajo Chapter, Nambe Pueblo, Crownpoint Navajo Chapter, Santa Ana Pueblo, Cochiti Pueblo, and Red Lake Navajo Chapter.

I have deep appreciation for my research assistant, Pablo Lituma, who helped immensely with the graphics and the citations. He has worked intermittently over the course of a few years on my project with me. He is a talented designer who helped me bring my envisioned graphics to fruition. Thanks to Diana Chávez for assisting toward the end of this project with tracking down bibliographic sources.

I want to thank my research team, my cousins Connie and Terrence Harjo, who both helped me carry out my survey at Mvskoke Festival. I'd like to thank the Mvskoke Festival staff for providing me with a venue to administer my survey. I'd like to thank all of the participants who responded to the survey, whether in person, online, or in mail-outs. I am eternally grateful for the feedback. Thank you to my aunt and uncle, Nettie and "Lil" (Jim B. Jr.) Harjo, for keeping and taking care of my daughter, who fell ill while I was administering my survey at Mvskoke Festival. Thank you to my cousin C. J., who has never failed to keep me laughing and was one of the first to take my survey. And I'd like to thank

Freda Fields and all the community folks who let me run my survey questions by them in order to understand what would work and what wouldn't.

Thank you to my family and friends whose radars I disappeared from as I worked on this project. Thank you for all your support and understanding, and for receiving me back into the fold of the family. I also want to thank my other two uncles: John, who provided me a place to live at one time, and my uncle Chubbs (Frank). All of my father's brothers have supported and teased me like I was their own daughter. Thank you to my parents, Duke and Ellen Harjo, for lifelong support, encouragement, and unconditional love, and for providing an exemplar of love for the community. My dad was my de facto co-principal investigator on this project, always willing to listen to me sort through my project, offer suggestions, and translate Mvskoke words for me—he was the first person to raise my consciousness. My mother was my constant cheerleader and provider of sage insight. Thank you to Daniel, my partner in life: I appreciate your love and support. Our shared cultural knowledge and language, coupled with your willingness to listen to my ideas as I sorted through them, has been immensely grounding.

I want to acknowledge the life, love, kindness, and energy that Jeannie Coffey shared with the children and youth of Sapulpa. I have the deepest gratitude to my cousin, Robert Coffey, for sharing his beautiful mother.

Finally, I want to thank my daughter Hotvlkuce for her support and remarkable patience as I have wrestled with and written my ideas and somehow still kept us alive! Thank you for being willing to venture out and capture pictures for this project. She has taken care of me as much as I have taken care of her during the writing of this book. She is a bottomless well of joy in my life. This work would not have been possible without a network of kinship relations and their hard work to beat down paths for younger Mvskokvlke to journey even further with their dreams and wishes than ever imagined. I give all the credit back to my kinship network, and any errors and oversights all belong to me.

Mvto.

SPIRAL to the **STARS**

Introduction

Renegotiating Mvskoke Knowledge

We watched television every day at my grandfather's house, before cable, when there were only four channels: ABC, CBS, NBC, and PBS. We watched *The Price is Right* and *Wheel of Fortune*. Hosts Bob Barker and Pat Sajak crooned at us while we sat in Grandpa's HUD home, situated in a Creek housing subdivision, with a gravel-dirt road leading in and out.[1] Their voices droned from his console TV, which looked like a piece of wooden furniture; I only knew a handful of people who had a "fancy" TV like that. With game shows humming in the background and the smell of sliced USDA luncheon meat, *commodity Spam*, frying in the skillet in the kitchen, Grandpa would tell me medicine stories. Some seemed unfathomable—but I believed them and believe them still. He would start by telling me I needed to be able to take care of myself, before going on to teach me medicine songs and instructing me on contemporary uses of Mvskoke medicine. As times change, our needs change, and I learned from my grandfather that the songs and medicine shift to meet our current needs. One song he taught me was meant to be sung in a pawn shop when you want the proprietor to negotiate in your favor! The song's purpose wasn't to unfairly sway interactions but rather to make you heard and understood. Thus Creek values and ways morph into new manifestations and applications. Our ways are not bound to "traditional" use, and I think our relatives would think it was ridiculous if we refused to benefit from our knowledge and lifeways in the current day. The purpose of this story about my grandpa is to demonstrate a renegotiation of knowledge and its use as a tool. Our medicine does not stand still either, and its use is not frozen in time.[2] In this book, I share other Mvskoke stories with a commitment to prioritizing the theories that come from the lived and felt experiences of Mvskoke communities, and practices born out of necessity and love.

The primary argument of this book is that Mvskoke communities have what they need at their disposal; everyday community practices are deep, rich, and meaningful, and have sustained Mvskoke people through many moments and in many places. Community practices are articulated through Mvskoke relationships, knowledge, power, and spatialities. Despite the eliminatory work of the settler state, these Mvskoke practices, like those of other Indigenous and marginalized groups who are targeted by settler colonialism, have managed to fly under the radar undetected. Mvskoke communities have sustained the spaces to dream, imagine, speculate, and activate the wishes of our ancestors, contemporary kin, and future relatives—all in a present temporality, which is Indigenous futurity. Mvskoke futurity carries out a form of Indigenous futurity while honoring the lived experiences and knowledge of the Mvskoke community. Mvskoke experiences, practices, and theories generate four concepts fundamental to Mvskoke futurity: *este-cate* sovereignty (Indigenous kinship sovereignty); community (and body) knowledge; collective power; and the imagining, constructing, and accessing of Mvskoke spatialities.[3]

Examining Mvskoke community through the lens of futurity enables us to step out of clashes over grievance claims for a moment and speculate about the future that our ancestors desired and that we desire, and about how to create something that our future relatives will want and need. The notion of futurity challenges a conventional reckoning of time and the future, and pushes us to create right now—in the present moment—that which our ancestors, we, and future relatives desire. As community builders, we often ask tactical sets of questions to develop a concrete plan, and then tell people that they are going to have to sit and wait, knowing that conditions will not improve in their time: their dreams will be for someone else. In other words, we tell them "not yet." We cannot say "not yet."[4] I am not eschewing a long view of community; I am merely saying that futurity does not have to be limited to a future temporality, in which we have to wait to create and get to the place where we want to be. Indeed, there are a range of ways in which we are already enacting Mvskoke futurity to shift community conditions.

Shifting conditions and community contexts require us to renegotiate Mvskoke lifeways and practices. Sharing the story of my grandpa's pawn shop song illustrates the ease with which renegotiation of Mvskoke knowledge and practices can occur. *Spiral to the Stars* recognizes Mvskoke ways of knowing as a legitimate source of power and recognizes that Mvskoke people embody, enact, and share power and knowledge in multiple spatialities. My operating definition of *futurity* is the enactment of theories and practices that activate our ancestors' unrealized possibilities, the act of living out the futures we wish for in a contemporary moment, and the creation of the conditions for these futures. This is futurity: it operates in service to our ancestors, contemporary relatives, and future relatives. I employ futurity as an analytical tool throughout the book.

Mvskoke poet, musician, and playwright Joy Harjo's poem "A Map to the Next World" urges us to think about Mvskoke futurities—the other possible worlds to live in that refuse elimination at the hands of settler colonialism.[5] In her poem, Harjo takes the reader through the prevailing world conditions and wonders about a map to the next world, offering suggestions of looking inward—the map is written into us. As a Mvskoke person, I consider Harjo's poem a call to action, a call to conceive of a map to the next world. This is a significant endeavor that requires renegotiating Mvskoke knowledge—something we have always done. This book is just one idea for constructing a map, using futurity as an analytical tool. As an Indigenous mapper and cartographer, I develop way-finding tools that I will unpack in each chapter. I put into action my community knowledge and academic training to imagine tools that communities can use to operationalize their knowledge without requiring so-called experts to identify their areas of genius. However, before delving further into Mvskoke futurity, it is necessary to provide some background on Mvskoke people, and then trace a quick timeline of how they have organized themselves.

Mvskoke People

Pre-removal

Mvskoke people previously lived in a complex of tribal towns primarily in present-day Georgia and Alabama along major rivers. They are descendants of Mississippian people, who existed across the eastern half of the United States.[6] Other tribes from the southeastern United States, notably the Cherokee, Chickasaw, Choctaw, and Seminole tribes, "view themselves as lineal descendants of ancient Mississippian culture who practiced Southeastern ceremonialism."[7] The

Mississippian people are said to have ascended to prominence approximately between AD 800 and 1500, and were primarily agriculturalists residing and farming on fertile river soil near the Mississippi River and its tributaries; their ceremonial life was evident in the construction of great flat-topped temple mounds.[8]

LeAnne Howe and Jim Wilson argue for the sophistication of Mississippian people, citing Claudine Payne, who states, "Mississippian people farmed maize extensively; lived in societies known as chiefdoms led by hereditary rulers; conducted long-distance trade in copper, marine shell, and other valuables; resided in towns, villages, and farmsteads; built monumental architecture in the form of earthen, flat topped mounds; conducted warfare, often fortifying their towns with stockades; and shared religious and iconographic traditions. When the first Europeans (the Hernando de Soto expedition) arrived in Arkansas in 1541, the people they encountered were Mississippians."[9]

Mvskoke is a language and a nation of tribal towns. *Muscogee* is often used to reference the language, but more recently the tribe has publicly begun to refer to it as the *Mvskoke* language. *Muskogean* refers to a family of languages in the linguistics field. Thus, Mvskoke people derive from a group of closely related, homogeneous tribal towns that were mostly of Muskogean linguistic stock.[10] Today, Muskogean languages are spoken by Mvskoke people in Oklahoma. In the southeastern homelands of Alabama and Georgia, Muscogee is intentionally spoken by the federally recognized tribe—Poarch Band of Creek Indians—and passively spoken by the general public by way of the legacy of Muscogee place names. Mvskoke people's cultural and governance practices closely resemble those of other Indigenous nations within the Southeastern Ceremonial Complex such as the Choctaw, Chickasaw, Cherokee, and Seminole, all of whom practice stompdance, the Green Corn Ceremony, and stickball. In pre-removal times, Mvskoke people consisted of fifty or more autonomous tribal towns. However, they moved into larger collective formations as needed for negotiation, trade, warfare, and the maintenance of the balance of power: "The confederacy's towns were divided into red/war and white/peace groups."[11] The collective of towns expanded and contracted and consisted of a mixture of people of varying linguistic stocks and dialects, with ceremony and culture operating as a common denominator: "With the assistance of advisors, a *mekko* governed each town. Creek clans and towns met once every year. During the early eighteenth century the Creek population of more than twenty thousand occupied at least fifty towns."[12]

The *etvlwa* (tribal town, plural *etvlwvlke* or *etvlwas*) became recognized by the U.S. government and other governments as a regional political unit. This led to internal strife within the etvlwvlke. Alexander McGillivray, whose father was a Scottish trader married to a Creek woman, and who was educated in a Western system, organized the Upper Creeks as a regional political unit.[13] These subunits of the etvlwvlke became known as the official Creek Nation. This angered other towns—the Lower Creeks in particular, who were often left out of negotiations, and who pushed back.[14] These regions were areal units that operated as political economies, maneuvered by the Upper and Lower factions as a form of community development, to negotiate the movement of trade and goods through their regions, but also to raise capital to settle debt. In some cases, factions would negotiate without the knowledge of the other faction, which caused strife when one group learned that some of their territory had been negotiated in exchange for trade movement that would not benefit them.[15]

The signing of the 1790 Treaty of New York was led by McGillivray. There were no Lower Creeks involved in the signing. Vast land tracts were ceded, and there were stipulations in the treaty that Creeks were to learn farming, etc. Just years after the signing of the Treaty of New York, McGillivray died, and Benjamin Hawkins, an Indian agent in Creek Territory, worked to assimilate Mvskokvlke to Eurocentric values and practices. He was adamant about having Creek people visit him at his office because he had created what he viewed as a "model town of the plan for civilization": a town morphology that had a main street, in contrast to the town square morphology to which Creeks were accustomed.[16] Hawkins promoted Christianity and other assimilative practices aimed at eliminating ceremonial practices. The federal government viewed and treated Mvskokvlke not as multiple etvlwvlke—that is, not as different important town sites each with their own leaders—but as one nation with a principal leader or leaders.

Post-removal

After the Andrew Jackson–era federal government dispossessed Mvskoke people of all their aboriginal lands, they were removed to Indian Territory, an area set aside by the federal government to contain tribes they were displacing and house tribes already residing in the region. There the Mvskoke people reorganized a government, proclaiming a council hill under an oak tree. The tree that witnessed this sacred event still stands in what is now the Creek

Nation Council Oak Park, and it marked the impetus of present-day Tulsa, Oklahoma. The Civil War unraveled the Mvskoke people's work of rebuilding, however, and they entered into their final treaty with the federal government in 1866. By this time the etvlwvlke's political power had devolved and been taken up by the formal central Creek government, which functioned to represent the etvlwvlke.[17] The following year they established a government modeled after the federal government's bicameral system, with two houses: the House of Kings and the House of Warriors. During this second formation of the tribal government, the Mvskoke people selected Okmulgee as their capital—it remains the capital of the Muscogee (Creek) Nation (MCN) today, and the Mvskoke council house still stands today in the main square of downtown Okmulgee. While the Mvskoke people were undergoing a political transformation into an institutionalized government, the social organization of etvl-wvlke shifted toward more dispersed agrarian communities, with ceremonial grounds and churches. This was a turn away from the precisely planned town morphology of the Southeastern etvlwa, which had, for example, a central area for activities surrounded by dwelling structures. As Isham and Clark explain the shift from etvlwvlke to Christian agricultural communities, "Through the late nineteenth and early twentieth centuries mainstream pressures gradually transformed many of the forty-seven tribal towns from ceremonial grounds into rural agricultural communities. Each of these centered on the Baptist Indian church, among Upper Creeks, or the Methodist Indian church, among descendants of Lower Creeks."[18] A palpable tension still exists today at times between Church and stompdance factions. However, despite what appears to be a shift in how the etvlwa is spatially and socially organized, the tribal town values and knowledge are still practiced in a plurality of spatialities—at the stompgrounds, in church, and at sports tournaments, to name a few. Federal government policies have continually battered Mvskoke ways of knowing kinship, community, and land.

Allotment

The Dawes Severalty Act of 1887 was an assimilation policy aimed at shifting the Mvskoke epistemology of land from a collective to an individual venture. The policy divided the entire Mvskoke land base into parcels and allotted some of the parcels to Mvskoke families to develop homesteads and assimilate into property-owning agricultural life, like their white settler counterparts. The

Curtis Act of 1898 dismantled the authority of tribal courts and tribal governments, another blow to tribal sovereignty.[19] Although MCN did not formally disband, there was heavy governmental oversight in the installation of its chiefs.[20] However, a strident opposition formed to these injurious policies meted out by the settler government. Chitto Harjo (Crazy Snake) led a movement to refuse the individualistic land practices imposed on Mvskoke people by the federal government and to honor old Mvskoke law. This movement, known as the Crazy Snake Rebellion, also called for a re-centering of traditional or ceremonial ground leadership and government, situated at Hickory Ground. The "Snakes" held council at Hickory Ground and sought to restore old Mvskoke law; they reinstated the Lighthorse force to patrol and maintain order.[21] Chitto Harjo's ongoing movement incited fear among the local whites, who sought mob justice. In 1909, local authorities barged into Hickory Ground in search of a thief who had stolen meat from a nearby smokehouse, leading to a violent gun battle, which dampened the Crazy Snake Rebellion and its wishes for Mvskoke people to "defend by force their rights to self-government and equality" against white settlers.[22] While white settler policing suppressed the Snakes' movement for territorial and political sovereignty, a fuller version of Mvskoke sovereignty would reemerge later in the 1970s with the court case *Harjo v. Kleppe*.

During this same era of allotment and assimilation, between 1889 and 1906, settlers were flooding into Indian Territory; the apparatus for their entry was the Oklahoma land rush.[23] Settler laws dismantled collective Indigenous lands and futures and at the same time built settler dreams. In 1907, Oklahoma gained statehood. Since that time, Oklahoma tribes have persisted through many devastating eras of settler colonial policies—boarding schools, the federal relocation program, federally appointed leadership of the tribe, desecration of grave sites, and the ongoing failure of the federal trust relationship that governs Indian lands, to name a few.

The Oklahoma Indian Welfare Act of 1936 enabled tribes to reorganize as constitutional governments. In the 1930s and 1940s, three tribal towns that were part of the Mvskoke confederacy—Alabama-Quassarte, Kialegee, and Thlopthlocco—organized as separate entities, obtaining charters and becoming federally recognized tribes.[24] During most of the 1900s, MCN was subjected to excessive governmental oversight in both appointing and approving its chiefs. MCN was federally recognized in 1970, and in 1976, in the landmark case *Harjo v. Kleppe*, the United States District Court ruled that the Curtis Act had only dismantled MCN's territorial sovereignty, not its political sovereignty—this meant that Creek National Council had never been stripped of its powers, and it remained the official government body.[25] Today the current geopolitical grouping of the Mvskoke confederacy that was removed to Oklahoma is as follows: there are four federally recognized Mvskoke peoples in Oklahoma— Alabama-Quassarte Tribal Town, Thlopthlocco Tribal Town, Kialegee Tribal Town, and Muscogee (Creek) Nation.

Community Futurity

My primary focus in this book is the many iterations of community among Mvskoke people, such as ceremonial grounds, Mvskoke churches, organically formed Mvskoke communities, and the Mvskoke chartered community, which is an official designation in Muscogee (Creek) Nation. The chartered community enjoys advantages such as brick-and-mortar community centers and funding from the tribe in the form of a block development grant. Mvskoke community centers also host Elderly Nutrition Programs that feed their senior citizens or elders, and others have gaming operations and other businesses to provide a revenue stream to their community. These sites also provide the space for communities to convene, visit, and build networks of relationality.

Many of the shifts in Mvskoke communities, and their reemergence in different iterations, are responses to settler colonialism. Settler colonialism is not a temporality that has passed; it is a far-reaching structure that persists. The logic of settler colonialism shapes how both nation-state and tribal governance function; it changes how we imagine the ways in which our families and romantic relationships operate and should be structured. Settler colonialism shapes our ways of knowing, managing, and exchanging land. Settler colonial structuring of land and laws renders Indigenous girls and women subhuman and rapeable with impunity, as exemplified by the ongoing issue of missing and murdered Indigenous women and jurisdictional land issues related to prosecuting perpetrators.[26] Its institutions, laws, and practices work to slowly and insidiously eliminate Indigenous people and other groups that are not white and heteronormative. Settler colonialism has a far-reaching impact, and it operates as expansive dispossession.[27] Further, it works to dispossess Indigenous communities of their futures—futures imagined on their terms within their ways of knowing.

Throughout this work, I spatialize futurity, which involves recognizing the spatial forms, or spatialities, that futurity creates and/or operates within, and the ways in which these futurity spatialities operate in relationship to one another.

Spatializing futurity helps us to see that Mvskoke community is shaped by many spatial and temporal realms and manifests in material form with great complexity. Spatializing futurity is grounded in Indigenous methodologies that resist settler colonialism. The focus on futurity in this work holds promise for recuperating the unactivated possibilities of our ancestors whose lives and imagined worlds have been cut short by the accumulation of violences, large, small, and micro-, produced by the ongoing structures of settler colonialism.[28] Futurity is the invocation of many temporalities and spatialities to form an imaginary that is constructed from energy, kinship, community knowledge, collective power, and geographies produced by many iterations of Mvskoke emergence.

Questions about the future pertain to Mvskoke elements of life that include but are not limited to the medicine ways that protect our health and spirit, corn to make sofke, hickory to make stickball sticks, stompgrounds to dance at, and Mvskoke language to speak with Hesaketvmese (Maker of Breath) and with relatives. Community futurity work is about understanding prevailing approaches of how we comprehend and put into action that which our communities care about and desire. As I grapple with how this happens, my work teaching Indigenous geographies and community action at the University of New Mexico has provided an excellent place to think and practice community futurity alongside our Indigenous students who share similar community concerns and aspirations to honor the teachings and knowledge of their kin, both human and nonhuman. As well, the students often leave the places where their families are concentrated and move to a city for work and school. Collective action and thinking related to Indigenous communities can transpire in many locations, and the Indigenous community is not spatially limited to the reservation or government-assigned lands.

Before there were formal rules, regulations, or structures that articulated how chartered communities recognized by the Muscogee (Creek) Nation (MCN) would operate, sites of community in Sapulpa, Oklahoma, occurred in less formal settings: houses, churches, stompgrounds, and even Walmart! In its early days, the Sapulpa Indian community did not have a place to meet, so community members gathered at the local laundromat to talk about what they envisioned for their community.[29] The general attitude of the community was, "Let's imagine what we want and get it done." In these informal meetings, laughter and goodwill were always present. Kids, myself included, dashed all over the place, chasing each other on the lawn of the Sapulpa Indian Clinic, while the savory aroma of grilled hamburgers and hot dogs wafted through the air and a crowd of Mvskoke and Euchee adults visited, laughed, and hashed out their dreams. They ate grilled food, chips, potato salad, and watermelon, with a local Mvskoke elder at the helm of the grill, preparing thick and juicy hamburgers for the crowd. These informal gatherings were how the community came together. Everyone brought something, including cakes and pies, his or her appetites, and humorous stories to share. Sharing community planning conversations over coffee is, in essence, a means of having control over one's life and community. In a way, it is the way in which the community sees itself traveling to and arriving at both a current and future destination.

Today, the Sapulpa Creek Indian Community is a chartered community, complete with a brick-and-mortar community building that houses an MCN-operated Elderly Nutrition Program and an executive board that governs and oversees community activities. Community meetings are held at a dedicated time and place, carried out according to tribal rules and regulations outlined in title 11 of MCN's legal code ("Communities Emetvlhvmkvke"), and guided by *Robert's Rules of Order*.[30] Typically, the executive board and a handful of community members show up for the meetings. I am even a bit intimidated to enter such a formalized version of a community gathering. However, as of December 2017, the community turnout is growing, and currently upward of twenty to twenty-five people attend.

Mvskoke people have always exercised forethought and intention with regard to their communities. However, prevailing governance structures, as well as the resources that a community may assume are necessary to build communities intentionally, can become entrenched with formality. Formality can become so burdensome that it forecloses the possibility of communities imagining and enacting their wishes and discourages community work. Further, formality can reproduce normative settler colonial governance structures that shift power from the collective of everyday folks to the elites, putting decision-making in the hands of a few. Nevertheless, Mvskoke people maintain their communities in other ways, through celebrations, storytelling, social relations, and myriad other practices. These practices maintain a future, past, and present for the informal community—that is, futurity. Collective practices such as celebrations and more casual community gatherings are ways in which to come to know and build a network of relationality. For example, stompdance is a practice through which the community ensures the future of the tribe by setting aside time for young people to learn the dance, the songs, and how to become community leaders.[31] This routine of providing a learning and practice space creates an undisrupted line of future singers and dancers. We practice, perform, and realize a future that includes stompdance.

However, this is nothing new: Mvskoke people have practiced forms of futurity that have maintained and reproduced their communities and settlements for thousands of years. Mvskokvlke have maintained and reproduced aspects of their communities and settlements ranging from food and shelter to social interaction and spiritual, cultural, and political practices. One illustration of Mvskoke futurity can be seen when we look at the element of fire and its connection to forethought and planning. Blazing stars millions of light-years away flicker back signals in the form of constellations that dance and shift into different choreographies as the Earth makes its yearlong journey around the sun. Tilting toward and away from the sun, Earth never halts its annual trip, nor does it stop its daily rotation on its axis, making day and night and serving as a guide for Mvskoke practices. During daylight, for instance, the people plan for their future needs and gather firewood to use for food preparation and the stompdance fire. We also use fire to plan future agricultural seasons, employing prescribed burns to restore fertility to the soil.

Mvskoke practices of futurity directly connect to the persistence of the etvl-wvlke, or tribal towns, which are the primary political, spiritual, and cultural milieux in which Mvskoke activities have been carried out. The tribal towns forged by fire have continually maintained themselves in fluctuating form. The etvlwa has been iteratively shaped in response to a continual stream of political economies over time and space; in its present form, chartered MCN communities, stompgrounds, and Indian churches function as the de facto etvlwa. Additionally, the Alabama-Quassarte, Thlopthlocco, and Kialegee Tribal Towns represent three federally recognized etvlwas that have persisted despite Indian removal. These tribal towns share a jurisdictional area with the MCN in Oklahoma. Today's community-building efforts devote intentional forethought to building on and sustaining that which enables a community to propagate, which is the intention of Mvskoke tools of futurity. Our community practices maintain Mvskoke community in continual movement: throughout this book the reader will see a people that is perpetually moving in order to be part of the contemporary moment.

Early on I discovered and appreciated social engagement, and this sustained me in a school system where I did not feel valued or understood. I watched my parents and extended family involve themselves in community work—in mainstream discourse it would be characterized as community organizing, but that is not what we call it. I did not hear the language of activists or activism: we speak of fighting for your people. The Mvskoke community does not engage much with oppositional politics and tactics, such as protests that target Mvskoke decision-makers within the community, in part because one of the decision-makers might be your relative, or quite possibly the relative of your best friend.

The central intention of this book is not to practice oppositional politics or advance grievance claims; instead, this book considers how Mvskoke people create places and communities that we care about by recognizing our stories, kinship moments, and ways of convening collectively. Also, it considers how we think about our short-term needs and the long-term goals of sustaining our communities.[32] This book's intentions involve (re-)centering our attention and efforts on our worldviews, livelihoods, and lifeways, despite the politics of subjugation and the practices of institutions informed by settler colonialism.

As part of recognizing Mvskoke knowledge, I share Mvskoke narratives to help understand and unpack the meaning of various theories within the context of my community. In the pages that follow, I step through a series of stories in which I am continually understanding, practicing, and renovating ideas of futurity. Spiraling through space and time, Mvskoke spaces—such as sporting events or impromptu conversations in Walmart—and places—such as a community building or stompgrounds—are in a dialectic conversation. Intersections of space and place generate impactful ways of understanding, both new and old, and ultimately generate a way to be in the world now and in the future. These iterative spirals of praxis are also a practice of futurity.

Methodological Trajectory

I will now trace a series of personal narratives that led to the turn to futurity in this project. Each of these narratives relates to the building of a repertoire of tools I used in community work: actions, approaches, and methods that have evolved over time. These experiences begin with taking part in informal community gatherings as a child. These meetings were the impetus from which Sapulpa Creek Indian Community emerged as one of the first chartered communities. The community did not have a designated community building but met in various places over the years. In these meetings the community collectively conceived a future, brainstorming and carrying out small fundraising activities to get there, such as selling food and soda. This happened at a very local scale. Many of my friends' parents participated in the leadership activities of Sapulpa Creek Indian Community, making it a win-win situation: when our parents gathered in the community, we had to go, but we were not required to sit through the meetings, and this provided us opportunities to gather and play.

While the Creek communities functioned informally, MCN was on the rise as well. Traveling with my parents while they took part in meetings in the early years of MCN's contemporary (re)formation of the 1970s, in which Mvskokvlke elected their leadership and ratified a new constitution after decades of federal government control, I attended alongside them, sitting and soaking in the political activities, but when possible I bolted outside to play. During smoke breaks I stood near the adults, pretending not to listen. During this time, more federal resources were made available to the tribe for development, and more resources seemed to mean more meetings and more formality. Oakridge School, south of Okmulgee, was the site of the meetings before today's fully developed tribal complex (campus) existed. The tribe used various office spaces and still does—for example, the MCN Health Administration's offices are located in Lackey Hall at Oklahoma State University's Okmulgee campus, while MCN's Behavioral Health and Contract Health offices are located downtown. Thus, I had access to both informal and formal types of community-building as I was growing up; although at the time I was only passively involved, I am still able to reflect on this embodied knowledge and gain instruction from it. These foundational experiences provided examples of loving and serving one's community. Because of these early phases of community observation and learning, my role in community-building developed into active involvement as I moved into young adulthood. The impetus for this new period was a set of community grievances surrounding a series of deaths and development projects proposed on valued Indigenous lands.

The first set of tools in my repertoire focused on student and community protest and providing support to grieving families. When I was attending Haskell Indian Junior College (HIJC)—which is now known as Haskell Indian Nations University—in Lawrence, Kansas, four young Indigenous men lost their lives in four separate events. Cecil Dawes, twenty-one years old (Cheyenne-Arapaho/Mvskoke/Seminole), and John Sandoval, nineteen years old (Navajo), were found dead in the river in two separate incidents.[33] Christopher Bread, nineteen years old (Kiowa/Cherokee), was found dead in the ditch of a country road. Gregg Sevier, twenty-two years old (Mvskoke), was distraught and suicidal in his room; after his parents placed a concerned call to the police, they lost Gregg

to two police bullets through his heart within one minute and thirty-six seconds
of the Lawrence police officers' arrival. The first three deaths occurred in the
span of a year from 1988 to 1989, and Gregg's death was in April 1991.[34] The
weight of four deaths was too much to bear in the relatively small and close-knit
Indigenous community in Lawrence. The young men's deaths are a deep wound,
even decades later. All these young men are zero to two degrees of separation
from other Indigenous families and communities—in the expansive kinship
network that is Indian country, everyone is connected and kin. Christopher
Bread's mother, Marilyn Bread, later shared haunting words with a group of
young Indigenous women that intimated the impact of losing her son: "You
never forget how your children were as babies, you always remember them as
they were when they were little, that is how I think of him."[35] I thought I understood what she meant, but only when I was a mother did I finally comprehend
an inkling of her grief. For students on campus, these were frightening times.
We were scared for our friends' welfare and our own, and publicly we wondered
if a serial killer was targeting young Indigenous men. The local fraternal order
of the police replied in their newsletter that the "serial" in the cases was "cereal
malt beverage," a reply that ratcheted up tensions in the community.[36] There
was an inquest of the officers who shot Gregg Sevier, and the local Indigenous
community and students attended it. We organized, made signs saying, "Cecil,
John, Christopher, Gregg, who is next? Me?" and marched from Haskell to
the Douglas County courthouse—we needed answers. We deployed collective oppositional power; it was a small bit for the moment, though it was not
enough, for further incidents of white male violence against Haskell students
continued.

Protesting was a means to express our frustration, and it gained the city's
attention during this tense time; however, as I began to acquire academic training in geography and planning, my ways of understanding community and
place were reshaped based on the conceptual frameworks of these fields. The
next community methodological tools I learned were technical analysis and
cultural geography approaches. New ways of understanding provided me multiple perspectives on Indigenous and community issues, and I employed them
in comprehending the impact of a proposed transportation development project
adjacent to HIJC.

Haskell Wetlands, located south of the main campus of Haskell Indian
Nations University (HINU), was threatened by the planned building of a major
thoroughfare through it, which was approved for development by the Army

Corps of Engineers. Using new ways of examining a site, I understood that the construction of the thoroughfare would have environmental and cultural implications. Environmentally, the air, water, and sound quality would be affected, which would have an impact on the living beings in the ecosystem. In terms of cultural geography, Haskell Wetlands serves as an important site where knowledge is experienced in a range of ways. The wetlands' connection to emotive knowledge can be traced back to the school's inception. The wetlands were and still are a place where Indigenous students go to pray, or to weep in abject loneliness.[37] Haskell has a long and storied history of students leaving their communities of origin to attend school there; the school started in 1884 as an off-reservation Indian boarding school, and it had an outing program whereby students learned trades and were "assimilated into white society, but only as wage laborers."[38] The wetlands are where those with broken hearts, from being separated from family or other causes, sought comfort. In the early years of Haskell, some even fled, dying of exposure near the Wakarusa River.[39]

Further, the wetlands are a contemporary sacred site used by multiple tribes in several ways. In 1994, a multi-tipi Native American Church (NAC) meeting convened at the entry to the wetlands to celebrate an amendment to the Freedom of Religion Act that protected medicine used in NAC meetings. Students and local Indigenous communities conduct sweats there, and after the wetlands became a target for transportation development, Stan Herd, a local landscape artist, marked the site with sacred symbols, mowing designs into the grass: a medicine wheel, a water bird, and a bear paw print (figure 1).[40] Each of the cardinal directions is marked with a column of stone that bears witness to prayers, tobacco ties, and other prayer offerings left behind.

This site represents the production of culture and felt knowledge across many generations, by many Indigenous nations from throughout the United States. Faced with the threat of development of a traffic corridor, I drew planning analysis from my community work repertoire and worked to raise awareness. At the time I was unaware that I was tackling community organizing and grievance claim work. Although the issue of transportation development in Haskell Wetlands picked up momentum as the years passed, the road was ultimately constructed, opening in the fall of 2016, over twenty years later.[41]

The next set of tools for carrying out community work that I encountered was Geographic Information Systems (GIS) mapping. While attending the University of Kansas, I applied for and earned funding through the Bureau of Indian Affairs' (BIA) national tribal GIS center at the time, the Geographic

FIGURE 1   Haskell Wetlands Medicine Wheel, Stan Herd. Photograph © Jon Blumb.

Data Service Center (GDSC), as a cooperative education student in the field of GIS. The GDSC paid my tuition and books, and I worked for wages at their service center in Lakewood, Colorado, every summer until I graduated. One aspect of this experience that I appreciated was the kinship bond I deepened with my father's oldest brother—my uncle John, who worked for United Airlines after having left his home in Oklahoma through the federal relocation program. He moved through United Airlines' hub cities, taking opportunities in Chicago, Cleveland, and Denver. During my summers I lived with him and my aunt Lynn, and I heard family stories from which our collective memories are built. Some of the stories were coarse, but they were still humorous, and they focused on his life with his brothers in Okemah, Oklahoma, as children before their mother and infant sister passed. I received two streams of education that summer—family and place narratives about rural Okemah, and tribal GIS mapping.

   During the 1990s, the GDSC served Environmental Systems Research Institute (ESRI) mapping software and GIS training to Indian country. It operated as the central site where tribes could access GIS; it housed a supercomputer that tribes dialed into, as well as a remote sensing unit that provided satellite imagery to them. The operation was primarily staffed with contract workers, with only a handful of full-time government employees. This, apparently, was one of the reasons the BIA was investing in teaching more Indigenous students: to pipeline us back to Indian country. During my summers as an undergraduate I trained in these offices, learning GIS firsthand, working on digital soil maps for the Blackfeet reservation, attending national trainings and workshops in our facilities, mapping an MCN housing subdivision, and meeting Indigenous professionals working in GIS. I invested many years learning GIS and applying spatial analysis in caring for land. My GDSC experience coincided with the threat to the Haskell Wetlands, along with a threat to another sacred place targeted for transportation development in Macon, Georgia: the Ocmulgee mounds, an important site for Mvskoke people (figure 2). Reports filtered back to MCN of a proposed road through a site where artifacts existed—our artifacts—and I heard a radio interview with one of our elected officials who was considering a cash settlement to permit its construction. This moment was the impetus for me to think about our physical, spiritual, and emotional ties to

FIGURE 2 Great Temple Mound, Ocmulgee National Monument. Photograph by Laura Harjo.

land. It required me to make space to think about this urgent issue, and I have never stopped. How could we sell off permission to desecrate our patrimony? I could not fathom this, and existing theories were not helping me think it through. While I continued using Western mapping tools for delineating and understanding place, there was another aspect I was missing, yet I didn't know enough to know just what was missing. There was knowledge operating that I didn't have the language for.

In their respective work, Tanana Athabascan scholar Dian Million and Michi Saagiig Nishnaabeg scholar Leanne Betasamosake Simpson both argue for a felt knowledge and pedagogy of the land, which I conceive of as the spiritual and emotional connections to ancestral lands that I share with my relatives—past, present, and future.[42] Land reveals to us how we are to carry ourselves as Mvskokvlke (people from a marshy area) and how we are to relate to one another—with *vnokeckv*, which means love that cares for and tends to the needs of the people, something more than hetero-romantic love, a compassionate love.[43] Thus, it is of paramount importance to turn to our stories about place, land, and practices—all stories, even contemporary ones, and even those geographies no longer in ancestral or rural lands—and take note of how these elements of relationality and vnokeckv are in communication with us. While Joy Harjo's poem "Map to the Next World" points to the land and kinship to instruct us, Leanne Betasamosake Simpson's work deepens the instruction that the land provides, and also offers a loving example of engaging with one another.[44] Simpson's story about Kwezens, a young Anishinaabe girl who is guided by a squirrel to maple syrup, illustrates both the teachings of the land and the ways in which the extended family offers Kwezens nurturing and support. Kwezens experiences a form of whole-body learning that is acquired through a process of being with the land—a story of coming into knowing that Simpson calls knowledge "given lovingly by the spirits."[45] The interaction with human and nonhuman kin in this Anishinaabe story resembles Mvskoke ideas about energy exchanges. Using a Mvskoke framework that understands all interactions between entities as energy transfers, we can understand what kind of energy is produced in our relations with the land, spirits, and family—giving, nurturing, and supporting.[46] Simpson suspends her lovely narrative for a moment, asking the reader to consider what would have happened if Kwezens's knowledge gift of maple syrup, offered by the land and spirits, had been received in a context ruptured by settler colonialism.[47] What if her mother had been subjected to violence that rendered her unable to provide loving encouragement or place a supportive touch on Kwezens's back? What if her extended family were unable to believe or support her, having their spirits quelled by the settler violence of boarding school, or the trauma of a murdered uncle or a missing aunt, or a grandmother mired in deep grief?[48] If we read this narrative through the Mvskoke lens of energy transfers, we can see that the traumatic impact of settler colonial violence would diminish the quality of the energy transfers in her family and render them unable to share, exchange, or produce the energy that makes Kwezens well, happy, and understood.

Thus, another tool in community work is an understanding of our relationality to one another and to the spaces and places we inhabit—as well as the legacies of settler impact upon these relationships.[49] Land teaches us and brings us together; combined with spatiality, this provides a multilayered methodology that opens a wider range of possibilities, especially in relation to the often-contested lands that Mvskoke people have connections and claims to.

My final story in this series of brief narratives of community-building and action has to do with the way I have renegotiated my thinking and practice of mapping, which for over a decade was situated within GIS and the practice of reducing complex phenomena to points, lines, and areas for spatial analyses and grievance claims. The way that I was trained in mapping never quite fully aligned with the Indigenous community context or its cultural geography. I saw Western approaches of cartographic representation and Indigenous spatialities as separate because I understood the ethical implications that mapping Indigenous spatialities posed—especially cultural and embodied knowledges. Thus I was wary of integrating the two. In some ways I likened my GIS work to playing a video game—it was fun to me, but it was separate from the more important community knowledge that I was pondering. I was living the cultural geography aspect of my work, but I did not have the conceptual tools of Indigenous methodologies to integrate into the work.

I spent six years at Cherokee Nation, leading a department that provided spatial research and analysis to the tribe. I found the work meaningful because of its aspect of relationality, and I often relayed to staff that we must get things right because someone's grandma, aunt, or uncle was counting on us. In my role as the tribe's GIS administrator, I oversaw the development of data, maps, and spatial analyses used in legal claims and for tribal and community development and health. Often the development aspect involved determining where to distribute limited resources so that they would have the most impact and serve the largest proportion of the community. Selecting development sites entailed analyzing the catchment areas of clinics, casinos, tag offices, etc. to understand where to leverage the most resources. This work kept us busy. However, a major pivot point in my work came when I spoke at and participated in the International Forum on Indigenous Mapping: Mapping for Indigenous Advocacy and Empowerment, organized by the Indigenous Communities Mapping Initiative in Vancouver, British Columbia, in 2004. The conference had two major tracks: (1) mapping for advocacy, which involved Indigenous groups providing maps as evidence supporting appeals and grievances that target the state apparatus, an approach that primarily uses a Cartesian coordinate system, a system of spatial ordering that renders Indigenous spaces and place legible to the state; and (2) mapping for empowerment, which encompassed mapping traditional knowledge and places for the intergenerational transfer of knowledge or for internal management of cultural resources.[50] In the first case, advocacy was to an outside entity, arguing a credible and meritorious claim, while in the second case, empowerment seemed to function internally and community knowledge already carried credibility and merit. For example, the Seri of Mexico showcased a map made from a quilt that denoted important places and sacred animals.[51] Being exposed to Indigenous mapping methodologies was a pivot point for me because I realized that the large bank of GIS knowledge that I had invested my time in (I have even dreamt about cultural GIS databases) was technical and rational—and not superior. I was a technocrat, using so-called expert-driven methods and approaches to tribal and community work.[52]

In contrast to technocratic approaches, the International Forum on Indigenous Mapping was in some ways illustrative of the bridging of the divide I perceived in my work between mapping and Indigenous knowledges. Over time, my community mapping work has become less about the technology of mapping and more about the ways in which the practices of community mapping and participatory mapping build relationality in a community. This turn to participatory mapping has resulted in a pivot away from being a GIS techie to being a participatory methods facilitator, relaying approaches that accomplish two goals: making mapping more accessible to a greater number of Indigenous people, and centering the members of the community as the experts on their own community, space, and place. I have found that Indigenous participatory mapping is powerful and creates wide bridges between community values, worldview, and knowledge. Seeking a path toward fighting for the legitimacy of knowledge of community members has emerged as my preferred mode of inquiry and practice. My mode of inquiry continues to evolve, because I find it unconscionable for academia not to accommodate or understand the value of my grandfather's pawn shop medicine song. If I am not here to honor and create the conditions for beautiful moments—everyday Mvskoke interactions—then in my eyes the worth and value of Mvskoke community work is lost.

Furthermore, the technocratic approaches that I worked within focused on appealing to the nation-state and incrementally building communities based on permissions, clearances, and actions on the part of the nation-state. This type of appeal to the politics of recognition can often shape community action efforts: to illustrate, I will connect my community-building narratives to the politics of recognition and discuss how my previous community action work is situated. The methodologies used in the types of community action endeavors I have chronicled are focused on subnational geopolitical entities—as was the case with appealing to Douglas County with regard to the deaths of the four young Indigenous men, and to the county or to tribal council members with regard to sacred sites in Lawrence, Kansas, and Macon, Georgia. Indigenous communities advocated their formal and informal claims before decision-makers. Such claims are bound up with making a community's oppression legible to an entity or individual that holds power to act upon the claim. Appealing claims to a state agency, such as the Army Corps of Engineers or the public school system, often places the final decision-making power about rectifying an injury in the hands of the very entity that did the injuring and creates a dynamic that grants this entity an authoritative position. From this authoritative position, they have the power to choose whether or not they wish to recognize the claims of an Indigenous nation, which can be especially problematic if the Indigenous community or nation has not organized their arguments and the elements of their community in ways that the state can read and recognize.

Notwithstanding this situation, Indigenous nations have found success using technocratic methods within the politics of recognition to secure dimensions of their community from erasure, and have found such methods useful in mapping claims—for example, the Cherokee/Choctaw/Chickasaw $40 million riverbed settlement. In 1970, the Supreme Court established the three tribes' ownership of the Arkansas riverbed.[53] The tribes negotiated the settlement, however—the Cherokee, Choctaw, and Chickasaw Nations Claims Settlement Act of 2002—to fully address the resources at stake: land, gravel, oil, and gas that had been taken and used without benefit to the proper owners, the three tribes.[54]

Under my direction, our GIS department mapped the lands.[55] Producing evidentiary maps for the tribes' legal counsel required staff, as well as mapping software, and involved dealing with a complex land nomenclature—for example, the historical riverbed high-water line and the current high-water line—to depict how the river meandered over time; lands that lie above the waterline are considered made land.[56] It was on this land that the squatters used the three tribal nations' resources. Such claims require considerable resources and expertise.

Despite "success," grievance claims such as the Arkansas riverbed settlement require a capitalist space economy, "which is productive of the very socio-spatial inequalities" that Indigenous communities are working to overcome.[57] The onus is upon Indigenous groups to either lodge credible claims against the state or to defend themselves against actions of the state. There are two pursuits here: one is appealing to the structures that create the problem in the first place, and the other is crafting reductive spatial representations of the Indigenous community. The first pursuit is existence in a constant state of survival and action in response to larger structures that are producing the inequalities; the other is the production of narratives directed at the state apparatus for use in grievance claims that are stripped of the complexity of Indigenous communities, spaces, and places. In the first pursuit, Indigenous groups hurtle through the politics of recognition, arguing before the state in ways and in language that the state will understand. A politics-of-recognition narrative requires Indigenous people to discuss themselves in terms of Western knowledge and taxonomies of land. These are hollowed-out narratives about Indigenous places that over time become naturalized stories and commonly received knowledge. Consequently, when communities structure their accounts within the terms of the politics of recognition, narratives of poverty, income, educational levels, etc. are retold and retrenched, sustaining a simplified and damage-based narrative about the community.[58]

The unfettered propagation of simplistic narratives can be put in check by community work, and their propagation can be countered by crafting Mvskoke narratives. We resist persistent narratives of subjugation every time we tell our community stories. No matter how big or small these stories are, they are an act of refusing and refuting the politics of recognition.

Spiral to the Stars refocuses and centers on elements that are anchored in the community, such as social relations, the recognition of relationality with all forms of kin, ways of knowing rooted in people, practices, and spatialities, and the dynamism felt when we collectively engage with these elements. *Spiral to the Stars* deals with four primary concepts: este-cate sovereignty, community knowledge, collective power, and emergence geographies. These are community-building tools that communities can use without waiting for permission to recognize, conceive, and enact their community-building efforts.

Thus the goal of this book is to explicate a set of tools for creating and building communities, spaces, and places for the grandfathers, grandmothers, aunts, uncles, moms, dads, cousins, daughters, sons, brothers, and sisters, along with our relatives who are now ancestors, the stars that hold their energy, and the plant and animal nations. This roll call is the community. *Spiral to the Stars* sorts through and grapples with practicing our future, continually renovating our idea of future, and determining how to get there—this is futurity. Futurity is the practice of engaging with ways of knowing, performing, and celebrating who we are, valorizing and creating new ways and theories constructed with community knowledge, and creating explicit paths or maps to get us to the place we want to be, so that we choose our future and our future does not choose us.

As I embark on this project of articulating tools that build communities, I wholly own up to the limits of my knowledge. I represent my own experience, however flawed and disjointed that may be, and do not stand as an expert on being Mvskoke, only on my own experience. I am witnessing and speaking to the world as I see and imagine it through multiple lenses that consider experiences of gender, generation, and being a HUD home kid, always in transit between the city, the country, and ceremonial and governmental spaces. *Spiral to the Stars* is not meant to silence or drown out others but to join a conversation about and with Mvskoke people. In the words of Mvskoke scholar Craig Womack, "It is a point along a spectrum, not the entire spectrum" of the Mvskoke experience.[59] In this positionality, I recognize that my experience is a female experience moving across many types of spatialities. There is a plurality of narratives, as we see when we read Mvskoke writers such as Craig Womack, Earnest Gouge, Jennifer Foerster, Joy Harjo, and Arigon Starr, whose narratives are informed by their own embodied experiences and positionalities.[60] I can only speak from my own experience; I draw upon several Indigenous scholars to formulate ideas, and I draw upon a community-based Mvskoke survey that I conducted to surmise others' conclusions.

As Craig Womack discusses, Mvskokvlke must do the best we can in telling our stories with what we have at our disposal.[61] Indeed this is true: it might be fragmented, but the intention of enacting Indigeneity is fully present. This Indigeneity is renegotiated—for example, we dance in sneakers, not moccasins. It is "lived, practiced, and relational."[62] I am not an expert on all things Mvskoke, but this work is informed by my experiences with my family, community, and Indigenous nation. My knowledges are intertwined with critical disciplines— Mvskoke knowledge with geography and spatial thinking, critical Indigenous studies, and Indigenous feminist theories. While these bodies of knowledge are not explicitly Mvskoke, the production of knowledge does not happen in a vacuum. For this reason, it is important for Mvskoke communities to speak and live their truths from a plurality of unique perspectives.

Futurity

Futurity consists of living out the futures of our ancestor relatives. Maintaining continuity in practices and values and renovating them as necessary, creating communities we wish to live in in the present moment, and considering future relatives are ways of enacting futurity right now, and everyday people can perform and are performing this in a range of spatialities. I speak of futurity as the means by which Mvskokvlke garner greater insight into and control over how they wish their communities to develop, but it is of interest how they (re)imagine and re-member a space-time continuum of the past, present, and future that is modulated by human and more-than-human relationships. I will provide a brief overview of some conversations related to futurity and situate my work. Indigenous futurity and futurism are growing and taking shape in a number of ways, such as recognizing settler futurity and the ways that settler practices and ideologies are normalized and enacted in Indigenous communities. Within Native American and Indigenous studies, futurity is used as a lens to understand how settler colonialism operates to ensure that its own time-space continuum continues into the future without breaking, and it is also used to consider a future temporality in which Indigenous communities decolonize setter epistemologies and (re-)center Indigenous epistemologies.[63] Scholars are disrupting settler futurity in refined ways: for example, within educational systems, Indigenous scholars are thwarting pedagogies that impose a settler future at the expense of Indigenous ways of knowing.[64] Native Hawaiian scholars are applying practices that disrupt settler futurity to ensure futures for their communities.[65] Indigenous scholar Grace Dillon is an important figure who first conceptualized and coined the term "Indigenous futurism," employing science fiction storytelling that collapses the divide between technology and the sacred.[66] Her work is paradigm-shifting, and it continues to make and hold space for Indigenous narratives and Indigenous young people, punks, goths, techies, nerds, gamers—anyone feeling like outliers in their home community. The work of Cherokee scholar Brian Hudson integrates culture with technology, using terms such as *cyberpunk*, which is the notion that "information wants to be free."[67] Hudson posits that the author of the Cherokee syllabary, Sequoyah, was a cultural hacker with open-source aspirations, and argues that the creative digital disseminators of the syllabary are enacting *Cherokee cyberpunk*, which we see in the art and technology work of Roy Boney and Joseph Erb.[68]

Lenapé scholar Joanne Barker employs an Indigenous futurity lens to read Debra Yepa-Pappan's artwork. Yepa-Pappan's digital collage is a nod to *Star Trek* entitled *Live Long and Prosper*. Barker posits the emancipatory nature of Yepa-Pappan's work: it offers Indigenous women and their communities "multiple possibilities of past, present, and future in ways that refuse" being frozen in time as relics—we can be fans/fangirls/fanboys/fanfolx who like *Star Trek* or *Star Wars*.[69] Anishinaabe scholar Elizabeth LaPensée employs futurity in her art; she is a game designer who integrates gaming technology with Indigenous stories, which has been a current vein of interest at Indigenous Comic Con.[70] Although the gaming and comic industry is dominated by males, Arigon Starr has successfully self-published two volumes of the comic *Super Indian*, writing the narratives and illustrating and lettering the images.[71] LaPensée authored a graphic novel and co-edited, with female comic book author and illustrator Weshoyot Alvitre, an anthology of works that shapeshift the story of Deer Woman into one of Indigenous female futurity.[72]

Within the Deer Woman anthology, Mvskoke scholar Kimberly Robertson focuses on aunties—this is a term that both Robertson and Jenell Navarro use in their creative work to refer to a radical kinship-making practice in which nonblood kin are relied upon for support, love, and relationality, especially within the diaspora. Robertson draws upon a radical kinship network in Los Angeles to create her fiction vignette "Las Aunties." This piece illustrates the wider network of kinship the young protagonist relies upon in the absence of Mvskoke consanguinity and unpacks the unique life path and experiences of the chosen aunties, each of whom provides a unique set of tools of futurity for the young protagonist.[73] Robertson also creates zine-like collage work, echoing the aesthetic of Wendy Red Star's art, that layers kin-space-time constellations of each auntie. Robertson narrates her piece from the point of view of her daughter and describes her drawing upon a network of aunties who can help her de in a plurality of ways that ensure Mvskoke futurity and Indigenous feminist futurity—thus she insists, "In Aunties We Trust" (see figure 3).[74]

A time-space envelope is a conception used by twentieth-century geographers to understand and delineate spatialities related to a region and temporality.[75] However, I prefer to use the term *kin-space-time envelope*; I conceive of it as polyvalent and avoid thinking of it as a container. Kin-space-time envelopes function to unblock interactions typically fixed across spaces. The time-space envelope concept is often used to understand social relations within the processes of globalization, such as political, cultural, and economic impacts connected to an area or geography.[76] However, I am renegotiating its use and employing it with an Indigenous knowledge system. A shift toward Mvskoke practices of kinship and knowing the world yields an imaginary that connects with many forms of kin, sites, and temporalities. Kinship takes primacy in a Mvskoke imaginary, while an imaginary that gives primacy to Western notions of time makes our world linear and chronological. A kin-space-time envelope can be a memory, but not solely in the sense of recalling a scene or a vignette; it also provides instruction for how to be in the world, or it invokes a sense of responsibility in the person recalling the memory. For example, if I look to the stompgrounds, outside of the main dance area, I may have a particular memory of my mother sitting in a lawn chair, fanning herself in the muggy summer heat, talking with other shellshakers, telling jokes, and laughing. That memory of social relations is a kin-space-time envelope that reminds me to be joyful in my interactions with kin. Kin-space-time envelopes provide advisement for how to be in the world. An Indigenous kin-space-time envelope considers ancestral practices that we draw upon to renovate, reinvigorate, and sustain our bodies, psyches, livelihoods, and communities. A kin-space-time constellation is a network of kin-space-time envelopes. A constellation then operationalizes multiple dimensions—for instance, the spirit world, the practices of ancestors, cosmology, ceremony, and the everyday social reproduction of the community.

The work of the Indigenous futurism and futurity authors mentioned is related to thinking about how we (re)imagine our communities and epistemologies in the face of prevailing technologies and conditions. Their foci differ, however—the educational system, the narration of Indigenous sci-fi, the (re)appropriation of horror narratives, Deer Woman, technology, art, gaming, coding, virtual reality, film, animation.[77] The means of practicing futurity varies as well—writing and illustrating stories, coding and programming games, rendering animation, capturing and editing analog and digital photos and video—but

FIGURE 3 "In Aunties We Trust," collage by Kimberly Robertson.

the creation always involves the use of one's hands.[78] Through storytelling, art, and the self-publishing of community-based knowledge, all of these cultural workers are creating futurity in the present moment, dreaming of a (re)imagined future where narratives about Indigenous people are more complex and aligned with lived, felt knowledge. The work of relationality and of creating and disseminating narratives in a range of ways is compelling, and it informs my thinking on tools of futurity and kinship. The quality of kinship connections propagates into the quality of community narratives and knowledge—whether full and rich or only surface-level, lacking depth. In my own work, which imagines a spatialized notion of futurity, I perform this imagining through both analog and digital means—an individual drawing a map biography of their life is just as powerful as visiting the sites of our forcibly abandoned etvlwas in Alabama and Georgia via a digital mapping fly-through of the land.

I choose to focus on futurity because it is a more robust concept than future. A focus on the future is a focus solely on a temporality to come. However, futurity means that we do not have to wait to see hopeful possibilities materialize in our communities. Mvskoke people are performing futurity in everyday spaces, and this is powerful. The everyday practices of Mvskoke kinship relations generate a set of emergence geographies, which I explain in chapter 4. In this book I continually work to spatialize futurity; therefore, my notion of futurity focuses on Indigenous spatialities and the relationships, knowledge, and power of transformation enacted by them. Further, I write about activating Indigenous spatialities through both intentional and unintentional knowledge production in everyday life, as well as the vision that collective activities can produce. Inhabitants of Indigenous spatialities are already engaging in relationality and mobilizing their collective and embodied knowledges to imagine, dream, and create a Mvskoke imaginary that is lived out in emergence geographies. Futurity is space, place, and temporality produced socially by people, including relatives located in the past, present, and future. It invokes many other temporalities, other spaces, and yet-to-be-imagined possibilities: it is a practice of conceiving imaginaries. Indigenous futurity places us in conversation or in a dialectic with the unactivated possibilities of our past, present, and future relatives; these conversations include spaces and places that are rich with meaning and experience.

Kin-space-time constellations can be moments connected to time, spaces, and places—for example, they can be connected to a continuum of community responsibility to uphold Mvskoke systems of care and not allow them to cease. Hence, the responsibility and desire to stompdance operate simultaneously; we provide past, present, and future stewardship to the dance because it provides for our past, present, and future care. The stompdance is a collection of kin-space-time envelopes—a kin-space-time constellation. These kin-space-time envelopes are represented in practices such as dancing, stargazing, listening, eating, visiting, and letting go of grudges. For an example of what exactly a kin-space-time envelope looks like in practice, we can first consider stargazing: we are observing the same stars as our ancestors. Another example is listening to the songs: we can ponder whether our ancestors, and hopefully future relatives, desire the lighthearted feeling of hearing stompdance songs. In one last example, our Green Corn is our new year—a time for renewed outlooks or second chances. Therefore, after a round of dancing or a shared meal, one might feel the lifting of a year's worth of disappointments or a reconnection with kin we feel have slighted us—this is the continuance of a treasured form of recuperation of community and self. Surely our ancestors felt such physical and emotional experiences while dancing hundreds of years ago—and our future relatives will enact this, though it might perform something different for them. Stompdance is a system of care whose meaning is predicated on the subjectivity of the observer or practitioner of the constellation of practices. Poet Rupi Kaur writes, "i am the product of all the ancestors getting together and deciding these stories need to be told."[79] This statement identifies and names submerged agents of futurity that reach to and from the spirit realm. These junctures are memories, practices, and writings through which ancestors and unactivated possibilities speak.

In an everyday example, the pawn shop also draws on kin-space-time envelopes. As a person scans the shop and work tools catch their eye, it might evoke a memory of their father or aunt repairing a car, or they may be reminded of a teaching about how to use a car jack to change a flat. As I look to ethnic studies scholar Sharon Luk's work, she draws upon Hortense Spillers's "intramural protocol of reading," and I use this to understand that we read these spaces as kin-space-time-envelopes based on our standpoint, or subjectivity of the moment.[80] The pawn shop song is an example: it draws from our kin, perhaps from a song used in 1783 in diplomacy practices in Alabama, but based on my standpoint in the kin-space-time juncture or envelope from which I am reading, this song is a pawn shop song. That might change tomorrow or in twenty years, when it will be read according to different conditions and a different subjectivity.

The spaces and places and all the entities that produce them—people, non-humans, flora, fauna, spiritual entities—all embody energy. For better or worse, then, these kin-space-time envelopes can "hold" resilience and trauma. Futurity is a constant renegotiation of past, present, and future, time-space junctures that are transitory and ever in flux. Because daily conditions and circumstances shift, so too does our perception of the kin-space-time envelopes we draw upon. Thus kin-space-time envelopes are flexible and relative to one's positionality. They hold the potential to retrieve memories and help us understand the possibilities both enacted and unactivated in these moments. Further, the individual or community that does the imagining has the possibility of synthesizing any number of kin-space-time envelopes to open and conceive new possibilities.

Rethinking Indigenous Community

The word *territory* has a very specific meaning related to geopolitical containers within the Western spatial imaginary of nation-states.[81] Peoples are relegated to fixed and bounded spaces. Futurity can help us rethink such notions. As a key to the making of meaning, resistance, social movements, and imaginaries, futurity moves across and plays out on many potential scales—a regional set of processes, the body, a household, star constellations, soundscapes, or smells-capes.[82] Hence the idea of futurity and Indigenous space and place does not relegate us solely to the places where the federal government has "assigned" us. Some of our (re)emergence and migration stories are based on our responses to acts of settler futurity that include Indian removal and relocation; however, we also carry other such stories that are based on movement of our own choosing. Those stories have yet to be conceived, written, and told. Mvskoke people have generated Mvskoke community, even beyond our eleven-county tribal jurisdiction. Thus, conceptions held by Mvskoke and other Indigenous communities disrupt commonly received notions of fixity of place.

It is imperative to renegotiate how we conceive of the Indigenous community, particularly in our current moment, because we do not stay fixed in our communities of origin. People are constantly in movement, for school, work, and other pursuits. However, as a result of settler colonial eliminatory policies and practices, Mvskoke people have continually renegotiated and recalibrated our practices of what it means to be a community. As mentioned earlier, Mvskoke people once lived in autonomous tribal towns, but dramatic upheavals have resulted in our renovating how our community looks and functions. It is crucial that we refuse a valorized narrative of fixity because we have not remained fixed in place. Rethinking the Indigenous community allows us to step back and consider the ways in which Indigenous community surfaces; in doing so, we refuse the eliminatory logics of settler colonialism. Another approach to rethinking the Indigenous community is imagining unactivated possibilities—disrupted dreams.

As far as unactivated possibilities, we might ask: What if Mvskoke people hadn't been traumatically removed to Indian Territory? If Mvskoke people return to places like Ocmulgee Old Fields, located at Ocmulgee National Monument in Macon, Georgia, or visit tribal town sites, what can we know? What can invoke us into action, into dreaming of a Mvskoke imaginary in the past and in the future? These are unactivated possibilities. Although the federal government has forced us to live under its rule and seemingly foreclosed our ability to imagine other possibilities outside of our fixed eleven-county area, it has not foreclosed all of our possibilities. We may no longer "own" the land at the sites of our communities of origin, our etvlwas, but we still own the memories, as well as kin-space-time envelopes that hold knowledge and stories about our ways of planning our places, our views of the constellations, and our negotiations with alligators and humidity. Finding and returning to our places enables us to speculate with our relatives, to gather information based on all our senses, and to be in a place that shapes a felt knowledge that we can embody and draw upon with our speculating and imagining.

Social relations across temporalities structure how the Indigenous community develops, and futurity holds spaces to create our own narratives that are informed by the memories of our relatives and tribes. Many versions of the Mvskoke community have been authored as a continuum of coming into being—as emergences, migrations, perceived futures, and renegotiated present moments. All of these narratives hold the possibility of being taken up now or in the future; regardless of the temporality, the community can author new ways of being in the world. And there is power in the invocation of kin-space-time envelopes. Cree scholar Karyn Recollet invokes the enactment of community dance practice, the round dance, in the city as an active form of resistance to and protest against settler colonial violence.[83] Here we see the idea of jumping scale from the community of origin to the urban context, in opposition to the oppressive global system of settler colonialism.[84]

We can experience the act of drawing upon a kin-space-time envelope by playing and listening to recorded stompdance songs in places where stompdance is not carried out, such as while driving, in places distant from the stompgrounds, or in one's household. The songs activate felt knowledge and experience tied to locations. Songs hold memory, functioning as kin-space-time envelopes, and this can support resilience and thriving too. The night sky holds Mvskoke kin-space-time envelopes that continue to be accessible: we see the same constellations that our relatives gazed at, and I would surmise that our relatives after us will access the same star systems and gain direction and draw power from them.

Futurity is an action; it's a practice. The actions we take today enact our relatives' futurity: we both live out the futurity architecture of our ancestor relatives and frame a futurity for our future relatives. Futurity is a practice that invokes our ancestors' and relatives' unactivated possibilities in our present lived moment, and it imagines future possibilities. Even possibilities we thought were gone or extinguished can be revived in the imaginary embodied by futurity. Futurity can exist in the metaphysical realm or the spirit realm. For example, missing and murdered Indigenous women and girls (MMIWG) are often portrayed with extinguished lives and futures. However, futurity enables kin in the present moment to activate possibilities that their MMIWG relatives were not able to physically carry out. The energy of MMIWG provokes us to action in myriad ways: to create art, to dialogue, to pause and remember the women and girls, to pause and think of the places and conditions that engender violence against Indigenous women and girls. This is different from a legacy. Futurity can mean that yet-to-be-conceived possibilities are invoked in us by the memory, energy, and personal narratives of these murdered and missing Indigenous women and girls.

Indigenous futurity serves the community, and it imagines and constructs the worlds we want to live in. (Re)imagining is a decolonizing methodology. Indigenous futurity (re)imagines where the community is and who the community is; it speculates outside of the prevailing conditions to understand and realize the delayed or unactivated possibilities of our ancestors and current-day relatives. However, it also provides space for conceiving renegotiated Mvskoke imaginaries that, as Womack argues, innovate on tradition and initiate new ways of life.[85] Furthermore, through the act of (re)imagining community we can realize that we are living out the unactivated possibilities of relatives. The realization of unactivated possibilities through tools of futurity empowers the community. This methodology is decolonial in nature because it allows community members to draw upon all the senses and all the realms, such as the physical and the metaphysical, to dream and craft the communities we want to reside in. In the next section, I share my methods and place them in conversation with Indigenous methodologists.

Methods

Indigenous methodologist Shawn Wilson contends that "the purpose of any ceremony is to build stronger relationships or to bridge the distance between our cosmos and us."[86] Indeed, at the core of Indigenous methodologies lie considerations of relationality with all entities. In his book *Research Is Ceremony*, Wilson writes a letter to his children explaining his research journey. With a similar focus on relationality, I included my cousins Connie and Terrence Harjo in this Mvskoke research journey as members of the research team. Further, I engaged in a feedback loop with community members, family, friends, and MCN staff, constantly checking in with them about the best way to structure the project's research design. Ultimately, I was guided by an ethical obligation to the community, something that Wilson refers to as "relational accountability," meaning that the methodologies are shaped by and relative to a community context, and that furthermore they are carried out in a respectful, reciprocal, and responsible way.

Linda Tuhiwai Smith's seminal work *Decolonizing Methodologies* has forged a path for other Indigenous researchers to operate in ways that honor their communities of origin; Smith's book legitimizes community knowledge systems, while arguing the problem of Western research paradigms imposed upon Indigenous ways of knowing the world.[87] Smith provides twenty-five Indigenous community projects that can function as decolonizing methodologies. These endeavors can serve as points of departure to formulate a fuller community engagement, and in my own methodologies I build upon Smith's projects of "imagining" and "creating."[88] Asking Mvskoke community members to speculate about the future of their communities and lifeways is a form of *imagining*—that is, conceiving of a Mvskoke imaginary. Smith suggests that Indigenous communities *create* their own solutions—in my methods I use four methodologies that are shaped by the context and knowledges of the Mvskoke community.[89]

One of my methods was a survey that was reviewed many times before it went live, which is a concrete form of relational accountability. In designing the survey, I formulated it within the context of the Mvskoke community; as such, it asks community members to imagine a Mvskoke future twenty years and seven generations from now. The community context shaping the survey instrument carries out and endorses Maggie Walter and Chris Andersen's idea of Indigenous statistics that are shaped through an Indigenous methodology—in this case, by Mvskoke futurity.[90] The survey was carried out because there were not enough resources to conduct research with the depth and breadth that extensive interviews could provide. In the post-survey process, Mvskoke people wished to share insights beyond what they had provided in the survey—there was a degree of trust and rapport established from the outset when the survey was administered. For example, I provided respondents with a map of MCN chartered communities to review as they were filling out the survey. Through the course of this conversation, common connections to communities, relatives, and families became evident, which correlates with Wilson's idea of relationality. Indigenous scholar Andrew Jolivétte contends that radical love is "a fundamental aspect of a sacred research justice agenda and requires that we see research participants as members of our family."[91]

I also employ the work of Mvskoke scholars and artists and read these as texts that illuminate the written experience. Miho Kim reminds us of inequality in research and the ways that marginalized populations experience exclusion and disempowerment predicated in part by lack of access to data—also, I would argue, to narratives about themselves and their experiences in mainstream sources. Ultimately, what is at stake here is providing a platform for people to speak about their experiences, which I attempt to do with the survey, interviews with Mvskoke people, and the writing and sharing of Mvskoke stories and wishes. There are too few contemporary narratives about Mvskoke people.

I also employ self-reflexivity in my grappling with the subject matter and in my analysis. For example, I do so by reflecting on my trajectory of building my methodological repertoire. Further, I use the words of Yakama scholar Michelle Jacob: "I have engaged in reflexivity—not to be narcissistic but rather to make possible 'dimensions to the research undertaken that provide a fuller, more accurate, and more meaningful picture of everyone and every-thing involved.'"[92] Jacob employs researcher reflexivity in her analysis; my methods employ a dialectical loop to grapple with assessing community data.[93]

Finally, these methods are an act of resistance, flouting the notion of capitalist practices that divide work from fun, as illustrated by the ways that the research team laughed and teased each other. In forming my research team, I purposefully selected my relatives, as a gesture meant to dismantle elitist notions of research and capitalist practices of research productivity; also, the fun that we had doing this research is an act of generative refusal of capitalist approaches to labor.[94]

Mvskoke Tools of Futurity:
Their Necessity and Sequence

Working within the politics of recognition is not always the most fruitful way of proceeding; it can require extensive resources to prepare and defend claims within the federal legislative process and the court system. In my experience, I have witnessed a room brim with energy as people begin to share their knowledge, ideas, concerns, and dreams—there is a form of relationality at work. In some ways, this kind of work is sacred: it invokes the spirit and embodied knowledge of the participants. I am heartened and inspired every time I see a community group—whether a formal community group or the university students that I work with—get encouraged as they realize the fullness and might of their power and their ability to act, and when I see the ways in which they begin to trust in their own knowledge and produce knowledge together. They then use this community knowledge to coalesce and invoke a different kind of power—not a hegemonic type of power, but a collective power that cares about kin and community and that is used to make one another's lives and community better. This works in opposition to commonly received ideas about power, such as authoritative power. Finally, community groups stage their power, knowledge, and collective action spaces, which manifest in myriad ways. It seems to me, then, that there is a process through which people can realize their own power. The people are their own resources and can do it for themselves.

This book proposes four tools of Mvskoke futurity, in the form of four methodologies that are theorized and emerge from Mvskoke practices: (1) radical sovereignty or este-cate sovereignty, (2) community knowledge, (3) collective power, and (4) emergence geographies. Each of these concepts bears on a community's map to the next world, which is to say that they serve as way-finding tools enabling a community to dream, speculate, and realize futurity and the lush promise. This book explores these four tools to provide ways for community members to do their own community-based way-finding work. Each one of the tools of futurity provides a way of understanding the Mvskoke experience and crafting theories that emerge from that experience. Although I speak of Mvskoke futurities in all four tools, these can be extended to refer to Indigenous futurities more broadly, and some dimensions will work for other communities as well, not solely Mvskoke or other Indigenous communities.

Furthermore, because there are common thematic threads that run through the four tools of futurity—such as movement, interstices, felt knowledge, and community—they overlap in many ways and do not adhere to strict categorical boundaries. For example, movement is an element present in all four tools: within the Mvskoke experience, we have always been in movement, from our origin and emergence stories to removal from our communities of origin to Oklahoma; there is movement in our dances, and we are still in movement today. Interstices are in-between spaces, which can include the space that is produced between the material and metaphysical worlds, something that is present in the work of Mvskoke writers. In these interstitial spaces, dreaming, imagining, feeling, and remembering take place. For example, there are some stompdance leaders whose songs make one feel like one is in an interstitial space—somewhere between the material, the metaphysical, and the stars. Another recurrent theme throughout the book is felt knowledge, because these tools of futurity engage with past, present, and future knowledge that is experienced and known by the ancestors and relatives. Ultimately, these concepts are not four separate buckets; instead they are flexible enough to serve the varying circumstances of the community and of the user. Futurity is active and constantly being renegotiated; these tools of futurity offer means to transition to other ways of enacting and producing, outside of the logics of settler colonialism, places we wish to inhabit.

Returning to the idea that tools of futurity are way-finding tools that operate to create a map to the next world, this book is organized to teach the tools in a series of steps. It is arranged in an order that demonstrates how power, knowledge, and agency continue to grow in magnitude as we proceed, with each tool of futurity building on the next. The sequence is the following: first comes radical sovereignty, which enables us to realize that everyone carries the power to act. Next is community knowledge, which is the coalescing of Mvskoke people and their knowledge to form a theory to make sense of the world. Subsequently, the concept of collective power spirals together with the previous two tools to formulate and perform actions. And finally, emergence geographies are the spaces and places that Mvskoke people carve out, despite forced removal and land dispossession, to produce the social relations that they need to thrive. They are spaces and places that are produced repeatedly, such as the MCN tribal complex, or produced out of renegotiated approaches to social relations, such as softball tournaments or online community interactions.

Radical Sovereignty

In the Muscogee word *este-cate*, *este* means "man" and *cate* means "red," which translates to "red man." *Este-cate* is a vernacular term used to recognize an Indigenous person as kin, regardless of gender; the term *este-cate* grounds sovereignty in practices of kinship. For example, when greeting one another, Mvskokvlke might say, "Hey, este-cate!" or when seeing other Indigenous folks in an urban setting, Mvskokvlke might recognize them as kin and say to their family "Hey, look, este-cates!" To explain the tool of este-cate sovereignty further, first I want to explain the word *radical*. I use this word according to Indigenous scholar Leanne Simpson's definition: "a thorough and comprehensive reform, and I use this term . . . to channel the vitality of my Ancestors to create a present that is recognizable to them because it is fundamentally different than the one the settler creates. I am not using the term to mean crazy, violent, or from the fringe."[95] Radical sovereignty or este-cate sovereignty is a type of sovereignty that predates the contemporary notion of tribal sovereignty—we have always practiced it and continue to do so. However, it is not articulated through the politics of normative governance systems but rather through the poetics of Mvskoke community. For example, all entities embody energy, and this matters because the way in which we treat other entities can tamper with, support, sustain, strengthen, undermine, or hinder their life forces. It is important to consider relationality in our engagements with both human and more-than-human entities. Through this relationality, social relations between blood and nonblood kin are forged, which creates the conditions for energy and relationality to construct futurity at the most fundamental level. Then, energy and kinship are operationalized to act and do not require permission from normative governance structures. Radical sovereignty or este-cate sovereignty is born from Mvskoke vernacular spaces and experiences. Many forms of radical sovereignty exist, and este-cate sovereignty is one such form; it is understood and known through daily lived experiences, which means that everyone has this tool at their disposal. In subsequent discussions in this book I will refer specifically to este-cate sovereignty: this is a type of action and freedom realized in everyday and vernacular spaces against the grain of the politics of settler colonial elimination. Therefore, este-cate sovereignty is a tool to find our way back to the ways in which community is already performing sovereignty and enacting energy and kinship governed by love for the community.

Community Knowledge

The second way-finding tool is community knowledge. Community knowledge builds on este-cate sovereignty because este-cate sovereignty is a focus on individuals and communities realizing the level of autonomy and self-determination they have always possessed. Community knowledge is understood as knowledge acquired from daily lived practices, but it is understood in many other senses too, and there is a feedback loop with the spirit world as well, through prayer and conversation. For example, the Green Corn Ceremony goes back further than can be remembered, and its practice embodies many types of knowledge. This knowledge empowers the community.

Collective Power

The next way-finding tool is collective power. The practice of community knowledge can be felt, and recognizing that is powerful; however, the collective can also mobilize community knowledge into transformative action. So, in terms of collective power, there is an inherent kind of power that re-energizes community, and there is another kind of collective power that is action—action to transform, a kind of action that changes conditions. Re-energizing power is that which renews community; this is a form of vnokeckv—decolonial love.

Emergence Geographies

The final way-finding tool is the idea of emergence geographies: these are spaces and places within which the production of community decolonial love and transformation takes place. Emergence geographies make space for Mvskoke ways of being in the world, and they renovate where Mvskoke spaces and places can exist.

The use of futurity methodologies is not a strictly linear process—as in, use this way-finding tool first, then this one, etc. However, they are organized to correspond to what I posit as a Mvskoke idea of conscientization. I ordered the chapters in a sequence that I imagine a Mvskoke person might follow to emerge into the power of self and community. First, we recognize the embodiment of power, agency, and energy in all beings, a principle that we have always enacted despite the nation-state. There is a belief in oneself, or confidence in oneself, a building of self-esteem, a notion that we are just as good and that we have the authority to self-determine the directions and futures of our communities. Then with this confidence comes the sharing of self with others, and this is community or Mvskoke knowledge production, which we begin to see our role in. As a result, we see that we act with others, whether through dance or other collective action—we enact collective and transformative power. Finally, these agentive processes are carried out in spaces and places. Despite the federal government assigning them to an eleven-county area in Oklahoma, Mvskoke people continue to emerge in a multitude of spaces and places. Furthermore, within MCN's eleven-county area, our communities are present but often under the radar of the settler government. The four tools of futurity provide the means by which community members can perform their own community-building work and produce Mvskoke futurities—Mvskokvlke imagining and performing their past, present, and futures.

Spatializing Futurity

Since the tools of futurity are processes of relationality, they are carried out in a location, or are connections to a spatial imaginary in which meaning, memories, and desires are shared among community. For this reason, spatialities are a common thread throughout *Spiral to the Stars.* Indigenous spatialities are needed because Western spatial imaginaries are not complex enough to imagine and carry out Indigenous futurities. Because spatialities are at stake, I use spatial language, speaking of geographies, space, place, kin-space-time envelopes, and scale.

Mvskoke spaces are social spaces that are not placed within measurement geographies of Cartesian mapping but instead connected to multidimensional spatialities: terrestrial, virtual, spiritual/metaphysical, and celestial realms. These realms constitute the geographies of our kin across many space-time configurations. Bringing a kin-space-time lens to Mvskoke geographies makes a Mvskoke space. I use space to discuss geographies that are rife with opportunities to apply analytic lenses. The spaces are relational; they are open to change predicated on the positionality of the individual or community. An envelope is a spatial object that is relative and changes. Kin-space-time envelopes unblock bounded spatial interactions. The kin-space-time constellation is a cluster of kin-space-time envelopes that offer new spatial configurations, which we need as Mvskoke people to live and be in the world. Examples of Mvskoke spaces are funerals, family reunions, and impromptu games of basketball or softball.

Mvskoke places are locations that are imbued with meaning to a community; however, places can be provisional and relational to the social relations that drive the meaning of place. Mvskoke places exist as a palimpsest, a layer of spatial meaning covered by several layers of settler geographies of place. For example, in the Mvskoke homelands of Alabama and Georgia, several layers of settler places obscure Mvskoke places, and the memory and cartographic representation of etvlwvlke have been covered with counties and municipalities named after white men. Mvskoke places are situated within measurement geographies and imbued with particularity, time, and location, such as a tribal town location or ceremonial grounds. Mvskoke places are also multidimensional. Mvskoke space and place can also be invoked through the body. If we turn to the work of my daughter Hotvlkuce Harjo, we see the invocation of a Mississippian-era kinspace-time envelope. Hotvlkuce is a punk-identified visual artist who invokes ancestral knowledge and practices in her artwork to offer a site of futurity.

My daughter reflects on the workings of Mvskoke space when conceptualizing her artwork. She looks to community knowledge in an urban space of the diaspora, invoking her grandfather's teachings and memories. Drawing on a deep study of Mississippian art, she stylizes facial markings in a contemporary context, living the futurity of her Mississippian ancestors as a punk (see figure 4, "Mississippian Black Metal Girl on a Friday Night"). She awakens Mvskoke space and brings it to her life and body, using tribal ancestral markers—tattoos—to grapple with her way of being and expressing herself. Her way of being combines both space and place in a dialectical and processual interchange, activating the unrealized possibilities of her ancestors.

I return throughout the book to the concept of scale, and here I turn to how it fits into the project of futurity. In previous writings, I have used geographic scale to articulate the different sites at which a local community might either place grievance claims, imagine social justice, or create social relations.[96] Scale functions in different ways, and I do not mean it as an index in a hierarchy of fixed geopolitical units; rather, scale requires us to examine the processes that created the geopolitical units. The scale of the Mvskoke community is produced through relational processes rather than territorial processes. The production of scale is often used to understand the ways in which capital moves, or Western and settler formations of territory, or territories' relationship to the larger global political economy. Indigenous community scales are instantiated in myriad ways. It can be useful for communities to understand political and economic geographies in order to advance liberatory claims. For example, if a

FIGURE 4 "Mississippian Black Metal Girl on a Friday Night," ink illustration, Hotvlkuce Harjo.

local community group finds itself in a position in which local entities such as the city or county government do not wish to listen or respond to grievances, they might choose to jump scale to a national or international policy- and/or decision-making body—for example, they might take claims to the United Nations Permanent Forum on Indigenous Issues. This idea of jumping scale means that a local community bypasses more local systems of governance to seek action and support in other places. Scale is useful to a community that wants to spatially strategize its emancipation. Here I wish to examine how scale is produced through relationality and through social processes that transcend the terrestrial realm and geographic positions of x, y, and z, or latitude, longitude, and altitude. Indigenous community scales are instantiated in myriad ways.

I examine how to build on the notion of scale in a different way that refers to jumping scale to the spiritual realm, and across time and space in ways that place the community in dialogue with ancestors and future relatives. In this case "jumping scale" valorizes processes of relationality. This concept of scale builds love and relationality across many realms and temporalities. Jumping scale can also be a community organizing strategy: for example, when performing a power analysis for a community issue or campaign, such as one related to the school-to-prison pipeline, students of color might find that they are overcriminalized in the school system and that they do not have the power to influence the decision-makers in their school. Jumping scale in this case means identifying several other supporters or allies for their cause. They might locate their supporters via social media or by drawing in other decision-makers such as a city councilor or state legislator—in this way their ability to influence decision-makers to intervene in the pattern of overcriminalization has swelled. Their power has jumped scale. Where they have grown a base of power that can challenge decision-makers, they have also jumped scale within an ordering of political power; they have bypassed local power to reach decision-makers who can make sweeping policy changes regarding subjective disciplinary practices in schools. Jumping scale does not solely function to grow a base of supporters to mobilize toward a cause. The late geographer Clyde Woods, in his seminal work *Development Arrested*, uses scale to elucidate how the planter class in the southeastern United States has persisted across time and space, rising to political power and legislating racialized laws that have subjugated people of color in the Southeast.[97] Woods conceives of blues epistemology as a means by which Black people sustain their worldview, history, and futurity—in a similar turn, *Spiral to the Stars* conceives of an imaginary shaped by Mvskoke knowledge and theories.

Indeed, scale is helpful to community because it explains where phenomena are impacting the community and where to take action. Scale explicates spatialities from which responses and actions to these phenomena might be staged at distinct levels, such as the scale of the body, the scale of the household, the scale of the county, or the scale of MCN. Furthermore, at the outset of this introduction, I discussed the renegotiation of Mvskoke knowledges and practices, and it is important to think about a spatial language for understanding this renegotiation and how, where, and why it takes place. The Mvskoke individual living in the city without access to practices such as stompdance or traditional games still perpetuates other Mvskoke values and practices; they still enact Mvskoke community even if it is at the scale of a single person and their body. Scale works with emergence geographies to help understand the spatial imaginary of relationality and kinship that operates in the Mvskoke community in ways that draw upon a network of spatiotemporal locations.

In *Spiral to the Stars*, I examine tools of futurity—este-cate sovereignty, community knowledge, collective power, and emergence geographies—from a perspective of scale: commencing with the body, I move onward to the collective level where knowledge production, power, and geographies are staged. The first tool, este-cate sovereignty, is articulated at the scale of the body. The second tool, community knowledge production, consists of community members coming together to share, produce, and analyze knowledge. The third tool, collective power, again involves many people coming together, but geographically this can be broader than a single community, addressing many different spatial realities: action might be staged within a single community building, or in three or four stompgrounds or churches across the region, or across international boundaries, such as in the case of the *Walking with Our Sisters* moccasin installation. Further, collective power might extend beyond the traditional community when it involves studying star constellations and Mvskoke star stories. With the final tool, emergence geographies, a number of scales are produced from lived experiences of Mvskoke people that function as both context and product.[98]

Each tool helps a community find its way back to practices of relationality and kinship making and operationalize these practices into autonomy and self-determination. Each helps a community find its way back to knowledge that is felt, embodied, experienced in the community, and placed into action for the community, and to the spaces and places in which this knowledge is enacted. Material, ephemeral, metaphysical, and virtual spaces are all geographies in which these ideas and actions are staged. Each tool has the potential to operate either unintentionally or intentionally: for instance, everyday Mvskoke practices such as speaking Muscogee words like *mvto* (thank you) or *honka* (boogeyman, monster, malevolent spirit) that are part of one's language repertoire could be an unintentional practice of futurity, while gathering a group of people to conduct a community engagement activity is an intentional practice. This book is meant to convey both unintentional and intentional practices so that communities might see how they are already doing work that they might not have been aware of and also draw upon purposeful methods for strengthening their communities.

Sequencing the concepts of futurity in this way is a pedagogical move for teaching them, with each concept building on the next. First comes understanding one's positionality and the fact that there is richness and value in it. Also important is understanding one's capacities related to autonomy, kinship building, and self-determination. The second step is recognizing that community knowledge and felt knowledge are just as important and valid as positivist models of knowledge production. Third comes finding that self-determined, felt knowledge can be collectively tapped to generate informal and formal actions that shape community. And finally, the fourth step involves the places in which all of this gets staged and realized—the geographies of emergence.

Organization of the Book

The primary claim of *Spiral to the Stars* is that communities already have what they need to live, shape, and imagine many modes of futurity. Therefore, the methodologies of este-cate/radical sovereignty, community knowledge, collective power, and emergence geographies—the naming and claiming of the spaces needed to enact all this power and possibility—are the tools of futurity for Mvskoke communities and other communities that strive for resilience and the living of full lives. This work aligns with Jolivétte's idea of sacred methodologies of Collective Ceremonial Research Responsiveness, which consists of at least three components: radical love, transformative justice, and collective action.[99] The book is organized into five chapters, with chapter 1 taking on the problem of formal sovereignty and how the prevailing emancipatory practices that are based upon it can be problematic as well. In this chapter, I introduce este-cate sovereignty, which situates power and self-determination at the site of the body in the community. In chapter 2, I shift the ontological and epistemological renderings of community, land, methodologies, and knowledge away from the settler colonial framework and toward an Indigenous worldview. In chapter 3, I explicate three distinct axes of power or spheres of influence, beginning first with transformational power or Indigenous community power, based on similarity and on creating places and futures through means such as recognizing felt knowledge and creating nonmarket economies in the community. The second kind of power I talk about, which includes prevailing concepts of power, is oppositional power. This type of power is predicated on countering a dominant narrative or appealing to a settler institution or normative governance structure. Finally, there is oppressive power, which is predicated on power asymmetries, particularly at work in Oklahoma to thwart MCN's planned development. In chapter 4, I introduce a Mvskoke story of emergence as a way of understanding how Mvskoke people, place, and communities are continually (re)emerging and moving. I explicate the Creek community survey I administered at Creek Festival and provide a closer reading of agency at the levels of tribal nation, community, and self to understand how communities are invoking este-cate sovereignty and carving out transformational spaces. In chapter 5, I grapple with the question, *What is to be done?* How do we imagine futurity and what kind of tools can we apply that invoke este-cate sovereignty and refuse settler colonial practices, while embracing Indigenous and Mvskoke ways of knowing to decolonize our ways of engaging with community and create a beautiful path to a lush place? Finally, chapter 6 contains community-based methods that carry out the tools of Mvskoke futurity. It provides a series of methods that can be used by a community to begin to enact community-driven modes of futurity. These tools can provide opportunities for individuals and communities to realize their own power and agency. The process of carrying out these methods in community also produces and reinforces kinship connections.

HICKORY TREES AND CORN SOUP

I am from neon green fireflies blinking in the night, from John Cope's dried
   sweet corn and Williams Chili

I am from oak and hickory trees, green hills, streams, fresh summer willow
   arbors, all-night ceremony, NDN street games, and jewelry making

I am from thick damp night air carrying the songs of the ancestors among
   harmonizing turtles, and a glowing fire

I am from fluffy grandiose trees creating a canopy of refuge from the hot sun
   and hard rain

My grandmothers, Lena Wind and Julia Hardridge, dynamic Mvskoke matri-
   archs who died young, before their children could know them as elders

Their spirits embolden me in my walk, steeling me with protection and courage

I am from laughter, jokes, and smiles, and rambunctious family convenings

From Mvskoke humor, with instructive punch lines

I am from the Etvlwas (tribal towns)—Alabama, and Tvskege that flourished in
   the woodlands before the destroyers arrived

I am from Yvhv (wolf) clan, the Mvskoke grandfather clan, gifted with the
   responsibility to care for the people

I am from drawing your curtains at night to shut out watchful malevolent
   spirits and mean medicine

I am from the Mvskoke songs and prayers of my people, uttered long before I
   was born

I am from sokhv, vce, corn soup, grape dumplings, and wild onions

I am from every few Fridays, my parents loading up the trunk of a gold Pontiac
   Catalina with clothes and the TV, riding, drinking Bubble Up soda and
   listening to K-Tel compilation cassette tapes in a tape recorder for several
   hours to go home from Lawrence to Weleetka

From my mother, Ellen Harjo, a ribbon dancer and shell shaker bringing me to
   Kellyville stompgrounds, and imprinting Mvskoke songs and her song on
   me, from which I flourish

From my father, Duke Harjo, a Mvskoke statesman, his quiet strength, kind
   instruction, and vision for the people, sitting with him at community and
   tribal meetings, and him transferring to me a way to move and be in this
   world

—Laura Harjo, 2015

CHAPTER 1

The Lush Promise of
Radical Sovereignty

"Hickory Trees and Corn Soup" presents my experience and practice of being Mvskoke, not as an academic, artist, or author, but as a crusty kid from Sapulpa, Oklahoma, playing softball in the streets with other Mvskoke kids, dog-paddling in the murky waters of Polecat Creek, or rooting around for reusable gems at the city dump, all while happily sharing in taunting humor.[1] These are examples of daily lived experiences from an MCN housing subdivision neighborhood. Although not all the places mentioned—the streets, the creek, or the city dump—are part of the experience of all Mvskoke people, they are part of my experiences and those of the kids I grew up with. At first glance, these experiences may seem insignificant and banal when viewed through the lens of legal discourse or Western conceptions of self-governance or sovereignty. However, Indigenous scholar Scott Richard Lyons defines sovereignty as "nothing less than our attempt to survive and flourish as a people," which grounds sovereignty within the community.[2] Community-grounded sovereignty is illustrated in these practices of appropriating space in the street, creek, and city dump; other tribal members too practice their own versions of what I call "radical sovereignty" or "este-cate sovereignty" in the interstices of everyday life—that is, the in-between spaces of MCN and all other iterations of Mvskoke spaces, places, and informal sites. Other versions of este-cate sovereignty practices might look radically different from my own representation—they might consist of gathering and chopping wood, noodling for catfish, or hanging washed clothes on a clothesline. Radical sovereignty does not have to wait for the nation-state to recognize it or deem it legitimate. Instead, it is embodied in being Mvskoke and practiced without permission from anyone.

Radical sovereignty or este-cate sovereignty is constituted by Mvskoke actions that recognize the power and self-determination necessary to perform and create vernacular practices and geographies. Although I agree that the notion of formal tribal sovereignty is necessary in order to block the dispossession of Mvskoke land, gain fair access to health, education, and housing, and ensure the security of one's body, I still insist that tribes and Indigenous communities have always enacted and continue to enact a form of este-cate sovereignty bound up in local community knowledge and practice. Our flourishing as a community derives from an embodied and collective practice of este-cate sovereignty. Through this practice, we make our past, present, and futures.

Our past, present, and futures are constructs of the lush promise, which is a phrase from Joy Harjo's poem "Map to the Next World."[3] The lush promise is a Mvskoke imaginary that is shaped by and carries the hopes, dreams, and wishes of the people to live a life that is full. Each of the tools of futurity serves a specific function in finding our way to the lush promise, starting with este-cate sovereignty. Through este-cate sovereignty we recognize our personal and community-grounded self-determining practices, which are bound up in ourselves and our connection to our kin.

The lush promise is a goal that communities unceasingly work toward, and it requires remembering and renegotiating Mvskoke narratives and practices that provide for a full life in the current moment. The lush promise is not informed by a singular notion of "the" Mvskoke culture and values, but by many versions. Based on one's experience and aspirations, the lush promise is multidimensional, multisensory, and multispatial. The lush promise might take on a multitude of forms for various individuals. My notion of a lush promise might not be your notion of a lush promise. A Mvskoke imaginary is not confined to our minds; it can structure our daily practices. The Mvskoke imaginary consists of the dimensions of social relations with humans and nonhumans across time and space; these relations stretched across time and space produce the spaces and places that we call community.[4] It is not my job to tell people what Mvskoke culture and values should be; here I am simply bearing witness to my story and the way I conceive of the elements of este-cate sovereignty and how they structure Mvskoke community.

The lush promise is informed by Leanne Simpson's idea of decolonial love, which involves living a life that is full.[5] Mvskoke people already carry experiences, knowledge, and practices that render lives full. Examples of ways in which individuals and families can live a full life include being in good relationships with humans and more-than-humans, grappling with and recuperating from trauma and grief, engaging in spiritual practices, and reproducing Mvskoke lifeways. The definition of a full life can vary across a range of individual experiences—what is a full life for one person might not be a full life for another person. However, there might be dimensions of a full life that individuals can agree upon, and the collectively agreed-upon dimensions might form a community imaginary of the lush promise. The lush promise can shift over time based on conditions and needs: as with the pawn shop song at the outset of the book, our uses of knowledge are renegotiated, and so too is the Mvskoke imaginary of the community. Mvskokvlke have imagined a plurality of ways in which the community must manifest under the prevailing conditions of a series of spatiotemporalities.

Este-cate sovereignty renovates conventionally received ideas of tribal sovereignty and draws upon the profundity of Mvskoke epistemologies to structure sovereignty. Este-cate sovereignty is a type of sovereignty that Mvskoke people have always practiced, one that predates settler colonialism, and Mvskoke people still practice it in new and renegotiated forms in their daily life. This other way of knowing sovereignty can be carried out by individual community members to perpetuate their community.

Because one's physical body carries este-cate sovereignty, a multitude of Mvskoke experiences or subjectivities generate many possible forms of este-cate sovereignty. For example, one person might sew and make their family's clothes, while another might be an artist who produces silkscreens of other possible worlds; regardless, both the garment maker and the artist are taking action without waiting on a formal structure or entity, such as the federal government or tribal government, to give them the green light or permission. Each person embodies their assemblage of resources and carries the capacity to act by employing these embodied resources. Embodied resources, experiences, and capacities encapsulate futurity; a community can mobilize these to fulfill the lush promise. The extent to which one can act upon and realize these capacities based on one's abilities is both agency and self-determination.

Recognizing and mobilizing one's agency and power unlocks a variety of possibilities. We are constantly and effortlessly performing este-cate sovereignty whenever we recognize the way that energy, kinship, and agentive power operate in our everyday spaces. As Mvskoke people, our experiences shape our senses of ourselves and are a consequence of the teachings of our relatives and our experiences with, in, and outside of our communities. But though Mvskoke epistemologies structure our communities, we should not lose sight of the fact that settler structures are operating as well. Communities normalize and, for better or worse, reproduce these settler ideologies. For example, we might reproduce hegemonic, authority-wielding types of power over others in meetings or interpersonal interactions, or believe that our community knowledge is not as valid or as good as that of "experts." Therefore, while settler ideologies are naturalized, and we receive them and mobilize them to our slow "demise"—or rather a sort of low-intensity elimination—este-cate sovereignty reminds us that our Mvskoke ideologies are more powerful and present than we might recognize and that they can subvert settler ideologies.[6]

Our experiences form our subjectivity, and our subjectivity shapes our wishes, our actions, our ways of knowing the world, and our ways of performing in the world. Therefore, this subjectivity shapes our material communities—for example, Mvskoke people embody practices of este-cate sovereignty in our sociocultural use of space. Even though our settlements no longer look and function exactly like our pre-removal etvlwas, our use of space in our ceremonial grounds and our Mvskoke churches still operates in an approximate semblance, which I discuss more in chapter 4, "Emergence Geographies."

Este-cate sovereignty is our awareness of our Mvskoke subjectivity and recognition of powerful dimensions such as human and more-than-human energy and decolonial love for the community—which is connected to the belief that you create for the community and your relatives. I posit that one way of emancipating ourselves and our communities from settler ideologies and practices is the cognizance and practice of our Mvskoke subjectivity in everyday places: we can mobilize the elements that form us as Mvskoke people into an array of actions. Energy and decolonial love are powerful, and Womack argues that Mvskoke people employ a form of radical resistance that he calls a "Red Stick" approach: this approach re-centers Indigeneity and rejects the notion that white supremacist ideologies are more powerful than Indigenous ones.[7] Mvskoke people are empowered when we embody strong will, look inward instead of outward, and push back against settler practices that operate to extinguish our fire—in a metaphorical sense as well as in the literal sense of the fires at our ceremonial grounds.

Our senses of self are shaped by an iterative process of experiences, and tracing my journey of community work reveals an iterative process in which I have been reshaped by a repertoire of community experiences and tools. Other community members and communities have their own timelines that they can trace and reflect on. The actions they chose based on their care for and responsibility toward community and Mvskokvlke are examples of este-cate sovereignty. Este-cate sovereignty is a type of personal as well as community sovereignty that locates power at less formal scales, which might be in a local community or an online community. In these locations that circumvent authority, power resides. One form of este-cate sovereignty that Sarah Deer writes about is bodily sovereignty, which reimbues Indigenous bodies with integrity in the face of the settler state's actions to usurp original Indigenous governance structures and compromise the bodily sovereignty and autonomy of Indigenous people, in particular Indigenous women.[8]

The concept of este-cate sovereignty I am suggesting is comprised of Mvskoke principles of energy, relationality, felt knowledge, and vnokeckv (intentions of a non-hetero decolonial love). The tenet of energy means that we recognize the power and life in all things; relationality means that we make kinship connections and come to know and recognize our responsibility to our kin; felt knowledge refers to the fact that we carry an archive of experiential knowledge that can empower us or trigger us into submission. The intention of love and responsibility doesn't require extensive resources and isn't constrained to a particular place or territory. It can mean providing a meal to someone, or opening space for young people to play basketball, or providing instruction in something they wish to learn, such as the creation of comic books or computer coding. Finally, Mvskoke individuals, families, and communities carry out este-cate sovereignty every day in our communities and vernacular interstices; we only need to look through an intentional lens of energy, relationality, and felt knowledge to observe and locate moments of este-cate sovereignty. Este-cate sovereignty is enacted in our material world. However, it too can jump scale and place us in relationality within spiritual and metaphysical interstices. One example of jumping scale is related to the unexpected death of my father: after his death I maintained a dialogue with him and with my other ancestor relatives, imagining their unactivated possibilities, their legacy, which I needed to pick up and carry in my unique way in the present temporality.

In October 2014, my father, surrounded by his relatives, drew his last breath at the intensive care unit of Saint Francis Medical Center in Tulsa. Holding on to him in his hospital room as he transitioned to a spiritual realm, I knew that his energy was transcending the earthly scale, moving from material to metaphysical. His energy was traveling the Milky Way.[9] Subsequently, I spent every night for the next year standing under the stars armed with tobacco and prayers, contemplating what it meant to be Mvskoke. A stream of ancestors was entering and exiting my thoughts, dialoguing with me; I remembered their stories and puzzled through what it all meant, struggling to piece through familial futurity. I tried earnestly to remember everything Mvskoke that had ever been conveyed to me in word and practice, scared that I would begin to forget stories and instruction. I could no longer simply ask my dad to retell a story or tell me how to say something in Mvskoke. Some nights, clouds obscured the stars; my smoky conversations with Hesaketvmese (Maker of Breath) and my relatives still billowed skyward, and I continued drawing upon kin-space-time envelopes and dialoguing with relatives in the spiritual realm. During that year, I watched the three stars of Orion's belt trek across the night sky with the seasons through fall, winter, and spring, until they finally disappeared low in the western sky. I reflected on how when we transition from material to spiritual form, political fights no longer matter. The tribal government, appeals to the nation-state for fair treatment, the honoring of claims, the politics of recognition are no longer at stake in that realm. There is no court of appeals in the spirit world. Thus, what does it mean to decenter our communities from these institutions framed by normative governance? We constantly urge the nation-state to honor grievance claims. However, if we imagine our relatives not as subjects of the state but as the protagonists of a star story, or of a modern-day migration from the country to the city, to the in-between places, it changes the energy of the experiences that fill the spaces of our lives. They fill with love, energy, power, and self-determination. That is este-cate sovereignty, and it is a form of sovereignty that those who labor for freedom can embrace. A Mvskoke person does not stop practicing este-cate sovereignty once they step beyond federally delineated boundaries. Nor do the community or ceremonial grounds cease to be self-determining even if there is no affiliation with the formal tribal government. A Mvskoke person continues to embody the wisdom, knowledge, and people of the larger Mvskoke group. In this manner it is more about how you treat people and carry yourself than about citizenship in an imagined governance structure. The act of drawing from our relatives who have transitioned to a spiritual realm transcends a settler ordering of space. Indigenous communities should not wait for permission from nation-states or other formal governance sites to enact who they are and practice the Indigenous lifeways central to their existence.[10]

One of my actions of futurity was a refusal to speak to anyone. During my year of nightly star watching and prayer, I was in direct dialogue with my relatives. In part not wanting to be distracted by the fast pace of social media, where everything posted is cast as having a degree of urgency that requires all of your attention and energy, I shut down my accounts or simply stopped logging in. I was carrying an undocumented archive that was still fresh after having spent an entire summer traveling Creek Nation with my father, and I tried to remember stories and conversations about the tribe, community and our responsibility to it, and sense of place. In part, my embodied archive is my father's, constructed from the stories he told me of being young with his four brothers, John, Norm, Chubbs, and Lil, playing alongside their horse-drawn wagon as they traveled to a Mvskoke church, or of vaccinating cattle outside of Okemah when he was a young man. Further, I had an open line of communication with the spirit world through which I was having conversations with my ancestor relatives, which sharpened my focus in thinking about Mvskoke futurity. The Mvskoke imaginary is grounded in our ancestors' and relatives' embodied archive of narratives and knowledge, or what Don Fixico calls "Third Door knowledge," which is knowledge produced by and for Mvskoke people.[11]

When we dialogue with ancestor relatives, there is energy present, something that is explained by many Mvskoke authors. The late Mvskoke author Joan Chaudhuri, née Hill, claims that a Mvskoke way of being in the world is animated by energy in all things.[12] Fixico too argues that there is spiritual energy in all elements.[13] Within a Mvskoke belief system, Chaudhuri argues, our time existing in material form is animated by a transfer of energy among beings, an important grounding concept for understanding the realm of community and all beings that inhabit a community. Energy is exchanged and sensed through interaction, conversations, and contemplation. We create a collective that is built from energy produced together. In community, the process of social relations—such as a community gathering to socialize or make decisions—snowballs the kinship energy of the collective into something greater than it was at the outset of the process. This energy moves in a continuum, and although leadership may change, we still dance and practice Mvskoke ways of being in the world. This energy extends across time and space and possesses the power to change our communities in ways that we desire. For example, my dialogue with ancestor relatives draws upon their energy and knowledge, which is not bounded by

material forms or by linear ideas of time and space. It is an act of jumping scale
to the spirit world and the cosmos. Further, the Mvskoke concept of energy,
which I will refer to throughout the book as simply *energy*, operates in informal,
vernacular, and ungoverned spaces, but this energy also extends into the stars
and reaches back to the intentions our ancestors set in place for us through
prayers to Hesaketvmese and through their collective ways of understanding
and deliberating matters of importance in the etvlwas (tribal towns). Mvskoke
cosmologic stories tell us that when our physical bodies cease breathing, our
energy travels through Orion's belt to the Milky Way, the source of all energy,
the next place.[14]

Este-cate sovereignty draws upon knowledge that we carry and feel. Indigenous scholars Craig Womack, Dian Million, Michelle Raheja, Jennifer Denetdale, Leanne Simpson, Audra Simpson, and Taiaiake Alfred direct us to inter-
rogate the role of Western scholarship in silencing Indigenous knowledges,
while working to reveal local forms of knowledge and experience through the
lens of decolonization. Indigenous feminist scholar Dian Million's theory of *felt
knowledge* provides a framework that opens up thinking by asking us to consider
what it feels like to be Mvskoke (specifically a Mvskoke woman), to live in a
Mvskoke community, and to have a range of human experiences that include
joy, laughter, celebration, pain, and loss.[15] The idea of felt knowledge brings the
importance of producing and enacting local knowledge into sharper focus.

Este-cate sovereignty refuses the nation-state, and I draw on Indigenous
feminist scholar Audra Simpson's "logic of refusal" in my own refusal to work
and fully frame this project within the normative systems of governance and
thought.[16] I refuse to work within a grievance model framework, and I refuse to
seek permission from the nation-state to enact that which sustains the conditions of possibility for Mvskoke people to flourish and practice este-cate sovereignty. This notion of este-cate sovereignty is not new, and neither is the idea of
nation-building that responds to the cultural and political context of a region.

Two schools of thought on sovereignty exist: one that proposes that tribes
honor the nation-states' rules of engagement and meanings of sovereignty, and
another that I argue corresponds to radical sovereignty, in which we have love,
agency, and power in our communities that work to honor and create relationality among all beings. The idea of tribal nation-building comes out of Harvard
University and primarily addresses the governance systems of tribes.[17] Advocates of tribal nation-building insist that constitutions and courts are sites where
"stronger governance systems" (a phrase commonly used at tribal conferences)

might be constructed. Immense resources are poured into navigating this form of sovereignty—Indian law programs, for-profit companies offering training on federal rules and regulations, and policy and law institutes and nonprofits that function as tribal nation advocates and watchdogs.

However, a radical turn in Indigenous sovereignty has become more pronounced during the early twenty-first century, predicated on ideas of settler colonialism, gender, sexuality, world systems, and global Indigenous peoples. I situate my work within this latter school of thought, among those who are discussing how to make things happen without the permission of the government and working to disrupt eliminatory processes of settler colonialism. I endeavor to make this project provide a road map for Indigenous peoples to enact este-cate sovereignty outside the state, outside normative systems of governance.

Furthermore, este-cate sovereignty serves as a route to valorizing Mvskoke ways of being in the world that sustain one's spirit, household, and community and coalesce into a Mvskoke nation. Through such practices, Mvskoke lifeways can be leveraged into transformative power, which is communities' ability to renovate prevailing ideas of sovereignty and achieve both the journey toward and the living out of the livelihoods they wish to see across many generations and spaces—in other words, futurity.[18]

Este-cate sovereignty builds upon antecedents derived from a worldwide Indigenous peoples' movement, which even today continues to develop in a variety of ways: it is a call to practice Indigenous laws on Indigenous lands as well as a resurgence of Indigenous practices and philosophies. There are several ways to discuss the Indigenous peoples' movement, and some of the earlier conversations have been situated in sociology. Within that conversation, the global Indigenous peoples' movement and development strategies are referred to as being from the Fourth World. While the "world" ordering is problematic, the way that it fits with radical sovereignty is that it is a category that does not bind people to delineated nation-state geographies.

I would build upon these initial ideas to conceive of radical sovereignty. First, the Fourth World is a realm of spiritual and cultural struggles against the nation-state, and it calls on practitioners to "assert Indigenous laws on Indigenous lands."[19] The use of this term attempts to organize peoples around similar sociopolitical conditions, which often means living under the rule of settler colonial governance systems and suffering from a host of issues, including premature death. According to the Indian Health Service, "American Indians and Alaska Natives born today have a life expectancy that is 5.5 years less than the

U.S. all races population"; furthermore, they die at higher rates from causes such as diabetes, assault/homicide, and self-harm and suicide.[20] Warne and Laji-modiere argue that historical trauma yields three primary types of stressors—gestational, childhood, and adulthood—which eventually lead to chronic disease disparities.[21] In particular, settler colonialism structures violence within the experiences of American Indian and Alaska Natives, such as unresolved trauma, boarding school experiences that involve physical and sexual abuse, loss of culture and language, and loss of traditional parenting, to name a few.[22] Adverse childhood experiences include physical and sexual abuse, neglect, the witnessing of violence, food insecurity, and family members in prison, while adverse adulthood experiences can include poverty, racism, toxic stress, and lack of role models—all of which are a result of systemic settler violence.[23] However, a resurgence of Indigenous ways of knowing and theories shapes responses to the settler state, and I contend that this resurgence can shape our community-based practices.[24]

Indigenous scholars have debated the question of sovereignty for the past few decades. Many problematize sovereignty and try to imagine a way of being in the world that is integrated into and works with existing governance systems; the Harvard Project on American Indian Economic Development is one such group that focuses on Native nation-building. Others imagine a world that is separate from settler colonial systems.[25] In many ways, this split echoes the ongoing problematic of sustaining Indigenous belief systems within a continuing settler project that constantly works to erase, silence, and eliminate Indigenous peoples.

Prevailing modes of tribal sovereignty opt for an integrationist and incrementalist approach of working with existing governance systems, and the goal to build tribes' capacity in governance is derived from the work of the Harvard University project.[26] This approach seeks to move through federal governance systems to sustain the tribal government and land base. Many others, such as Kiera Ladner and Sarah Deer, recognize the flaws of settler-shaped tribal sovereignty and actively work to reshape tribal sovereignty in dialogue with their peoples' original instructions.[27] Creating a world separate from, or emancipated from, settler colonial systems is the approach that este-cate sovereignty builds upon in its re-centering of Mvskoke practices of energy, kinship, and decolonial love. Theories of decolonization and Indigenous epistemologies are antecedents for my proposed idea of este-cate sovereignty.

Remembering, Honoring, and Enacting

Many Indigenous scholars ground their work in the lifeways, practices, traditions, stories, and epistemologies of their respective nations and communities, including Craig Womack, LeAnne Howe, Taiaiake Alfred, Linda Tuhiwai Smith, and Leonie Pihama; Chickasaw scholar Jodi Byrd calls this "scholarship grounded within local and national knowledges."[28] For many Indigenous scholars, tribal knowledge is the point of departure when discussing their nations and governments. This is a common approach across the board, whether in Harvard's Native nation-building project or Taiaiake Alfred's approach to honoring the desires of Indigenous communities' ancestors.[29] Mvskoke poet Joy Harjo narrates in her work that Mvskoke people are bound up in the task of honoring their knowledge and relationships and recognizing when there is a breakdown in either one that keeps the people from re-membering a lush, full imaginary. In "Map to the Next World," Harjo laments:

> We no longer know the names of the birds here,
> How to speak to them by their personal names.
> Once we knew everything in this lush promise.[30]

Here she references the Mvskoke creation stories, acknowledging that in the beginning, in time immemorial, the Mvskoke believed humans could talk to the animals. The metanarrative of the poem describes the deep relationship Mvskokvlke once had with the natural world and the way this relationship has been disrupted. The poem forces the question: How will we get to the "next world" if we no longer fully map out the rituals and knowledge of this world? Harjo's poem suggests that we should trust in the knowledge of our ancestors and that individuals will have to find their way alone armed with their ancestral knowledge.

At one time Mvskoke people were in conversation with the animals, and perhaps there was a map in place to ensure the fulfillment of the lush promise. Today, however, we must renegotiate how we will be in relationship to the animals in both literal and metaphorical conversations. Harjo proposes trusting in one's personal energy and power while remaining conscious of the local knowledge that has sustained Mvskoke people since time immemorial. Knowing the birds by name, talking to them, and regarding them as kin are demonstrations of the ways in which Mvskokvlke value more-than-human beings. Mvskoke people had the knowledge to flourish in this "lush promise," which is the crux of the Mvskoke imaginary. Further, as a counter to the discouraging thought that maybe we don't have a map to the next world, she offers us the idea that we do have this map if we look inward to our own energy, power, and knowledge, and outward to that of our relatives and community—there is where we will collectively find the map to the next world, the map to the lush promise.

Mohawk scholar Taiaiake Alfred's work also supports the concept of mapping a path to the "next world." In *Peace, Power, Righteousness: An Indigenous Manifesto* and *Wasáse: Indigenous Pathways of Action and Freedom*, Alfred discusses the idea of recovering and regenerating Indigenous nations by honoring what a nation's ancestors wanted for their people.[31] He asks Anishinaabe spiritual leader Eddie Benton-Benai what sovereignty means to him. Benton-Benai responds, "Personally, I am sovereign. So, sovereignty isn't something someone gives you. It's a responsibility you carry inside yourself. In order for my people to achieve sovereignty, each man and woman among us has to be sovereign."[32] Este-cate sovereignty enacts what our ancestors would have wanted, but also what we carry within us.

One of the bases of este-cate sovereignty, then, is never to lose sight of the fact that it is embodied, it is felt, it goes where we go and is not bound to a geographic area, and, as Alfred's treatment of sovereignty suggests, it is enacted by individuals. This differs from the idea that the tribal government enacts sovereignty, not the people. How, then, can an individual's Indigenous nation enact this type of este-cate sovereignty?

Alfred further argues that community leaders are revolutionary and should "symbolize and activate the hopes, dreams, and ideals of the young people of their generation."[33] This informs the argument that radical or este-cate sovereignty can draw upon community leaders of the type Alfred describes—in the current moment this might mean heeding the millennial generation's unprecedented access to technology and to powerful tools of social and political movement building.

There are two dimensions of this argument for community leaders that relate back to este-cate sovereignty—one is what we mean by "community" and the other what we mean by "leader." Within the context of futurity and este-cate sovereignty, community can take many shapes and forms—it does not have to stay fixed to a geographic location. For example, some communities of Mvskokvlke come together based around affiliation or identity as Mvskoke people even when they aren't in the same place or don't live within the boundaries of the tribal nation. This is illustrated by the Mvskoke community groups that come together outside of the eleven-county jurisdictional boundary of MCN, such as the Muscogee Creek Nation New Mexico At-Large Mvskoke Community. It is also illustrated by online Mvskoke community groups such as the Muscogee Word of the Day Facebook group. Next, with regard to the notion of a community leader, a leader does not have to mean someone who delegates tasks and spurs people to action; it can be an individual who demonstrates astute ways of relationality, kinship making, and love for their community.

While most scholars typically look to youth, elders, and ancestors for action, wisdom, and knowledge, radical sovereignty means that everybody carries a set of resources to act as "leaders." This means that locally based practices and ways of knowing can be accessed in service to the community. Harjo's poem "Map to the Next World" is one example of epistemological guidance on the local and community scales. When epistemological guidance comes from many kin-space-time envelopes, this stretches relations across space.[34] The late geographer Clyde Woods approached development by engaging local epistemologies of the Black community. The blues epistemology that he derived from the local Black population works to subvert the planter class in the Mississippi Delta, which historically had oppressed the Black population through slave labor, slave wage labor, and federal policies that guarantee a dispossessed future.[35] The local and regional orders of power may appear unsurmountable, but the blues epistemology that Woods offers is a community-generated worldview and methodology that allows people and communities to enact a form of emancipation despite institutions of planter class power. Woods's work, which finds the conditions of possibility in the epistemologies of local people, is directly related to ideas of este-cate sovereignty.

Prevailing systems of formal sovereignty are problematic in the ways they don't allow communities and tribes to have true self-determination in guiding and deciding on land transactions without Bureau of Indian Affairs oversight. Not only tribal professionals but even everyday tribal members can see the lack of oversight that they enjoy over their own tribe's assets. Community members from various tribes continually question the efficacy of formal sovereignty. While I was attending an Indian Land Tenure Foundation gathering, a Standing Rock Sioux Tribe council member stated that "sovereignty means that we are our own nations and make our own decisions." He questioned the practice by which tribal land transactions require the Bureau of Indian Affairs' approval. He ended his statement with a query for all attendees in the room: "What is sovereignty, really?!"

Cherokee Nation teaches a forty-hour history course that all tribal employees are required to attend.[36] One section of the course explores the ways in which tribal sovereignty has devolved by using a metaphorical bundle of sticks to represent the salient aspects of sovereignty. The course then traces historical moments and legislative acts and policies of the federal government that have slowly and insidiously eroded the robustness that tribal sovereignty theoretically possessed. Over time, the bundle has diminished, effectively thwarting a full and rounded practice of tribal sovereignty.

I provide a sketch of the limits and impacts of formal sovereignty in order to propose that we build on the work of broadening the meaning of sovereignty outside of legal discourse. I acknowledge that other Indigenous scholars are thinking about unique ideas of sovereignty—such as Raheja's visual sovereignty—and I situate my offering of este-cate sovereignty as an agentive community-based approach to living and being in the world that valorizes community worldview.[37] Eagle Woman calls this "holistic" sovereignty.[38] Using a community-based approach, I consciously leave the grievance model of sovereignty at the door. Encapsulated within "real sovereignty" is a theory of change based on communities' wants and needs. Real sovereignty is often initiated outside of the normative governance structures of municipalities, counties, and states.

Decolonizing Communities and Drawing a New Map

Drawing a new and decolonized map that guides us to a lush promise of recuperating our relationships and our knowledge requires a bold reordering that can absolutely happen at the personal scale and the community scale. This reordering enables us to decolonize governance systems by critiquing these systems and recognizing where they reproduce settler colonial ideals. Critical Indigenous studies offers several contexts and technologies to consider in the process of decolonizing. Scholars are mapping new ways to enact tribal sovereignty, organize globally, decolonize, and understand tribal relationships to the state.[39] These threads of scholarship converge to form a theory of este-cate sovereignty and decolonization. Within this larger theory, one perspective courageously disavows normative governance systems, while another recuperates governance systems by breaking all the bones that support their framework and using splints of decolonization to reset it. The work of Mvskoke legal scholar Sarah Deer, for example, does not destroy everything that is not Indigenous but instead works to shape governance systems according to Indigenous epistemologies.

In *X-Marks: Native Signatures of Assent*, Lyons introduces a typology for Indigenous scholarship regarding nation and sovereignty.[40] He discusses decolonization in terms of Alfred's concept of nation-building and nationalism, which does not propose completely destroying everything that is not "Indigenous." Rather, Alfred proposes the idea of having some community-derived guiding principles for the work of nation-building. In this way, Indigenous nations would still use governance systems, but they would use Indigenous epistemologies in understanding and directing their work.

However, Glen Coulthard suggests that actions of decolonization cannot look to the nation-state for legitimacy, because doing so reestablishes the nation-state as an authority over Indigenous nations and requires Indigenous peoples, in many cases, to ask for recognition from their very oppressors. In his article "Subjects of Empire: Indigenous Peoples and the 'Politics of Recognition' in Canada," Coulthard problematizes Indigenous peoples' desire for recognition by the nation-state.[41] His article chronicles the Canadian government's position on Indigenous self-determination. Again we see self-determination, one of the tenets of sovereignty, appear. Canada's treatment of Indigenous sovereignty is problematic because Canada is a settler colonialism–based nation, and Indigenous peoples cannot look to the state to deem them legitimate. The state is an oppositional force to Indigenous peoples, and seeking redress and recognition within the very system that oppresses Native peoples is futile. Moreover, Coulthard problematizes the state's notion of power and argues that Indigenous peoples should not mimic it as a model of power. One conception of power opposed to the state-based power that Coulthard implicates is Andrea Smith's idea of transformative power, which is cooperative and progressive.[42] In summary, Coulthard problematizes normative governance, considering it neither a site where Indigenous peoples should seek some measure of recognition nor a type of power to replicate. His work underscores why the Western legal and governance systems should not be the ceiling on redress for Indigenous peoples.[43]

In other ways, too, Indigenous peoples who operate within the politics of recognition via national and supranational political systems, such as truth and reconciliation commissions and the United Nations Permanent Forum on

Indigenous Issues, are entering into spaces in which hierarchical legitimacy is imposed on Indigenous groups in terms of who may and may not make an intervention on the floor. The ordering of interventions to be heard on the floor of the UNPFII makes for a "gentrified meeting."[44] Lebsock shares the following statement with the North American Indigenous Peoples' Caucus to UNPFII:

> Engaging in the politics of recognition is expensive and requires resources to travel. Further, who gets to represent and speak for all indigenous peoples in such venues rests on who has the resources to travel both nationally and internationally to do hemispheric meetings, and gives authority to random people who show up or those who have access to resources with no mechanism in place for a more democratic way of doing the work.
>
> For many years, Lakota delegations to the Permanent Forum have been concerned about the increasing amalgamation of positions within the "Global" and "North American" caucuses. Owe Aku International shares these concerns of our Lakota relatives. The "Global" and "North American" Caucuses are actually only those people who decide to show up on a given day, at a given meeting, or who can afford to travel to a given place for a "caucus" called by NGOs that may or may not be actually "authorized" to do so. In the working group on indigenous populations and again at the Commission on Human Rights, those of us around for a while may recall that joint statements were utilized, instead of what are now liberally called "Caucus" statements, because they actually reflected who was agreeing to specific language. . . . This is a classic form of colonization and actually reduces statements to the lowest common denominator (as in Western democracies). It also forces independent, sovereign, self-determined Indigenous nations and communities into censoring or fully suppressing their own concerns because it wasn't introduced by any of the plural caucuses now favored by the Permanent Forum. In turn, this actually results in the suppression of creative, independent problem solving consistent with ancient traditions that we are representing. By only giving priority to "group" statements and ignoring the inherent understanding within our cultures of independence, we are turning the Permanent Forum into exactly what states want; a rather impotent means to give the impression of participation of IPs based on predictable language in gentrified caucus meetings.[45]

This is a further example of the problem of both formal sovereignty and access to resources and participation in governance systems: the UNPFII privileges collectives of Indigenous groups and NGOs but does not recognize official representatives of federally recognized Indigenous nations. In this statement, Lebsock suggests that the UNPFII is operating as a colonized form of governance. He problematizes the ways in which the UNPFII prioritizes who can speak, privileging those groups most likely to coalesce into a larger collective. Thus, an individual representing a sovereign Indian nation would still be treated as though their concerns were less important than those of a collective of NGOs. This complicates the notion that UNPFII functions as a benevolent organization. Indigenous peoples are consciously critiquing this site of governance, an initial step toward formulating a decolonized notion of the Indigenous-United Nations dialectic. It also demonstrates that this site of governance does not afford the kind of redress one would expect from a global organization.

In *Forced Federalism: Contemporary Challenges to Indigenous Nationhood*, Jeff Corntassel and Richard C. Witmer argue that the order of power between tribes and states (e.g., Oklahoma) has devolved into a sharper power asymmetry, with states taking on more roles and authority over tribal sovereignty.[46] Their work adds another axis of analysis to critiques of court rulings. They address the political economy of regional processes and power, asserting that the federal government has devolved some of its power relating to tribes to the scale of state governments. In some policy areas, this devolution means that tribes are now forced to negotiate with state governments over issues such as taxation and gaming. This level of analysis demonstrates how the executive and legislative branches of the U.S. government have further impaired tribal sovereignty.

Settler Colonialism

Settler colonialism actively operates to foreclose Indigenous futurities, as illustrated by the heavy resources required to even sit at the meeting table, the gentrification of meetings, and patriarchal sign-offs on tribal land decisions. All of these things make tribal sovereignty a moving target. Colonialism can be defined as a practice and ideology that extends across time and space throughout the world and includes elements such as land regimes based on Western conceptions. Settler colonialism, then, is not a historical moment, but rather a hegemonic bloc of time that still persists today.[47] We are not in a postcolonial epoch. Our everyday ways of being in the world, which we take for granted, are shaped by settler colonial practices. Examining the ways in which settler colonial practices continue to influence and shape communities is a critical pedagogical project because it seeks to organize and work with the community without the express permission and authority of the settler state, the U.S. government. It is necessary to explicate various manifestations of settler colonialism. In his work *Settler Colonialism*, Veracini differentiates between a migrant and a settler and discusses the distinctions between colonialism and settler colonialism.[48] He defines these terms in the context of sovereignty and political agency. Veracini describes both the migrant and the settler as people moving from one place to settle permanently in another. What sets the settler apart from the migrant is that settlers intend to create a political regime that replaces the existing Indigenous polity and invokes some measure of sovereignty. This process occurs at the expense of the existing Indigenous population. A migrant, however, does not have the power to impose sovereignty on an Indigenous people; rather, the migrant is co-opted or assimilated into the existing regime. A settler colonial regime has consumed place and people, folding them into a structure of practices and institutions with no regard for how this may impact Indigenous populations.

Settler Colonialism in Oklahoma

Mvskoke people experience settler colonialism through the imposition of alien authority structures, the dispossession of land, the displacement of people, and the dismantling of matrilocal and matriarchal practices. The primary argument is that Indigenous people's communities and self-governance experience a wholesale foreclosure under settler colonialism, and the people are forced to assimilate into a settler colonial government and nation. They are displaced, disciplined, and constantly moved, whether to lands hundreds or thousands of miles away, to boarding schools, or to the city. Political economies derived from a settler colonial state shape their sense of place, what they formally call themselves (e.g., Muscogee [Creek] Nation), and what they informally call themselves (Mvskoke people). The word *Mvskoke* transcends all separation according to federal recognition or stompgrounds, and it includes, for example, Creek, Muscogee, Alabama, Quassarte, Thlopthlocco, Kialegee, and all tribal towns—even those that are rarely spoken of or clouded by time. All are Mvskoke people.

President Andrew Jackson was instrumental in violently removing Mvskoke people from places where they once dreamed, danced, prayed, birthed their babies, buried their relatives, watched the stars, and deliberated the futurities of their etvlwas. Beginning in the early 1800s, Andrew Jackson urged Congress to enact a federal Indian policy that called for the removal of Indigenous nations from the Southeast to make way for further white settlement and development of the region.[49] In 1830, the U.S. Congress passed the Indian Removal Act. Experts estimate that during this forced removal to Indian Territory, half of the Mvskoke people perished.[50] As I examine the idea of settler colonialism in Oklahoma further, it becomes evident that the United States is a country founded on genocide.

If we step back and listen to stories from the past, we hear how settler colonialism not only eroded tribal power but attempted to destroy whole peoples and their cultures. Settler colonialism's collision with Southeastern tribes, including Mvskoke (Creek), Cherokee, Seminole, Chickasaw, and Choctaw, is chronicled at the Cherokee Heritage Museum's Trail of Tears exhibit.[51] This genocidal act of transferring Southeastern tribes to Indian Territory in Oklahoma is portrayed in various parts of the exhibit, including a replica of a rifle with a bayonet used to remove Cherokee families from their homes and herd them into forts for holding, a video in which elders remember this tragic long march, and late Mvskoke stompdance leader Dave Wind's narrative of the military hunt for Mvskoke in hiding.[52] Wind describes how tribal groups in hiding had to silence children, sometimes smothering them, to stop them from revealing the location of the rest of the group. Another exhibit in a dim room lit with blue lights evokes nighttime or darkness. Overhead, stereo speakers pipe in the sound of a strong wind blowing as a background to voices of local Cherokees retelling their relatives' stories from the Trail of Tears. The exhibit features a sculpture of a mother and child lying on the ground. Visitors hear a child's voice telling his mother he is cold; he nudges his mother, trying to waken her, only to discover she is dead. These exhibits are sad, poignant portrayals of the federal government's removal of Indigenous peoples from their homes and homelands. They tell the history of how Indigenous people tried to elude capture by hiding in terror. If captured, they walked the fatal trail to Oklahoma.[53] These are examples of settler colonialism chronicled by contemporary Indigenous peoples residing in northeastern Oklahoma. They portray the suffering that tribes endured under settler colonial policies.

Settler colonial states didn't only attempt to cleanse Indigenous peoples from their Native lands through overt measures such as the Trail of Tears; other erasures were more subversive, such as parceling a large collective land base into individually owned plots. Another way in which colonial powers attempted to erase Indigenous peoples from their lands was disallowing them citizenship in their tribal nations if they did not meet blood quantum rules, thus reducing a tribal nation's population.[54] As recently as the 1970s, the U.S. government enacted overtly genocidal policies. Claremore Indian Hospital, for example, practiced eugenics on Native women of reproductive age, sterilizing them without prior and informed consent.[55] Approximately seven generations after the Trail of Tears—an overtly genocidal act—agents of the settler colonial state were still trying to erase Indigenous peoples from this land.

These historical events and their political motivations firmly establish the United States as a settler colonial state founded on genocide and slavery. The U.S. government's continued support of these laws and practices perpetuates tribal subjugation and leads to the question: If U.S. policies are examples of what nations should aspire to, why would an Indigenous nation model itself after the very nation-state that legally restricts Indian self-governance, undermines its cultural preservation, and marginalizes its right to exist? Moreover, how does an Indigenous nation move forward on its own terms outside the purview of the federal government but within the scope of its local Indigenous community? I examine these questions to conceive of tools that can break down the machinations of a settler regime within an Indigenous community.

Settler Sovereignty and the Politics of Recognition

The U.S. Supreme Court has played a key role in preventing tribes from fully enacting formal tribal sovereignty, and its rulings in the early 1800s actively set forth a reduced notion of tribal sovereignty within a settler polity—the U.S. government. Although the high court recognized tribes as sovereign entities, it declared that Native nations had limited sovereignty in three court rulings that still demarcate the breadth and depth of tribal sovereignty today. *Johnson v. M'Intosh*, *Cherokee Nation v. Georgia*, and *Worcester v. Georgia*—known as "the Marshall trilogy," named after Chief Justice John Marshall, who presided over the cases and authored the legal opinions—all were decided during a relatively brief period.[56] These dramatic rulings set a precedent for delineating Indian sovereignty and thus cementing the relationship between state and federal governments and tribal nations. In the *Johnson v. M'Intosh* case, Marshall used the doctrine of discovery—based on the Christian principle of terra nullius, which deems land not occupied by Christians to be empty land—to affirm that

European colonizers were the discovering nation who had a right to ownership of the land, while Indians only had a right to occupy the land, but not to own it.[57] *Cherokee Nation v. Georgia* resulted in an opinion that prohibited the state of Georgia from attempts to exert state authority and law over Cherokee land and territory; it was in this decision that Marshall characterized tribes as "domestic dependent nations."[58] In the *Worcester v. Georgia* case, Marshall opined again that Georgia laws did not apply to the Cherokee Nation; although this was a favorable ruling for tribes, President Andrew Jackson refused to enforce it. Furthermore, the ruling solidified Jackson's and states' commitment to removing tribes from the southeastern United States. Jackson emboldened states to enact Indian removal policy through Congress, which resulted in tribes being forcibly removed from their homelands; in the end, tribes' status as domestic dependent sovereigns failed to keep them in their original territory.[59]

The Marshall trilogy also "divested tribes of their foreign nation status"; the decisions devolved tribal sovereignty, removing tribes from a world stage of international law to a realm dictated by domestic law.[60] The U.S. Supreme Court, then, established the scope of tribal sovereignty so that it had less political power than the U.S. government but slightly more than state governments.[61] The court also ruled that tribes were not able to alienate land without the permission of the federal government, nor were they allowed to enter into treaties with any nation-state other than the United States of America.[62] From that moment forward, the federal government slowly chipped away at tribal sovereignty.

Several Supreme Court and Federal Court of Appeals rulings in the late twentieth century further reduced sovereignty. Two primary Supreme Court cases, *Oliphant v. Suquamish* and *Montana v. United States*, addressed tribes' ability to govern and prosecute non–tribal members within their jurisdiction.[63] These rulings established case law for subsequent cases when lower courts addressed sovereignty issues such as tribes' jurisdiction over the regulation of hunting and fishing, the ability to adjudicate both civil and criminal cases regarding non–tribal members, and the right to impose zoning on non–tribal members within tribal territories.[64]

These rulings determined the geography and the people over which tribes could exercise their sovereignty. These rulings animated the geographic aspect in three primary ways: (1) tribes' autonomy over their territories was reduced, and land transactions had to be mediated through the federal government; (2) non-tribal rights-of-way traversing a tribe's jurisdiction were considered to fall under federal and state jurisdiction; and (3) a land nomenclature of open and closed areas was enacted that moderated how and when tribes could invoke zoning laws on their reservations in areas where non-Indians owned land, which were deemed open areas.[65] The U.S. Supreme Court has consistently ruled that tribes have the right to govern and tax their citizens within their political boundaries, but the court has given tribes only limited ability to govern, tax, or prosecute non–tribal members; this continues to evolve.

Based on the theory and practices of sovereignty and the interlocking ideals of self-governance and self-determination, tribal sovereignty is a form of racialized sovereignty or formal sovereignty that is enacted across different geographies. Biolsi problematizes formal sovereignty as racist and posits:

> The kind of sovereignty being honored here is a profoundly limited one—limited, in fact, to the point that it does not make logical sense to many Indian people, is not really sovereignty at all from their point of view, and can only be understood as bespeaking a profoundly racist view of Indians on the part of Congress, the courts, and white people in general.[66]

The nestedness of various political jurisdictions and the racialized notion of tribal sovereignty, then, complicates tribal jurisdiction.[67] MCN, for example, crosses several county and municipal boundaries, in addition to state lines. William C. Canby contends that tribes are sovereign and did not need an alien authority to legitimize their power to self-govern; furthermore, tribes already possess the inherent power to form governments.[68] The federal government's Indian policies have imposed actions on Mvskokvlke that resemble the assembling and disassembling of the tribe; however, Mvskokvlke have functioned and continue to function as an array of self-determining and self-governing communities—their presence is an unbroken continuum of existence. In light of nested jurisdictions, states confer the power to organize cities and counties but do not have authority over tribal nations.

The average American citizen is often perplexed by the political power of tribes.[69] Given the political complexities these boundaries pose, it is not surprising that citizens do not understand tribal issues of self-governance. A discourse that arises in Oklahoma among non-Indians, for example, is the idea that tribes are afforded some type of special treatment.[70] Oklahoma's relationships with tribes, however, have largely been steered by the federal government. The most succinct response to local contestations of tribal sovereignty is that tribes have conducted their affairs as sovereign nations, as evidenced by the treaties made between tribal nations and other countries prior to treating with the U.S. government. Before European settlement and through the beginning of the treaty-making era, tribes lived and conducted themselves in North America as autonomous nations and were regarded as such.[71]

In the contemporary geopolitical context, a tribe only has jurisdiction over its own citizens living within its political boundaries. The U.S. Supreme Court has explicitly written non–tribal members living within a tribe's political boundaries out of this equation.[72] This reduced notion of sovereignty has led to "lawless" areas in which non–tribal members can take refuge.[73] Knowing that a tribe's criminal jurisdiction becomes complicated quickly, non–tribal members target areas on Indian land for criminal activity. Ultimately, the court limited the extent of tribal political jurisdiction to the reservation boundary only. In Oklahoma, the boundary delineated by MCN's 1866 treaty functions as the tribe's jurisdictional boundary. MCN affirms that its reservation was never dissolved.[74]

Formal tribal sovereignty is an impaired racialized ideal rooted in the doctrine of discovery and crafted by the U.S. Supreme Court over the past two centuries. As such, tribal sovereignty is severely diminished in the United States. It lacks consent between two nations and is a relationship of control: Congress is not required to gain tribal consent before legislating on tribal sovereignty, and tribes cannot choose to accept or reject a congressional decision; therefore, tribal nations do not control their futures in the context of the settler government.[75] Tribal sovereignty in the United States is nebulous and contingent upon the impulses of Congress; moreover, with each new congressional law or policy, the tribal-federal relationship changes, and consequently so do the rights and obligations of tribal governments.[76] This type of sovereignty can be likened to going fishing with a short cane pole and thread, while the governing nation-state carries an eight-foot graphite rod with heavy-duty fishing line.[77] The former is shaky and weak, while the latter is robust and strong. Meanwhile, the cane pole keeps getting shorter. If the U.S. government's legal definition of sovereignty is the ceiling for formal tribal sovereignty in the United States, then the country's Native peoples continue to function from a precarious position. Formal sovereignty cannot be the ceiling on how we realize and enact self-determined communities. We do not have to ask the U.S. government for permission to enact the thoughts, beliefs, and visions of our communities.[78]

I am not proposing that tribes enact the formal idea of sovereignty enjoyed by nation-states, or even the impaired notion of tribal sovereignty in the United States, although our tribal governments continue to find resourceful ways to thrive within this limited notion of sovereignty. Rather, I propose that tribal communities enact what I call "este-cate sovereignty," a way of self-governance that is shaped by and derived from the cultural practices of Native communities. Radical sovereignty cannot be measured against normative governance systems. It is neither the impaired fishing pole nor the sleek graphite rod. Instead, este-cate sovereignty is more akin to what Mvskokvlke call "devil's shoestring" (*vloneske*), a method of fishing in which one uses one's hands to prepare and place a traditional medicine plant concoction atop the water.[79] No other equipment is necessary; devil's shoestring stuns the fish long enough to grab them with your hands. Using devil's shoestring is an example of Mvskoke praxis. It is a local community knowledge and practice.

Practices of Radical Sovereignty

I have now discussed what concepts of este-cate sovereignty look like; I have also discussed the injured nature of tribal sovereignty, which requires that we pursue este-cate sovereignty more overtly, because it offers possibilities to shape community futurities in ways that settler-controlled tribal sovereignty cannot. A Mvskoke practice of este-cate sovereignty was at one time naturalized, and now we must wrest back these practices and generatively refuse the naturalized practices of the nation-state. To generatively refuse, according to Leanne Simpson, is to refuse while still creating something effective for Indigenous peoples.[80] The politics of recognition has shaped how tribes form their governments. However, tribes have worked to inform those practices with Mvskoke knowledge—for example, legislation that supports chartered communities, ceremonial grounds, and Mvskoke churches. This prompts other questions, such as how este-cate sovereignty can enable us to actively recognize and expand upon Mvskoke practices that build community and resist settler colonial concepts of sovereignty.

A community praxis that recognizes and enacts este-cate sovereignty helps to construct an architecture of Mvskoke futurity with close attention to energy, decolonial love, self-determination, embodiment, vernacular practices, and consciousness. Radical sovereignty is invested in bolstering Mvskoke felt knowledge that we all carry, found in spiritual energy, kinship and relationality, and vnoke-ckv (decolonial love). It is important, then, to carry out this complex of energy, relationality, love, and felt knowledge in ways that empower community and instill vnokeckv and responsibility to community.

Some initial ideas of what this might look like are described as follows. First, regarding energy, recognition of energy is accomplished by honing an aware-ness to facts and data collected through our senses and emotions. For example, we speak with our bodies, and body language is powerful. Are we taking on postures of authority and superiority by placing our hands behind our heads? Honing our awareness of energy and reflecting on the message and energy our body language sends to others can reshape how we treat others and expand our awareness of how others are receiving us. However, this is not limited to human interactions, because relying on a Mvskoke concept of energy means recognizing that all elements have spiritual energy. How can we decenter our ideas of community-building so as not to focus strictly on humans? The concept of decentering human needs and desires includes other entities in a practice of este-cate sovereignty. What if we make it okay to convene and talk with our spiritual entities and elements, which include Mvskoke narratives and Mvskoke places? What changes if we imagine these elements as having a stake in how a community grows? What are other ways of perceiving spiritual energy in our communities? Star constellations, observation of human interactions, the way people are invited in or closed out—these are elements of energy transfers.

Next, a praxis of decolonial love is based foremost on love for community, which is distinct from a heterosexual notion of desire-based romantic love. To love community is to work in service to one's community. There is a dimension of responsibility—that is, an intention of concern—and a dimension of care: that is, the act of tending to community. Kinship means that all can have a role in carrying out acts of decolonial love. Also, acts of decolonial love tend to the energy and relationality between human and more-than-human kin and operate to strengthen kinship networks. Hence, decolonial love structures the resurgence and amplification of community's spiritual and relational power. What are examples, then, of a praxis of decolonial love? Leanne Betasamosake Simpson posits the idea that decolonial love means living a life that is full. Everyday acts of living a full life might be a community potluck dinner or a meal with extended family. In my own experience, my grandfather always said, "Bring what you like [to eat]," and we still say this, because there is a felt and affective quality when you share things that you enjoy with another person: you are actively carrying out good intentions for their spiritual energy, as well as tending to a relational aspect of community and kinship.

Another practice of este-cate sovereignty is self-determination, which involves personal autonomy and power. When Indigenous peoples seize control and act, this is a hallmark of self-determination. Radical sovereignty is embodied, and it goes where you go, which means that it also transcends territory. Thus the ability to move beyond fixed places that foreclose possible subjectivities can open possibilities for conceiving of a notion of este-cate sovereignty. Radical sovereignty is found in vernacular spaces and interstices. Moreover, we find este-cate sovereignty practiced in everyday moments of cultural practice, ritual, work, fun, and leisure. The everyday performance of community is an act of resistance against Indigenous elimination. Singing, dancing, or convening at a sports tournament or Mvskoke church can all be examples of este-cate sovereignty.

Consciously enacting these practices invokes the production of a Mvskoke imaginary. The imaginary transcends space, realizes community autonomy, recognizes the worth of vernacular practices of community, refuses the politics of recognition, and recognizes, realizes, and engenders the power of Mvskoke energy and kinship. Peoplehood is not tied to a space, and este-cate sovereignty is not tied to the nation-state. Refusing a settler ordering of space decolonizes spaces and untethers tribal members from federal government–assigned geopolitical geographies.

Using one certain tool of futurity—the "Where I Am From" poem template—can help community members to cultivate a sense of este-cate (radical) sovereignty and understand how they are performing este-cate sovereignty as a community. This writing exercise tells us about one's experience with family, sense of place, and vernacular spaces and practices, and it enables the writer to recognize these elements of community and attach significance to them. This writing exercise turns away from the politics of recognition and actively fills spaces with Mvskoke ways of being in the world. The writer(s) can read their produced work for aspects of este-cate sovereignty—energy, kinship, power, agency, and autonomy. The writers' analysis of this work is meant to demonstrate what dimensions are in fact operating to maintain Mvskoke people. Furthermore, this reflective analysis demonstrates to the community the ways in which they are already living a life that is full—which is the crux of decolonial love.

The "Where I Am From" exercise provides a way for individuals to articulate the cultural, community, familial, and spatial dimensions that they hold valuable. The poems can be written in a group or individually. I wrote a "Where I

Am From" poem on my own and shared later. Other times people take the template and develop a poem over days or weeks, and still other times a group writes individual poems to be shared the same day. For example, after writing their poem, each person may read it to others and share information, such as an everyday household item. This tells the collective about the experience and practices of the person and their household. A Mvskoke person writing a poem is articulating Mvskoke futurity; because the practices of being Mvskoke are embodied, describing the practices through the use of the poem articulates knowledge that might be difficult to explain. When this is performed with a group, often a pattern emerges regarding what people care about, and a community can make their own realizations about what their collective values are and what they want to create or build upon what already exists collectively.

Tool of Futurity: Este-Cate (Radical) Sovereignty

In this project I introduce Mvskoke symbols based on Mississippian iconography. While they are derived from the Southeastern Ceremonial Complex, non-Indigenous archaeologists often interpret their meaning based on Western knowledge systems. With any meaning we apply—whether the interpretation is Occidentalized or Indigenous—the originals are too far back in time for it to be proven; the best we can do is make a case for a certain interpretation. However, if we return to the initial example that I provided of the pawn shop song, whose meaning and use has likely shifted over time, perhaps it was once a diplomacy song, or used to negotiate in local bartering. Comparably, Southeastern artists are (re)appropriating the symbols of the Southeastern Ceremonial Complex and their meanings in a contemporary context. I am inspired mainly by the dynamism and movement of the repeating lines in many of the icons, which are reminiscent of the sacred—our stompdance—and the cosmological—our dialogue with the celestial realm.

Concerning the four Mississippian-inspired icons in this book, this is art that I have produced by carving print blocks and creating block prints; drawing upon existing iconography, I couple the four icons with the four tools of futurity.[81] These icons that come out of Mississippian work symbolize the natural environment, such as the wind, and they can also signify the tribal towns and the fire that are central to Mvskoke ceremonial life. My artistic and ideological interpretation of the repeating lines in the symbols is that they suggest a reiterating performance of a dance. A stompdance is performed many times throughout the night, with a different stompdance leader singing. The dance itself creates a new spatiality with each new round. This spatiality forms a spiral—some spirals might have several rings, and some might have fewer. The inner ring consists of individuals who take a leadership role to sing and shake shells. The outer rings are often children: there they are less likely to get hurt if the dance speeds up, and at the end of the line they can dance as slowly as they wish, sometimes with a parent or grandparent dancing behind them with a watchful eye. Some of the outer rings also have young people who jump in as a group, laughing and moving arms in sync to demonstrate their youthful solidarity. The dance spiral has reiterating lines or rings, with particular rings operating as sites of generational and intergenerational performance.

The este-cate (radical) sovereignty symbol in figure 5 remains true to the repeating lines and dynamic flow of the Mississippian line work. This piece embodies the ideas of kinship and energy that lie behind este-cate sovereignty—there is an ever-flowing path of energy exchanged between people and other entities such as plants and animals. This relationality never stops, but sometimes we forget how to stop, listen, and sense the messages that the energy is sending. The repeating lines express a couple of ideas. First, they indicate that the notion of relationality and kinship making is repeated over and over across many kin-space-time envelopes. Second, each of the repeating lines represents a type of relationality within the Mvskoke community, such as person to person, plant to animal, person to plant, etc.

FIGURE 5 *Este-Cate (Radical) Sovereignty*, relief print, Laura Harjo.

In este-cate sovereignty, the constant flow of energy in making and maintaining kinship is always at stake. Within our constellation of connections to humans and more-than-humans—plants, animals, spirits—resides a sustaining power and life force. We should care about este-cate sovereignty because it is a source of empowerment for the community—for communities who have been researched, who have had questions asked of them for reports that have often yielded very little, and for tribal organizations that have been involved in protracted battles with the nation-state and its concomitant apparatuses, such as the Bureau of Indian Affairs or local county governments. Through este-cate sovereignty, Mvskoke people get to see how their daily lived experience has profound meaning, especially where this lived experience is carried out with the intention of love for both community and family. The intention of love behind este-cate sovereignty carries weight and meaning, and despite its potential dismissal as emotive, it has profound connotation. Love produces spaces and places that have sustained Mvskoke people through epochs of trauma—forced removal, genocide, and the dispossession of their land. Moreover, in times and places where there was no semblance of normative governance systems, Mvskoke people have sustained themselves through songs and connections to Hesaketvmese and produced sacred space during the Mvskoke removal for our relatives' spirits to travel to the next place. Este-cate sovereignty performs responsibility to kin with vnokeckv. Actions performed with love that maintain and create kinship connections despite the trauma of settler colonialism are este-cate sovereignty. There are some who might snicker at the emotive aspects, but suffice it to say that este-cate sovereignty maintains Mvskoke people through moments of life and death.

A (re)conception of sovereignty in which action, power, and agency are moved from the national scale to the scale of the body, household, and community makes possible a liberation at these more local and individual scales. Pulling power closer to the body can increase one's agency and possibility of action. Spatialities in proximity to the body can lend themselves to a sort of freedom. With this embodiment of power in the individual and community, new subjectivities are imagined, and Mvskoke-produced geographies such as stompdance, the fiddle dance, etc. emerge as sites in which the new subjectivities are formed and carried out. Conversely, there may be hierarchies of gender, race, class, ability, and sexuality operating in ways that obstruct individuals from acting in agentive ways. For example, the right to the security of one's body is enshrined in human rights policy; however, because of the way that gender, race, and class operate, a woman might not be in a position in her community to have her claims and wishes recognized. If she is in a community where domestic violence is normalized, then to act in an agentive manner might put her at risk of violent consequences for acting outside of the norms and rules of "allowable" behavior.

It would make sense to argue that because this notion of freedom and sovereignty is embodied, all Mvskoke people have the potential to achieve it. Freedom operates in the everyday, and we are already performing it. Therefore, everyone can conceivably begin to read and analyze his or her own experiences as acts of este-cate sovereignty, which is a form of freedom. I had to rely on this form of sovereignty in spaces that were hostile to Indigenous ways of knowing the world.

The act of recognizing and resisting settler ideologies—which manifest as practices that look to the nation-state for recognition of tribal concerns, or as intra- and intertribal gendered politics—is a form of este-cate sovereignty and a form of power. It actively refuses both settler practices and grievance claims to settler structures, and consciously endeavors to take up more space with practices of este-cate sovereignty that tend to Mvskoke energy and kinship. Este-cate sovereignty examines community practices for gender hierarchies in the community that silence some to the benefit of others—for example, refusing to hear what women or youth want in a community or pretending there is not a Two Spirit / queer (2SQ) constituency, while men have full agency to shape the community and its future.[82]

The cost of not knowing or realizing how we enact este-cate sovereignty on a daily basis is that we are left without fully realizing the power in our everyday experiences; it means spending our lives believing there is one way to enact sovereignty and clutching to a form of sovereignty for which the nation-state sets the language, the rules, and the stage. Under the rule of formal sovereignty, tribes are responsible for integrating their ideals of sovereignty—concepts such as food sovereignty and cultural sovereignty—into tribal codes and federal policy. However, este-cate sovereignty is the everyday practice of sustaining, empowering, and emboldening the Mvskoke community. Este-cate sovereignty is a principle for moving and thinking in the world so that we can see what is of value; it lets us see that what is in the everyday is not banal but profound, because it makes space in which to be Mvskoke and recognizes and resists settler colonial ideologies and practices.

Some of the more positive implications of este-cate sovereignty are that it recuperates and edifies from many perspectives. In a spatiotemporal sense, it denaturalizes settler colonial ideologies of space and place and the Western ordering of Indigenous spaces. It allows for spatiotemporal speculations that connect past, present, and future through spatial practices mediated by individuals and community, such as taking space, unfixing places and ways of being, and speculating on past, present, and future. Radical sovereignty works in ways that build people and communities up, honoring their vernacular experiences as full of meaning. In addition, the person and/or community (re)collects their power—the power they feel when with community at a softball tournament, a festival, a dance, or a church service. Este-cate sovereignty calls on those moments and resists the narrative of broken community, authored by outsiders, that becomes internalized and enacted by community members. When communities play, sing, and dance, this is a form of resistance that concretizes resilience. Radical/este-cate sovereignty operates where the este-cate is, and thus it is not fixed in place. Where the este-cate walks, sits, stands, dances, or runs, so too does este-cate sovereignty travel. Finally, este-cate sovereignty produces space for a personal and community practice of este-cate sovereignty—and inspires a whole community to speculate together on a present and a future. The lush promise operates in many ways—we have seen it, we already know it, and we are living it because it exists in the everyday. The lush promise can be unfixed from the Mvskoke territory defined by the settler government, for it is enacted in spaces where Mvskoke people are, regardless of geopolitical boundaries. The lush promise is in movement and emergence, which are Mvskoke practices of futurity.

Summary: Radical Sovereignty

In this chapter, I have defined este-cate sovereignty and its relationship to the lush promise; further, I have discussed these ideas against the grain of settler colonialism, the logics of which are in constant motion to eliminate Indigenous peoples. Este-cate sovereignty is a form of embodied and personal sovereignty comprised of energy, kinship, and felt knowledge. It can operate on many scales: on a personal scale, on a community scale, or across a region among Indigenous peoples who share common land and cultural practices.

I have identified the idea of a Mvskoke imaginary—the lush promise—and connected this to the concept of este-cate sovereignty. I provide examples of kinship connections to kin-space-time envelopes where empowering felt knowledge and memory dwell. Further, I present examples of the prevailing notions of sovereignty, in which the community reacts and responds to oppressive systems. Thus the community is continually shaped by that which it centers. I conclude by presenting este-cate sovereignty as a way of finding our way back to the dimensions of Mvskoke lifeways that make us full: energy, kinship, and relationality. It thus operates to (1) fill our lives with positive affect, (2) generate self-determined agency and power, and (3) problematize and fill the void of normative practices of sovereignty, especially with regard to land.

Este-cate sovereignty is a way-finding tool for recognizing and practicing the ways in which kinship making in the community sustains us, in order to find our way back to our empowerment. We should care about este-cate sovereignty because it is power seized on a daily basis, and in many ways we practice it without even being aware of it. It is important because prevailing ideas of tribal sovereignty are not working to their fullest. Further, it is critical because kinship, energy, and relationality are key components that structure community—or the geographies and relations that we wish to participate in. Este-cate sovereignty empowers the community by recognizing and mobilizing agency that is bound up in kin, and it also resists settler colonial structures and practices of elimination. It builds upon the everyday practices in the community. It is also a building block for the next concept or tool, described in the next chapter: community knowledge. Este-cate sovereignty enables us to see the power that we already have; community knowledge then further validates this awareness and places it in dialogue with other community members to help us find our way to the next world.

CHAPTER 2

Mapping Speculations
to the Next World

*In the last days of the fourth world I wished to make a map for those who
would climb through the hole in the sky.*
*My only tools were the desires of humans as they emerged from the killing
fields, from the bedrooms and the kitchens.*
For the soul is a wanderer with many hands and feet.
*The map must be of sand and can't be read by ordinary light. It must
carry fire to the next tribal town, for renewal of spirit.*
*In the legend are instructions on the language of the land, how it was we
forgot to acknowledge the gift, as if we were not in it or of it.*

—Joy Harjo, "Map to the Next World"

The act of recognizing the ways we produce knowledge, honoring its power, and activating it in service to the community functions as a way-finding tool to futurity and the lush promise. The primary argument of this chapter is that people and the collective represented by the community hold valuable knowledge; this knowledge is practiced, embodied, and only known from individual positionalities. Despite attempts by the settler state and its agents to eliminate Mvskoke knowledge and livelihoods, Mvskoke knowledge persists because it is embodied and because it is practiced collectively. Attending to embodied and practiced knowledge can have a role in revealing subjugated knowledges, helping us discern what community members care about and want to grow in their communities and the actions they believe will best serve in creating these things.

Thus, to speculate about the future and to produce a map to the next world, it is necessary to explicate how Mvskoke knowledge is produced and discuss how it can counter and decolonize settler colonial knowledge production and empower the Mvskoke community. By *empower*, I mean "empowerment that is tied to an analysis of power relations and a recognition of systemic oppressions."[1]

Speculation enables the community to draw upon their knowledge to recognize their current state and conceive of extending their communities in ways that they care about, now and in the future. Discovering the presence, power, and importance of embodied knowledge is an act of futurity as well as resistance, because it marks Indigenous knowledge as important and meaningful in the current moment and in the future.

If este-cate sovereignty informs us that Mvskoke people already possess the capability and the agency to create and envision their communities, then the map is a way-finding tool through which that very capability is articulated with Mvskoke knowledge and Mvskoke desires. In the epigraph above, Mvskoke poet Joy Harjo chronicles the emergence of Mvskoke people from the killing fields, where their land, life, and many ways of being in the world have been dispossessed, displaced, and extinguished.[2] The map is the way-finding tool used to examine critical tensions between the negative legacies of Mvskoke displacement from the Southeast, the shifting conditions and relationship of the tribal nation to the nation-state, and the desire to maintain Mvskoke ways of life. A map to the next world is a map of futurity. Made of sand, it is ephemeral and responds to Mvskoke conditions and needs. A map made of sand can be made by anyone and does not demand high-end tools, specialized cartographic language, or the technology of digital cartography. Rather, it can be guided by embodied local or community knowledge. The map as a tool of futurity, then, is created from wishes to maintain Mvskoke lifeways, including language, community, ceremonial grounds, medicinal practices, and values like vnokeckv (love), generosity, and reciprocity. The legibility of the map is for the people themselves and not any other authority or interlocutor.

Indigenous Knowledge Production

Recognizing the process of knowledge production is important because episte-mology, which is a way of thinking about or knowing the world, is constructed within a set of social relations and processes; a methodology is how you are going to use community epistemology to "gain more knowledge about your reality."[3] At the He Manawa Whenua Indigenous Research Conference in Hamilton, New Zealand, Veronica Tawhai, a plenary speaker, quoted Maori scholar Shirley Mutu, urging us to take up space first with Indigenous knowledge before proceeding to learn and teach settler histories. Often we argue and chronologically trace knowledge commencing with published theorists. However, I argue that starting with the Indigenous community means commencing with embodied knowledge and lifeways that have been practiced for longer than the academic knowledge often used as a "starting point" has been published.

Other paradigms that focus on subjugated knowledge create space for Indigenous knowledge. In the prevailing knowledge and methodological norms, there is a knowledge regime at work, one that is bound to the Enlightenment period and to truth with a capital *T*, accessed through positivist and scientific methods.[4] The researcher is cast as the expert, observing and examining a research object; the researcher is not in relationship with the research object, which is distanced from the expert. This sort of knowledge production also adheres to ideas such as research "objectivity" and "neutrality," and serves to shape prevailing ideas of knowledge production in the academy.[5] Critical theories such as feminism, critical ethnic studies, and critical Indigenous studies disrupt these naturalized processes and theories of approaching knowledge.[6] These critical theories have opened space for Indigenous research paradigms to be practiced despite other prevailing research paradigms, like rational planning, which privilege settler epistemologies and positivist ways of understanding and planning communities that are not equipped to function with Indigenous community knowledges.[7] This is crucial work for community and academic contexts where Indigenous people might otherwise struggle to be understood; however, it's just as important to make our knowledge visible to ourselves, which is the purpose of the work of Maggie Walter and Chris Andersen, who use Indigenous epistemologies with data and statistics.[8]

Indigenous knowledge production is invested in creating and maintaining relationships, mutually beneficial exchange (the win/win idea), collective memory, and knowledge that is practical and useful, helping to extend meaning-making within the community.[9] For example, knowledge production can be found in practices related to sustenance—when and where to plant, when to harvest corn, or when and where to find deer.

Mvskoke Knowledge

Mvskoke communities produce knowledge in a range of ways, which I will explicate in the context of Mvskoke authors, research justice scholars, and an Indigenous feminist analysis. I begin first with locating the various ways that

Mvskoke knowledge production presents itself; I then identify some Mvskoke knowledge production practices, and I end with a discussion of epistemologies of land and time. Knowledge production is important because Mvskokvlke are assigning value to the knowledge that is produced. Knowledge has a social location and is socially constructed, and the truth is an action—that is, the search to create understanding.[10] For Mvskoke people, there are a number of ways to recognize how knowledge is produced. It is produced through feeling an experience, daydreaming, observing elements of the physical world, and sensing and intuiting relational energy, metaphysical energy, and entities.

Felt Knowledge

One component of Mvskoke community knowledge is felt knowledge, which is experienced and embodied, and is a counter to academic knowledge production that is "structured to privilege non-disabled, White, heterosexual, middle class men" and that "subscribes to the academic pretense that biases can and should be eliminated because of their potential invalidating effect on the research."[11] Indigenous community knowledge production gets dismissed in the academy for not fitting with normative approaches of so-called bias-free and objective research.[12] The body is an archive of experiences where knowledge is also produced and held.[13] Particular bodies are imbued with privilege, while others are simply treated like they do not belong.

The body indeed operates as an archive. It experiences and keeps felt knowledge, embodied and practiced. Also related to energy and feeling is the knowledge produced through music and movement. Mvskoke songs and dance are acts of performance that trigger memories.[14] They are performance cartographies that hold memories, invoking knowledge and relationality and operating to open a range of kin-space-time envelopes to dancers and listeners.

Smelt Knowledge

Smell is also a stimulus that holds memories and produces knowledge.[15] For example, Golden Pride in Albuquerque is a restaurant known widely for its award-winning breakfast burritos, fried chicken, and smoked meat. Its food draws a lengthy line of cars that snakes behind the restaurant, from which one can smell meat smoking. This smell mirrors the smell of the cook fire at the stompgrounds; thus, even hundreds of miles away from the stompgrounds, smell as knowledge invokes the performance cartography of the stompdance spiral and related activities, such as the women cooking outside, preparing a Green Corn feast for everybody. Knowledge is produced through location; however, the knowledge does not stay fixed to that location, but travels and shifts to assist in making meaning. The felt knowledge gained through the olfactory sense invokes a connection between New Mexico and the stompgrounds in Oklahoma—and, I would surmise, a connection to the original Mvskoke etvl-was in Alabama and Georgia.

Dream Knowledge

Another example of knowledge produced in the original etvlwas and renegoti-ated in the contemporary moment is knowledge about supernatural beings such as Tie-Snake, a water being whose story we carried with us from the Southeast, where Mvskoke people originally lived along the Ocmulgee, Coosa, Tallapoosa, Flint, and Chattahoochee Rivers.[16] Knowledge about Tie-Snake continues to be produced but is not fixed to the stories' places of origin in Alabama and Georgia: Tie-Snake appears in contemporary fiction, comic book narratives, and traditional Mvskoke stories, making its way to Lake Eufaula in Oklahoma and to the outer-space Mvskoke Nation in Starr's graphic story "Ue-Pucase."[17] In Craig S. Womack's novel *Drowning in Fire*, the young Mvskoke protagonist, Josh, gets his leg tangled in a fishing line while hiding under a dock trying to trick his friends into believing he has possibly drowned. When his friends grow increasingly nervous, Josh relents and finally decides to end the prank and swim to the surface to surprise them, but the fishing line cuts into his leg, pulling him underwater; Josh slips off to the underworld of Tie-Snake. In a dream sequence, his visit with Tie-Snake is an instance of bending time and space: he relives the origin story of earthdiver, inhabiting a place accessible to very few, and he spends four days in the underworld in a period of a few minutes.[18] Tie-Snake warns Josh not to divulge what he has witnessed and provides him with a ritual that he can use to summon the water being when needed. Josh's dream comes during a near-drowning experience, and in this space, or interstice between material and metaphysical, Josh produces knowledge about and with a storied Mvskoke being. Here Mvskoke knowledge is located in a dream state and in the inner world of imagination and fantasies: throughout *Drowning in Fire*, Womack invites the reader into Josh's interiority as he grapples with coming of age in small-town Oklahoma, where the prevailing norms and mores conflict with his sexuality and feelings. Josh observes social relations and parses them through his daydreams—daydreams in which he takes flight or imagines a relationship with his crush. His acts of imagining, experiencing, and thinking in interstices help him to make meaning of his surrounding environment. He is actively producing knowledge in Eufaula, in Weleetka, and at Wheeler Park in Oklahoma City.

Observational Knowledge

Knowledge is produced and understood through observation. Fixico argues that Creek and Seminole traditionalists' process of knowledge production begins first with watching, listening, and waiting for signs.[19] Mvskoke people have produced knowledge about their relationships with the surrounding environment, the stars, and the metaphysical world. Observation of flora, fauna, and weather produces information as well, especially in times of climate change—at a local scale, the community can discern if the summer is blistering and dry, with fewer turtles. Locals paying attention to the weather might notice extreme weather events. The observation of animals can also speak volumes—noticing where and when they gather, where they travel for water, when they flee, when they are quiet, or when they are acting erratically. Observing a Mvskoke notion of energy as it is transferred and exchanged between people, more-than-human entities, and entities of the metaphysical world is a form of knowledge production.

Stargazing Knowledge

Mvskoke people have always been in dialogue with the stars. Knowledge is present in the stars; Mvskoke people have observed the planets throughout time and still do today, for instruction and renewal of their life force. The movement of planets indicates times to plant and times to hold Green Corn Dances, and constellations hold a place for Mvskoke heroes and narratives. As mentioned earlier, the three stars of Orion's belt are noted as the place we pass through when we leave our physical bodies, to travel to the source of all energy.[20] Star lore across the world is shaped and influenced by positionality—physical location on earth, and cultural and social location. Mvskoke people—Alabama etvlwa and Seminole—viewed the Ursa Major constellation as part of a canoe, as do other peoples from Bali, Okinawa, the Marshall Islands, and the Aleut Islands.[21] In the poem "Remember," Joy Harjo writes, "Remember the sky that you were born under, know each of the star's stories," which is a reminder that we make meaning through our relationship to the stars—specifically here, the position of the stars when one's spiritual energy is born into a material form.[22] This situates one within a larger realm than the immediately local, and within a truth larger than the rational, "provable," "replicable" truth. It opens spaces for a wider swath of Mvskoke organizing principles to be recognized and put into operation.

Cultural Worker Knowledge

Our Mvskoke cultural workers—poets, artists, dancers, musicians, and singers— open possibilities and show us how we (re)emerge today. Knowledge is art, and Mvskoke artists are producing art that renders our cosmologic knowledge and our ancient symbology from the Southeast, and that has practical uses for today. Mvskoke jeweler Kenneth Johnson produces jewelry that represents renegotiated Mississippian-era symbology, which I discuss further in chapter 3.

Knowledge is produced in many locations and can occur anywhere and everywhere, not solely in spaces deemed Mvskoke territory. It is located wherever the practitioner performs knowledge production; with this experience, they are producing Mvskoke space. Arigon Starr is a Mvskoke performer based in Los Angeles who carries her narratives to and fro along Interstate 40, a primary connector between Los Angeles and Oklahoma, working through her ideas for her creative projects while driving. Her travels take her beyond the I-40 corridor, and her Mvskoke stories and performance in the form of songs, acting, comic books, graphic novels, and theater flow to places beyond the two mentioned, but the primary argument here is that she is a Mvskoke person who is not fixed in place and who nevertheless creates and shares narratives in a contemporary moment in a variety of spaces, also producing new Mvskoke geographies.

Practicing Lifeways as Knowledge

Practicing lifeways is knowledge production, and Mvskoke knowledge is found in practices including stompdance, gathering as a community, worshipping in Mvskoke churches, speaking Creek, singing in Creek, dancing, and preparing ceremonial grounds and camps for dances. We can see there are myriad ways of enacting Mvskoke identity, which thus socially produce a range of Mvskoke epistemologies. Mvskokvlke make meaning in a context of community norms and mores, which might vary from community to community; whether it is an online Mvskoke community, urban Mvskoke community, Mvskoke church community, ceremonial ground community, or sports community, different epistemologies can be shaped and emerge from them. For example, there are different dialects and spellings of Mvskoke-language words that vary within MCN and in other geographies that Mvskokvlke inhabit. Thus Mvskoke people, like any other Indigenous group, can have various highly nuanced epistemologies. Mvskoke knowledge practices are present in song, art, stories, plays, comic books, film, books, star stories, stargazing, community dinners, and online community discussion boards, all of which are forms of Mvskoke energy and lifeways. The actions that Mvskoke people are performing are Mvskoke practices, which we can see when we read the Mvskoke phenomenon of the wild onion dinner.

Every spring is wild onion dinner season, when Mvskoke people converge on the local community center or Mvskoke church for fundraising dinners. It is rare to find restaurants in Oklahoma that serve wild onion dinner fare.[23] Community folks must rely on their local Mvskoke cooks to prepare wild onions with eggs, salt meat, fried potatoes, pinto beans, fry bread, and pie, which is the standard. These gatherings often have large communal tables where people eat and visit with one another, reaching out to strangers and easily pulling them into a conversation. A full range of topics include tribal politics, whether people think an elected official is carrying out their work honestly and fairly, and the harvesting or purchase of wild onions. People might not reveal their personal wild onion harvest site, but they might discuss the going rate for a quart of cleaned onions, or where one might procure onions. The dinners are a Mvskoke practice that draws people regardless of their ideological stances; regardless of which side of the tribal politics fence they stand on, everyone has to eat. While everyone might not have a taste for wild onions, there is often plenty of other food to choose from and plenty of social relations.

The community learns about the dinners through word of mouth and the MCN newspaper, *Muscogee Nation News*, which advertises the dinners. Tribal members can map out their plans to attend the dinners on a weekly basis. These dinners rely on Mvskoke individuals' organizing and coordination to purchase, prepare, and serve the food, as well as do the post-dinner clean up. The dinners' primary purpose is to raise funds for a community or a Mvskoke church. There is knowledge required in securing funds to purchase the food and in asking for donations; further, there is knowledge required to prepare Mvskoke dishes.

Even in serving the food there is protocol, and there is protocol in where you sit. If one were to sit back and observe, wishing to make meaning out of this space, it would begin to unfold: Who is sitting together? Are there any seats for elders coming in the door? Do you need to give up your seat? Do you see old friends or relatives you have not seen in a long time? The bottom line is that Mvskoke people come out in droves not only to eat their knowledge production, but to communicate knowledge through dialogue as well.

The wild onion dinners across Mvskoke land are locations where community dialogue takes place. Mvskoke dialogue takes many forms, and the practice of dialogue occurs in any number of situations: not only in conversational dialogue, but also in practices such as the call-and-response in the performance of stompdance, or in joking, teasing, and humor between family and friends. In the call-and-response of stompdance, the stompdance leader calls out a verse and the other men respond in verse. Caller and responder are producing a relational exchange, and this is a form of dialogue and of knowledge. This kind of song dialogue has a role in producing the stompdance spiral.

Joking and taunting humor is another form of call-and-response dialogue, as illustrated by the "your mama" jokes that I engage in with my family and friends—my personal favorite is "Your mama is so old her clan is Pterodactyl." This form of humor is not limited to "your mama" jokes, but also includes making fun of each other or "ragging" on each other, all of which operates as a callout to an individual who responds with their own joke. Each response in the dialogue gets increasingly biting until one person gives up. All of this takes place in a good-natured manner. Humorous banter produces a form of relationality and kinship; knowing someone well enough to crack jokes at their mother's expense indicates a close relation.[24] Forming a bond and a relationship is an important aspect of community dialogue. However, humor should be applied contextually. For example, there needs to be an equal power dynamic: when the real or perceived power dynamic is not equal, then it is just an insult. Mvskoke knowledge is in the community, co-created and developed in dialogue. Dialogue, whether according to formal or informal notions, produces knowledge. The tools of futurity and activities in chapter 6 are intended to produce primarily intentional forms of dialogue; they involve convening groups of people to discuss and share their knowledge. As I trace the many ways in which dialogue and knowledge production present themselves, I argue that Mvskoke ways of knowing or epistemologies operate to govern Mvskoke knowledge production.

An example of how Mvskoke ways of knowing govern knowledge production is illustrated in Mvskoke epistemologies of land. Mvskoke land epistemologies help Mvskoke communities understand the ways in which land is used;
the stories produced in our communities of origin are still carried with us and
produce new Mvskoke spaces. The epigraph from Joy Harjo's "Map to the Next
World" is instructive as a Mvskoke land epistemology because it reveals the way
original land practices and narratives operated in Mvskoke community.[25] A
Mvskoke land epistemology is created from elements of the land, relationships
to the land, stories of the land, and how it feels to be involved in all these aspects;
in other instances, it is created from relationships that are not place-bound, such
as relationships with people or stars. Based on these relationships, we imbue
meaning into communities that are not fixed on the land or place-bound. When
a community creates its map, it means identifying the aspects of community and
Mvskoke lifeways that we wish to maintain or renovate. Joy Harjo's poem coun-
sels readers to create a way or plan to carry forward the social and sacred milieu,
the fire, to the next rendering of our tribal towns, which is the next world. The
land tells us how to make a map, and those who know the land can instruct us.
However, we must acknowledge the gifts that the land provides to us, including
story, place, sustenance, and belonging. The land is not a static object; it is alive,
it is kin, and the epistemologies from the woodlands of the Southeast are just
as alive as renegotiated Mvskoke epistemologies from the southern plains and
from the concrete and glass sitting atop the land in Los Angeles.

The gift of land operates in multiple ways, offering life-sustaining elements—
water, food, fuel for fire. It also holds stories of place. Mvskoke stories that
emerge from land epistemologies include narratives of Tie-Snake when one
is near water, narratives about owls, and spirit stories when it is dark outside.
Stories of these entities inform us how to conduct ourselves in the world, or
are informed by historical moments, or are harbingers of death, possibly urging
someone to get their affairs in order or be cautious. Further, Mvskoke people
have stories about water and rivers that are born from these dynamic places
and give us instruction. We carried place names from the Southeast, and in
Oklahoma there are water-based place names such as Okmulgee, Weleetka,
Wetumka, and Okemah. These place names are reminders of the lush promise.

Mvskoke ways of knowing also govern concepts of time and collapse the
commonly received idea of a time-space continuum. In Western culture, the
birth and death of an individual often serve as bookends for a person's life.
Mvskoke people, however, like many other Indigenous peoples, remain in con-

versation with and in relationship to their ancestors. Cultural or spiritual values, for Mvskokvlke, mean answering to an elder or to our ancestors. This belief system allows us to have a type of kinship relationship with our values. Our values keep us "in check" the same way our relatives or ancestors keep us "in check," to take care of us and keep us safe, well, and happy. We have a responsibility to our ancestors and to the values that sustained them and brought them joy. If our collective values fail us, Mvskoke people readjust, the same way our ancestor relatives would have. In this instance, time is not modulated by productivity, nor by life; it is modulated by relationality.

In contrast to Mvskoke epistemologies of time, the settler colonial notion of time divides it into segments to support a bigger capitalist machine.[26] Moreover, settler colonial ideas of time are extremely gendered. In many Western societies, a settler colonial notion of time dictates, for example, that men and women should be in specific spaces at specific times. Men work outside of the home during the day, while women spend their time in the home supporting a male's work role; local scales are viewed as the realm of women.[27] Societies did not divide time into labor, leisure, or fun before capitalist regimes took hold in various Western nations.[28] Academic research in Indian country becomes problematic when it requires a quick question-answer interaction based on settler colonial notions of time. Sometimes it may take an entire lifetime to get an answer from an individual: if the receiver is deemed to be a good steward of the knowledge to be shared, then perhaps it will be shared. Taking an ethical approach to this dilemma requires researchers to adapt their methodologies to the pace of their participants. This approach can run counter to the "publish or perish" world of academia, as the turnaround time of participatory work is often much slower than that of standard academic methodologies.[29]

One example of a Mvskoke way of knowing time is related to the idea of starting on time. During a workshop that I conducted with Mvskoke and Cherokee participants, we did not start at the specified time. The cofacilitators seemed a little uncomfortable at the fact that it was already well past 9:00 a.m. and everyone seemed to be casually visiting with one another. Making kinship connections came first—establishing and cultivating relationality took primacy over starting on time. The same can be said about other Mvskoke community functions: in less formal sites, relationality is prioritized over all else.

Knowledge production, ways of dialoguing, and Mvskoke epistemologies are way-finding tools to futurity because they help us recognize our knowledge and share how we understand the world; we all understand the world through different lenses. This process validates who we are, what we know, and what we practice. Knowledge production relates to the Mvskoke imaginary in many ways—as a spiritual journey, a sacred journey, the production of relationality, the cognizance of knowledge from one's natal community, and embodied knowledge. Mvskoke scholar Victoria Bomberry writes, "We still have our words, language, memory, and imagination to help us through," insisting that Mvskoke knowledge production provides us with the tools to imagine.[30] Further, Joy Harjo shows us what it looks like to be in movement, traveling, and using the power of smell to remember and instantiate a kinship connection with more-than-human beings; in her first book of poetry, *She Had Some Horses*, she expresses the sense of a sacred and spiritual interstice that connects her to horses and to her relatives and other Mvskoke people who continue to love horses despite the draw to love their cars and trucks.[31] The relationality and energy between nonhuman and human within a sacred interstice connects to the physical and metaphysical realms. She writes, "There was the horse that came to see me once in the middle of a long drive north from Las Cruces, New Mexico to Albuquerque. I perceived him first by an ancient and familiar smell. Then I was broken open by memory when he nudged me, in that space that is always around and through us, a space not defined or bound by linear time or perception."[32] Harjo is producing Mvskoke space in her moment of relationality with the horse; in her relationality, she is in dialogue with him through his smell and spirit. In the in-between space, much like Womack's drowning/dreaming sequence, there is a sacred journey of remembering and feeling the embodied knowledge of her natal community—their stories, their practices, and their relationship to animals. Further, when she writes that she was "broken open by memory when he nudged me," her embodied archive is enacting, through smell and touch, a Mvskoke imaginary that invokes and spirals together the memories and moments of many kin-space-time envelopes of her relatives' relationship with horses, filling the interstitial space between her and the horse.

Mvskoke knowledge is not produced in the objective, detached manner in which "conventional" knowledge operates; instead it acknowledges the relationality of many realms and elements, such as those that Harjo experiences with the horse. Mvskoke knowledge production is a spiritual journey; it recognizes natal community and spiritual realms as sources of knowledge, and it recognizes how we embody our natal community and our spiritual realm. The knowledge is embodied and hard-earned through experience. Mvskokvlke do not easily divulge their knowledge and experiences to non-Mvskokvlke, especially to a state apparatus that does not treat their knowledge with dignity.

Mvskoke Knowledge Praxis

A Mvskoke knowledge praxis operates as a theory/practice dialectic that recognizes where, when, and how knowledge is created and practiced; further, Mvskoke knowledge praxis generates theory from community practices. Doherty argues that "praxis is the process of applying theory through practice to develop more informed theory and practice, specifically as it relates to social change."[33] A Mvskoke knowledge praxis is employed to deepen an understanding of Mvskoke ways of understanding the world and to inform our community practice, and I maintain that we continually recalibrate our theories and practices in response to practical experience. What's more, the continual recalibration process of a Mvskoke knowledge praxis provides us ways of transforming communities that (re-)center Mvskoke epistemologies.

Therefore, this book crystallizes one particular moment in time according to one person's positionality, but even these theories should be moving and in transformation as conditions change. As we gain fuller stories, as we fill out our knowledge, as we develop and create new possibilities and live and experience within those new possibilities, our theories and praxis will shift. We are always returning to community-generated knowledge that is gained from the lived experiences and practices of community, which subsequently generates community-based theories that shape how to build a community. We constantly reiterate this process of renovating theory and practice into an effective praxis. Knowledge production should be concerned with yielding theory and praxis that elevate a community's wishes and concerns. Here Brown and Strega articulate the purpose of the knowledge creation process:

> Historically, the knowledge creation process has been separated from concerns about praxis: theorizing about the political nature of knowledge creation has rarely been translated into transforming our research practices. This book is deeply concerned with research as praxis, so the authors in this volume move continually between theory and practice, reflecting on how innovative and critical research theories might be applied, and then modifying theories because of their practice experience.[34]

As this quotation demonstrates, knowledge production and the relationship between research and practice are constantly being renovated; practice and reflection on this practice can deeply inform Mvskoke theory. Mvskoke practice illuminates Mvskoke theory, and this was evident in my doctoral fieldwork when I checked the survey with the community before it went live and involved family in the research process. This illustrates the relationship between research and practice, which I discuss more at length in chapter 4. I used a variety of methods to administer a community survey, including distributing it online and printing it to bring to meetings and to a major festival. Further, I read the survey to an elder and populated the survey with his answers. From this I learned a few things: that people needed a place to dialogue, that they wanted to know that it was safe to share their personal opinions without worrying about implications for their current or future employment with MCN, that people have different abilities and plan to accommodate accordingly, and that particular age groups were present at the festival where I administered the survey during different times of the day. The times of day at which different age cohorts attend the festival shape a Mvskoke praxis for community knowledge production.

A Mvskoke knowledge praxis enables the community to recognize its embodied knowledge, to create and act in the present moment in ways that attend to a present temporality, and to activate our relatives' unactivated possibilities. Yakama scholar Michelle Jacob posits that a Yakama knowledge praxis is based in everyday practices and that Indigenous bodies are sites of critical pedagogy.[35] Further, Indigenous bodies have the potential to operationalize a vast array of knowledge to imagine another world and determine the actions required right now to realize the imagined community futurity. An important aspect of these praxis processes is that the community produces, owns, and exchanges knowledge and maintains agency, power, and authorship over it. Communities are making power as they realize their modes of knowledge production, dialogue collectively, and write their own stories from the point of view of Fixico's Third Door. Oversight, ownership, and control of their knowledge and its presentation and narration is power.[36]

In figure 6, Daniel McCoy depicts a Mvskoke vision of the search for utopia, which juxtaposes his father, an El Camino truck with plates that read "MVTO"—which means "thank you" in Mvskoke—a mobile home next to running water, and a temple mound from a Mvskoke etvlwa. McCoy states, "We had a very basic house on an allotment in Eastern Oklahoma. I had all the things you'd ever need. Now, when I hear about issues of sustainability, a

FIGURE 6 *Ceaseless Quest for Utopia*, mural painting, Daniel McCoy Jr. Personal collection of the artist.

kind of back-to-the-earth type movement, eating better, living better, I grew up with all that. I'm very thankful for that, but at the time I didn't want that. I wanted what I saw on television. I wanted to be like Elliott in *E. T.*, riding my bicycle in the suburbs or something like that. I just didn't have that."[37] Movement through time and space reshapes knowledge: McCoy now lives in Santa Fe and invokes a renegotiated knowledge of his community of origin, reflecting that he had everything he needed but in his younger experience yearned for something different.

Decolonizing knowledge and valuing Mvskoke knowledge are imperative. Community knowledge is embodied, making it sacred, and therefore it deserves ethical, decolonized handling. Previous work in communities has proven that there can be problematic practices within them whereby individuals arrive to extract knowledge.[38] The work may be referred to as community engagement or participatory work; however, simply using the word *community* does not translate into socially just practices. Knowledge can be produced in unintentional ways through the practice of Mvskoke lifeways, or it can be produced intentionally. In the latter, intentional method, knowledge production consists of approaches to which I will now turn. Decolonizing knowledge production requires us to reflect on the degree to which the work being carried out is truly participatory. Sherry Arnstein provides a framework against which participatory work can be measured—in particular, whether what is being called "participatory" is actually hollow and disingenuous, not engaging fully with a community.[39] She lays out a hierarchy within which groups involved in participatory work can situate their projects to understand the degree to which people are actually "participating," meaning that their concerns and wishes are shaping a community narrative.[40] Arnstein parses a range of "participatory" practices into three major categories: (1) citizen power, (2) tokenism, and (3) nonparticipation.[41] Though Arnstein was writing in 1969, her insights are still useful today in terms of community work. The approaches she identifies as nonparticipation are a substitute for genuine participation, and Arnstein argues that nonparticipation is when a researcher or outsider attempts to "educate" or "cure" a given community. Within the tokenism category is the idea that participants will "have their voices heard," and their concerns are listened to but not acted upon. The idiom "having one's voice heard" is problematic from two perspectives. First, it reduces people's desires to an object—a voice—which is a rhetorical move that abstracts their concerns, thus stealing their thunder or diminishing the force of their specific arguments. Second, to be heard does not necessarily translate to having one's desires recognized or acted on. Another researcher/community dynamic occurs when community participants lack the knowledge to flip power levers on to create transformation, and when, further, there is a lack of interest on the part of researchers or outsiders who convene the community participants. It is in such moments that community participation is tokenism—when researchers, politicians, or planners consult with the community without attempts to change the status quo.

A truer participatory practice involves individuals in forming and answering a research question, involves a community in a planning process, or creates the conditions of decolonial love and community recuperation. While all the tools in this book can be used to address research, planning, organizing, and other such forms of engagement, the locus of the kind of Indigenous futurity that I am proposing works to recognize the unstoppable energy of our kin. A powerful example of this is the *Walking with Our Sisters* moccasin art installation, spearheaded by Métis artist Christi Belcourt. She wished to create an art project that honored the Indigenous women and girls who have gone missing or been murdered in Canada, and eventually realized that she could not complete hundreds of moccasin vamps (tops) on her own.[42]

Moccasins are common to many Indigenous communities, and Belcourt made a call on Facebook for artists to create and share beaded moccasin vamps for the WWOS memorial project. Tracy Bear relays the story that Belcourt grew a little worried as the deadline date neared for the moccasin vamps, but, in the way that Indigenous epistemologies of time are bent by social relations, on the day of the deadline the post office was flooded with packages from all over. In a 2014 interview Belcourt states that she originally asked for 600 pairs and received over 1,700; she further states that some families never talk about their loss because it hurts too much, and so the moccasin tops she received beyond the 600 she asked for also represent unacknowledged women and girls.[43] Each stitch embodies love, care, and remembrance. All the artists who created the moccasin tops have a stake in honoring the women and girls—they view MMIWG as kin, or perhaps they have personally lost a daughter, sister, mother, niece, aunt, or cousin, or maybe they are Indigenous women and girls who understand the regime of settler violence we must inhabit daily. Belcourt notes that "as we go along the project becomes stronger and stronger."[44] This is a form of collective knowledge production and meaning-making: "it gives people a vocabulary to talk about [MMIWG] . . . [and] the main thing is to make it stop—stopping the murders."[45] Belcourt is speaking to a futurity for Indigenous women and girls and extinguishing the settler futurity that functions within a regime of violence.

This knowledge and act of cultural production and ceremony has been led by the community; as the WWOS memorial installation enters communities, certain protocols are carried along with it, but the communities that receive the installation also shape the experience to their own protocols. For example, some places might provide skirts to women if they wish to enter the space, or they may decide to arrange the moccasins in ways that represent their traditional symbologies; others have created self-care stations with aromatherapy and lotions, and many of the communities have had side events that provide the space and opportunity to discuss and sort through community grieving and community action related to MMIWG.

On the same topic, MMIWG, the Canadian government has chosen a different approach to participation. In early 2017, the National Inquiry into Missing and Murdered Indigenous Women and Girls was assembled, and its commissioners traveled and held meetings to provide space for communities to tell their stories. However, this process has been fraught. The inquiry was mandated and funded by the Canadian government. The commission has had a turnover of staff on the project, and participants have reported poor treatment by the commission or a feeling that the commissioners and staff are not equipped to handle a national project that is tapping into communities and triggering trauma and grief on a large scale.[46] If we examine these two community knowledge production events, there are two approaches: the WWOS project is reflective of a practice of Indigenous futurity, while the National Inquiry into MMIWG is situated within the politics of recognition. The WWOS installation has provided space to grieve as well as strengthen social relations in the community. In contrast to this, the National Inquiry into MMIWG has institutionalized MMIWG dialogue, and perhaps in some ways the overformalization of dialogue has made it overly bureaucratic and stifling. This process has been fraught and will need examination because much is at stake, and the question must be asked: What benefit will families and communities gain from a painful narration of the sacred knowledge and traumatic stories of their loved ones?

We decolonize knowledge by avoiding hierarchies and uneven power dynamics predicated on difference. These power asymmetries have the power to silence some while emboldening others. Power asymmetries might be predicated on community hierarchies related to being a stompdance practitioner or churchgoer; the asymmetries might also be related to ideas about gender roles and class position, identities related to blood quantum, or notions of status related to one's authenticity as a Mvskoke person. Hierarchies can function in divisive ways, but they can also operate in ways that allow knowledge stewards to keep vital cultural information safe.

The decolonization of knowledge production processes takes on considerations related to the avoidance of hierarchies, the achieving of consensus, uneven power dynamics, the indigenization of knowledge, safe spaces, sacred dimensions, and the recuperating and healing of community. Processes of knowledge production should avoid hierarchies that are intended to silence; however, not all knowledge is democratic. In some cases, hierarchies are in place to protect knowledge, and there are those who are initiated and deemed stewards of particular kinds of community knowledge. One example of an important use of knowledge hierarchies is illustrated with the Zuni Map Art Project: in this project the community worked with knowledge keepers and artists to produce coded maps of places.[47] The initiated might recognize a sacred viewshed, or multiple viewsheds that are stopping places along a path to a key cultural place—for example, in the journey to harvest salt. The Zuni Map Art Project has brilliantly determined ways to integrate Zuni symbology with representations of place, which encodes the maps with tiers of legibility. Thus, the map project does not democratize knowledge but filters it, to illustrate sacred spatial grammars. One must be initiated in Zuni ways of knowing in order to render the map legible.

Decolonizing knowledge also means not just pretending to work toward consensus in knowledge production. While professional practice is starting to take up the idea of decolonization, it can result in either unintentional or intentional trivialization of a community's practices. The rhetoric of being participatory and inclusive is just bandied about, and while it might sound like it is in the service of social justice, this does not get carried out in practice. As well, producing knowledge should involve finding or creating safe spaces for participants. In a community where a domestic violence dialogue workshop is conducted, for example, this might mean that women are provided a protected location where their participation and safety are not compromised.

Related to the need for safe space is a consciousness of uneven power dynamics and the ways in which power asymmetries emerge during knowledge production. For example, when cohabitating partners participate in a workshop or session, one person might defer to their partner to provide input for both of them. Deferential dynamics operate to deprive an individual of sharing his or her unique perspective and prevent the community from benefiting from a wide range of experiential knowledge. It might mean that the couple's dialogue is reflective of a gendered engagement with space, which propagates into a gendered imaginary.

The process of knowledge production can engender community recuperation and healing in ways that recognize gendered ruptures and long-standing grudges. Recuperation and healing take on many forms, and it is the community's place to recognize ruptures and conceive of healing for itself. However, healing can take on a material form; for example, when a group of people who have disagreed or quietly held grudges over the years find themselves sitting at a table in a participatory session to discuss and share what they hold most important in the community, that can mean recuperation and healing. Shared dialogue related to collective memory functions in amazing ways, and the walls of negative intentions can begin to dissipate.

While intentional processes of knowledge production might function tactically to serve a research agenda, plan, community planning process, or community organizing campaign, they can also function in ways that are not solely instrumental or toward a desired end. More-than-instrumental and futurity-minded practices of knowledge production extend and amplify knowledge through sharing—the sharing of experiences, narratives, and ways of carrying out practices like language, cooking, hunting, etc.

Knowledge production is a form of way-finding, which means reassociating our knowledge with what it has been dissociated from—our bodies, our senses, our feelings. In this case, way-finding involves recuperating and strengthening these knowledge pathways that remind us of the array of knowledge we carry in our bodies.

In this chapter, the action of decolonization is treated as a means of responding to the ongoing project of settler colonialism.[48] This chapter attempts to define decolonizing practices and to understand what decolonization looks like in action rather than just in metaphor. Community development and planning work or futurity work practiced with no awareness of one's contribution to the structure of settler colonialism makes it impossible to intentionally decolonize. However, recognizing the ways in which our practices and ideologies are complicit with settler colonialism, such as racialized practices of xenophobia or gendered practices of patriarchy, homophobia, and transphobia, has the potential to completely shift our vision of other possible worlds when this work emerges from the people in a way that both honors "the original instructions" of valuing all human and more-than-human kin and works to attend to the short-term needs and long-range goals of sustaining Mvskoke lifeways.

To decolonize is an action, and the nation-state has carried out policies that have shaped communities now and historically, regulating where people live. So, what exactly are we decolonizing if we are cemented to the idea that justice only looks like attempting to convince a nation-state decision-making body to recognize the arguments and truths that communities convey to it for the security of communities, bodies, and food? This is the politics of recognition, not decolonization. Decolonizing as an action can redefine the definition of community and what constitutes land by underscoring the ways in which land is known and understood. Recognizing the importance of local knowledge and local people is critical in creating a map to the next world, either by informal or formal processes.

Thus we focus on shifting the conceptual paradigm of why we carry out community planning. When we reform our thinking about community, its constituent parts, and its dimensions of power and knowledge, the ontological and epistemological ideas around community and land necessarily shift, resisting notions that fix them in place. Deadening space as an object simplifies ideas of land and community. In terms of community, I mean that we must move beyond the valorization of a narrow view of community as fixed to one geographic location. Within the prevailing conditions of the market economy, educational opportunities, and spatial mobility, Indigenous people do not remain fixed in place.

We must also rethink whether our work centers on oppositional grievance claims that appeal to the nation-state and its surrogates, or whether it is centered on the daily experiences and practices of recognizing and carrying out Mvskoke lifeways. Mvskoke lifeways engender balance in normative governance systems and community desires; however, maintaining a careful balance becomes difficult because of the ease with which one can become engrossed in the daily battles and preparation that grievance claim work demands. We must focus on this reality and consciously consider how much time and energy we spend fighting and advocating truth claims in a system that fails to recognize Indigenous peoples as sovereign nations. The more time we spend fighting and advocating truth claims within a normative government system, the less time and energy we have to invest in Mvskoke language, stories, songs, or dance.

For us to carry Mvskoke lifeways into the future, one course includes returning to the Mvskoke tenet that energy is transmitted from being to being, including plants and animals.[49] Ever cognizant of this transferred energy, a community imaginary or vision should open opportunities for positive energy transfers between many entities, including humans, plants, animals, water, and land. Local knowledge and ways of being in the world represent a kind of energy that travels in and across individuals, their families, their communities, and the Mvskoke people. An example of relationality between human and nonhuman is demonstrated when Joy Harjo writes, "My cousin Donna Jo Harjo was a champion barrel racer and knew how to speak with horses. She had to live close to horses or not live at all. They were her people as much as any of the rest of us."[50] This passage illustrates both kinship and energy exchange without words, which too is a form of dialogue.

Mvskoke logic can be used to read other frameworks, continually questioning and considering the energy produced by community-building efforts. And we can reflect on the quality of energy exchange and relationality in a community by asking: Does the energy sustain, invigorate, heal, inspire, encourage, reconcile, improvise, and nurture, or does it damage, humiliate, dishonor, judge, dispirit, embarrass, eviscerate, frighten, jeer at, or manipulate? It's important to constantly check the quality of the energy in the community, in the room, and among folks dialoguing, because embarking on the creation of a community imaginary means that we must pay attention not only to the end goal but also to the process of its constant construction and how other entities are treated in this process. I am not simply proposing that we treat everyone well; I am urging consciousness, which embodies how our actions and nonactions, through conversation, tone of voice, or body language, impact a wide range of others, including the nonhuman world. Indeed, our actions or absence of actions are energy transfers that have the power to include or exclude. And they have the power to make us forget or remember our connection to plants, animals, water, land, and stars.

Felt knowledge is a critical aspect of community experience, and if we fail to recognize what we feel, whether it is a connection to a horse or to others, what do we truly build or create? What are we missing when we refuse to employ such logic? Do we end up with a life not lived to the fullest? A community dream that's extinguished, or never envisioned? Or the perpetuation of premature death in our communities? Local knowledge and practices are necessary for carrying out a map to the next world, a map that is drawn from intentional community knowledge production.

It is important as well to include the logic of nonhuman kin in community. All entities within the community have a level of importance—and to construct community purely according to the vision of human desires puts us in slippery territory because there is the assumption that humans will take into consideration the needs of nonhuman entities. What we consider becomes implicit, and the implicit is sometimes too subtle for humans. Thus, when we identify plant and animal nations and nonhuman entities in the communities, community work takes on a different task; it is not simply the act of convening a group of people to ask them what they want. It means that one must triangulate with the needs of nonhuman kin.

The conceptual framework of decolonizing knowledge production is an active and living response to the politics of recognition. Crafting practices of decolonization is an ongoing project because settler colonialism and the concomitant framework of the politics of recognition are an ongoing violent structure. Thus, *decolonize* is a verb, an action, not a metaphor, and this project involves conceiving of methods and on-the-ground engagement with Indigenous peoples that move toward the next world they wish to inhabit.[51] Often Indigenous peoples get caught up in the politics of recognition, which anticipates that the current conditions of a community will continue to persist and that any policies born out of these conditions will always be useful. But the conditions do not stay the same. The politics of recognition shift like sand as we follow major federal Indian policies, including Indian removal, Indian allotment, and the assimilation / boarding school era. The nation-state has created policies that shape their communities and everyday lives, of which many examples illustrate processes to eliminate Mvskoke people. For example, in the early nineteenth century, in spite of the Supreme Court recognizing tribes' sovereignty over their land, the Indian Removal Act forced Mvskoke people from their communities of origin in Alabama and Georgia; in the late nineteenth century, the federal government parceled land into individual allotments and enumerated men as the heads of household; the land allotment prompted ferment, resulting in the Crazy Snake (Chitto Harjo) revolt. In the early twenty-first century, the failure of federal trust responsibility for Individual Indian Money (IIM) accounts resulted in one of the largest class-action settlements in the history of the United States.[52] Interventions according to the politics of recognition may work within the system of the federal government, through implementation of and slow changes to federal laws and policies related to Indian land. Interventions happen in other ways, too, such as encouraging land owners to write wills to ensure the transfer of land in ways that avoid fractionation. Land fractionation is the undivided interest in a land parcel that grows exponentially when individuals die without a will and the interest in the land is transferred to all remaining heirs.

Major historical moments illustrate the politics of recognition in relation to Indian land, such as the state-empowered doctrine of discovery and the Marshall trilogy of cases that came out of Justice John Marshall's Supreme Court. *Johnson v. M'Intosh* established the concept of right to occupancy: this case extinguished Indigenous title to the land, considering Indigenous groups to have the right to merely occupy land, but not to own it, sell it, or settle land claims. *Cherokee Nation v. Georgia* formally reduced the reach of Native sovereignty over the land that they inhabit and use by deeming Indigenous nations domestic dependent sovereigns with a lesser sovereignty than that of the United States. *Worcester v. Georgia* reinforced the federal government's primacy over tribes on their own lands along with the doctrine of discovery supported in *Johnson v. M'Intosh*, deeming that the federal government had the authority to settle land claims. These rulings are the foundation of the guiding principles of the doctrine of discovery, right to occupancy, Native title, and the placing of Indigenous peoples in a paternalistic relationship whereby land is held in trust, adjudication of land is the federal government's realm, and sovereignty is injured. These are the imperatives that shape the politics of recognition within which Mvskoke people and other Indigenous nations dealing with land and tribal governments must engage.

Further, continually responding to government-driven imperatives shapes perceptions of land and the networks of interconnectivity between plants, animals, water, wind, and people. The federal system of power valorizes individual and private ownership of land. The ways in which people proudly name and claim land ownership and surveil and secure their containers of land runs counter to Indigenous narratives about land, and narratives of ownership of land become the prevailing epistemology instead of narratives of relationship with the land. Furthermore, it establishes a framework within which Mvskoke ways of knowing and ordering the world are subjugated and must be filtered through and recognized within a settler colonial system of knowledge. For example, land becomes an object and is flattened into dead space instead of being part of a kinship relation that sustains our livelihood.

The federal government also functions in terms of a master/slave dialectic, whereby Mvskoke people cannot be recognized as self-determining subjects unless another self-determining subject recognizes them as such. In other words, within power asymmetries, including the nation-state, the United Nations, the subnational state, and even the tribe and community, we see a level of gatekeeping that entails those in power not recognizing others as empowered agents.[53] And to gain material resources or agents of power, groups appeal to the state or other decision-making bodies, encouraging them to recognize and act accordingly upon such claims. This is a grievance model of gaining resources and power, a primary characteristic of the politics of recognition.

The Failure of the Politics of Recognition

A contemporary example in which the grievance claim model obstructs Mvskoke futurity is the Hickory Ground (Ocevpofv) land dispute between MCN and Poarch Band of Creek Indians (PBCI). While Mvskoke people in Oklahoma are direct descendants of tribal towns in Alabama and Georgia, PBCI are also descended from Mvskoke people, but they still reside in southern Alabama; they gained federal recognition in 1984.[54] Legal scholar Ashley Ray reports that PBCI is derived from the Mvskoke people who assisted and accommodated the federal government with alliance against "hostile" Mvskoke groups.[55] PBCI thus ingratiated itself with the federal government and was rewarded with being allowed to remain in Alabama, avoiding removal to Oklahoma.[56] Hickory Ground, located in Wetumpka, Alabama, is a sacred site for MCN; it is one of eight parcels initially placed into trust by PBCI, and further, PBCI made assurances that they would care for the site and preserve it for all Creek people. However, this has become a protracted and contentious dispute.[57] According to the lawsuit, the Hickory Ground site has spiritual and ceremonial significance for MCN, but it spatially coincides with the construction of PBCI's expansion of their casino. MCN and a small Poarch Band group agree on the significance of the site and the need to preserve it; however, the formal PBCI governance structure contends otherwise.[58] Mvskoke human rights activist Suzan Shown Harjo shares the words of former PBCI tribal chairman Eddie Tullis: "Indian sacred lands can be protected, but not at the expense of Indian businesses." This is indicative of PBCI's attitudes regarding their shared stake in Hickory Ground.[59] Although this quotation is drawn from a 2006 article, today capitalist economics still takes primacy over cultural and spiritual significance. In a lawsuit filed in 2012, MCN maintained that PBCI exhumed fifty-seven sets of human remains from Mvskoke graves located in Hickory Ground in order to construct their casino expansion. These deceased Mvskoke people were direct lineal ancestors of MCN, and PBCI did this without contacting MCN in Oklahoma. In the lawsuit between MCN and PBCI, MCN is fighting for their spiritual and emotional ties to Hickory Ground and for their exhumed relatives.[60] In response, PBCI asked the court to dismiss the case based in part on case law from the Snowbowl case in Arizona. San Francisco Peak is considered a sacred site by Navajo Nation and other tribes in the region, and Navajo Nation filed a lawsuit to halt the use of reclaimed wastewater for producing snow for the Snowbowl ski area in a place they and other tribes deem sacred.[61] In the Snowbowl ruling, the court found that Navajo Nation could not demonstrate a diminishment of the sacredness of the site, and, drawing upon the Snowbowl precedent, PBCI argued that MCN could not prove a diminishment of sacredness in their own case.

At the time of writing, this case is still pending, and in December 2017, Mvskoke Media reported that the three plaintiffs—MCN, Hickory Ground Tribal Town, and Mekko George Thompson—and the defendant PBCI et al. requested "a stay in order to continue active settlement negotiations that have recently taken place between MCN and PBCI in an effort to amicably resolve the dispute."[62] This is hopeful in terms of resolving the dispute as kin; however, it does not change the fact that Mvskokvlke were removed from their resting place. On May 21, 2018, the MCN National Council unanimously approved the act NCA 18-007, which appropriates $276,500 toward legal and related costs in protecting "the Muscogee sacred site of Hickory Ground near Wetumpka."[63]

This case demonstrates the failure of sovereignty that is bound up in the politics of recognition. PBCI appealed to the settler for recognition and validation and refused to work with their kin, the MCN. Suffice it to say, there was an informal group of PBCI that supported MCN, which is an example of este-cate sovereignty—an act of recognizing one another as kin and negotiating a solution as such.

This is an example of two Indigenous groups of similar descent embroiled in a detrimental notion of the politics of recognition. MCN is concerned about its ceremonial ground site and about the burial ground that was exhumed for casino construction. Events that have transpired thus far place a higher priority on business development than on sites that are foundational to Mvskoke lifeways. It is ironic that a dispute between two Mvskoke groups is being resolved in a federal court and argued under the terms of settler conceptions of land and place, rather than drawing upon Mvskoke epistemologies. Further, MCN must make their felt knowledge—their spiritual, cultural, and emotional ties to the site and to the exhumed graves—legible and comprehensible to this court. This is a form of epistemic violence because it is incongruous with Mvskoke kinship practices, and it forces felt knowledge to be codified, objectified, and explicated in a court that examines it as constituent parts and weighs the merits of arguments and objects.

In some cases, tribes do have to operate within the politics of recognition to respond to immediate and genocidal threats, such as the dispossession of land, the desecration of sacred lands—as described in the Poarch Band issue above—or missing and murdered Indigenous women. The logics of settler colonialism are not solely an Indigenous issue, nor are the analytics with which Indigenous people respond to settler colonialism solely the provenance of Indigenous people. We can draw on the work of critical scholars of color—for example, the work of scholars like Clyde Woods and Ruthie Gilmore takes on empire building with a range of analytical tools that Indigenous communities can use. The conversation about dismantling settler colonial institutions and practices has been and continues to be a dialectical one, informed by many groups, in many places. Everyone has a place in sorting this through; there is much at stake as we stave off state-sanctioned genocide. However, the project of the people is not solely to work not to get killed and to keep our spirits from being squashed; it is to remember, embark upon, and sustain what should be an even larger project—the original instructions that guide us in achieving a full and rich life. This rich, full life is what our ancestors wanted for us; they asked for it before we were born, and we too should be asking for it for those not yet born.

If this is what we can expect from state-based politics, then what are the possibilities of the politics of decolonization? Is decolonization only about creating a considerable social movement? I posit that decolonization is not related to a discrete territory or set of prescriptive actions; instead, it is tentative and provisional because each Indigenous group is experiencing the world in ways that are particular to it. These particularities will shift and change; thus, if the politics of recognition demands a vast amount of resources to effect change to a structure—the nation-state, a federal agency, or a city, state, or county government—that does not fully recognize Indigenous peoples as human, then why are we wasting our time on this? Moreover, what does the politics of decolonization provide for communities, and how can we think of it in terms of a series of concrete actions that people can carry out?

Where there is settler knowledge production at work, Indigenous knowledge production can counter this. Countering the naturalized truth regime is crucial if Mvskoke knowledge systems are to prevail and operate to sustain the local community. Therefore, from a political and community-building standpoint, decolonization also means people deciding how they want their communities to function—that is, a Mvskoke imaginary. Decolonization enacts the Mvskoke tenet of energy transfer and centers local knowledge within all projects while being cognizant of and eliminating the reproduction of settler colonial logics. Settler colonial logics invoke Indigenous groups to seek recognition for grievance claims or turn toward an elite echelon of primarily hetero-male leadership that diminishes or fails to recognize the matters that affect women, youth, and LGBTQ2S people. A closer examination of recognition reveals the ways in which settler logics operate.

The politics of decolonization have not been fully realized in the United States under the rubric of self-determination. In the same ways that sovereignty has been reduced by the state, so too has self-determination. As mediated through and by the state, self-determination is compromised. There is a false idea circulated that tribal nations have full autonomy over their nations and their land. Tribes, however, need attorneys and government workers who

understand federal government policies and the rules of administering federally funded programs, and thus they keep on reproducing the administrative
aspect of a federally recognized tribal nation. If land is held in trust, then local
Bureau of Indian Affairs offices serve as the primary mechanism for oversight of
and authority over tribal land. Decisions and policies, especially about housing,
community, and business development, are routed through a labyrinth of rules.
Even the idea of a will as a mechanism for managing one's estate, one commonly
recommended practice, does not sit well. "The old ones believe they are jinxing
themselves, or betting against themselves," Cris Stainbrook, president of Indian
Land Tenure Foundation, states regarding estate planning and will creation.[64]
The state does not understand the original instruction or guidance of the people
by our ancestors, nor does it understand that these instructions complicate our
place within and navigation through the prevailing system. So much energy is
invested in these systems, but how much is invested in Mvskoke lifeways? The
Indian Self-Determination Act is often regarded as a pivotal point for tribal
planning and autonomy, but tribes have been performing community planning
since their time of emergence.[65] Mvskoke people can trace the spatiocultural
organization of their community across time, from the mound builders to the
etvlwas to the current iterations of Mvskoke ceremonial grounds and churches.
Common threads connect the use of space and reflect cultural and ritual importance. The meeting place, for example, serves as a prevalent focal point in sites
designed for deliberation and social activities. This way of self-organizing, then,
relates directly to contemporary planning and development. Mvskoke people
organize their community work in many ways to sustain the tribal town or the
etvlwa, the site of political, cultural, and spiritual presence.

   Analyzing community knowledge is important. Often the context of Indigenous communities is primarily constructed from secondary data collected by
the nation-state. There is violence in these research methods and construc-
tions, and in Indigenous peoples being abstracted into race categories within
state-generated census data. Non-Indigenous peoples are unused to negotiating
Indigenous knowledges like felt knowledge and the experience of engaging and
living as a member of a tribal nation. To further complicate the issue, academic
research is complicit with colonialism in the collective minds of Indigenous
peoples. After years of being poked, prodded, and formed into research objects,
as well as having the bones of Indigenous ancestors sequestered in museums
and research universities, Indigenous peoples consider *research* a dirty word and
a dirty thing.[66] Research is considered colonized because it draws on Western

ways of knowing the world, which tend to classify Indigenous ways of knowing the world as "other" or different. Research practices have focused on treating Indigenous peoples as objects. As an object of research, Indigenous peoples represent something to have authority over, to pose questions about, to build a framework about, and to create taxonomies about, all based on the researcher's understanding of the "object."[67] The researcher then considers themselves the expert on the object (i.e., Indigenous peoples), while the expertise of Indigenous peoples remains unacknowledged and invisible. Linda Tuhiwai Smith characterizes differences in attitudes between Indigenous peoples and academic researchers according to the following categories: *time* (there was previously no division of labor in terms of work and leisure), *response to researcher* (a researcher may get her answer in a day, a week, or over a lifetime), and *worldviews* (the researcher and participant might not have aligned worldviews).[68]

The practice of settler knowledge production is problematic because it tends to gravitate toward the academician or the expert who views the Indigenous community as an object to which to apply theoretical frameworks. However, it can prove problematic when the theories do not correctly fit because they are conceived outside the context and positionality of an Indigenous community.

Power Asymmetries / Knowledge Extraction

One problem with the colonial gaze of research is that it represents an uneven balance of power. A relevant example, though it is not drawn from an Indigenous context, is Rob Kitchin's work on people with disabilities. He notes that disabled groups of people are often invisible as an object of study and as members of society.[69] He posits that researchers working with disabled populations are often self-centered in their approach. Typically, according to Kitchin, researchers have a set of questions they want to have answered and will extract knowledge from the community to accomplish this goal, but their research may have no relevance to the community. This pattern is replicated in Indigenous communities and is a frequent complaint among community members. The relationship between the researcher and the communities being researched, as well as the methods deployed, reproduces larger institutionalized structures such as the academy. Western-based knowledge production is based on power relationships that posit the researcher as the expert on the world and the researched as a subject that can provide data to be synthesized by the researcher.[70] If an academic understands the basis of decolonized research, then they have an ethical obligation to the communities they research to enact it at every opportunity. Simply put, if a researcher knows that participatory methods will help a community and does not practice them, then that is a lapse in ethics. When a researcher says that they will involve a community, but then only includes community members by merely informing or consulting them without integrating their knowledge and ideas, this is an example of ethical slippage. This form of tokenism allows community planners to check the box of including American Indian / Alaska Native communities in the process.[71] While I cannot exhaustively list all the ethical considerations related to Indigenous peoples and research here, I will explore more deeply the Indigenous notions of group tyranny, time, and the ethical responsibilities of a community researcher or facilitator.

Among the approaches to knowledge production that foreclose the agency and power of a community are objectification and "helicopter researchers"—the latter are an issue of special concern for the Association of American Geographers' Indigenous Peoples Specialty Group.[72] These researchers hover over a community like a helicopter, drop down, gather what they need, leave, and never develop a long-term relationship with the Indigenous community in which they are working. They come for a short while to gather their research, publish their paper, and move on. A researcher should have a basic understanding of the meaning of familial relationships in an Indigenous community, both fictive and actual kin, before forging relationships there. The late Ojibwe elder and University of Michigan lecturer Hap McCue, for example, expressed his pain over coming to know and befriend a researcher, only to hear later that he was being referred to as a research subject.[73] This betrayal also relates to a researcher's lack of follow-up with the community. They should keep a community abreast of their project's progress and report their findings. Failure to do so may leave a community feeling used. Researchers must understand that when they work with Indigenous communities, they are implicitly making a commitment to that community. This commitment is often comprised of the creation of ties between planners and a community.

Implications and Foreclosures

The Western view of the world and some of the implications of Western knowledge construction are limited because they are produced from the positionality of white men, who are speaking from their experience. As the prevailing producers of knowledge within the academy, white men have shaped the standards upon which subsequent researchers must adhere according to their limited lens. Amrah Salomón J. contends that "colonial research as it adheres to Western universalism and white supremacist thought does violence to expansive and non-linear notions of and relationships to time, space, and the cosmos, severing the living from the past while advancing scientific disciplinary epistemologies that sever spiritual, erotic, bodily, and emotional ways of knowing."[74] Salomón is insisting that Western knowledge carries out a form of violence that targets our kinship networks as a source of knowledge production; this epistemic violence consequently is a form of settler futurity that gets carried out at the expense of Indigenous futurity. An example of Mvskoke ideas that diverge from a Western ordering of the world is illustrated in Mvskoke / Citizen Potawatomi artist Daniel McCoy's work *The Chain of Being* (figure 7). In the left-side panel is a centering of nature, animals, and the environment according to a Mvskoke epistemology; in the right-side panel is a Western hierarchical ordering of the heavens, angels, people, animals, and plants.[75] McCoy explains that his Mvskoke mother provided him with a way of understanding the world: "My mother told

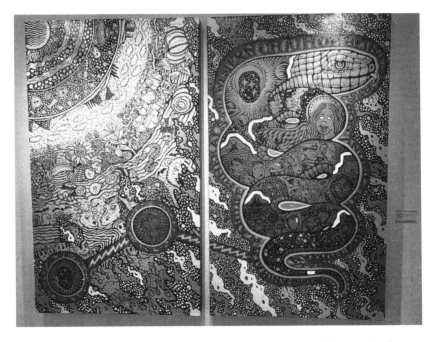

FIGURE 7 *The Chain of Being*, mural painting, Daniel McCoy Jr. Personal collection of the artist.

me years ago that eventually the impurities and pollution in the Earth will break apart and give way to a pristine, almost utopian landscape for all animals and ancient peoples to live upon again."[76]

Speculation is a form of action that empowers community to trust in their collective knowledge—their embodied knowledge—to conceive of what the lush promise means to them and how to produce it. Further, it provides a platform for the community to speak—to dialogue. To illustrate this point, in an intentional community participatory process, individuals who might not ordinarily engage in public speaking can develop some level of comfort within a group setting and share their knowledge.[77] Conversely, some participants may bully others with their point of view.[78] While an individual's silence at public forums may seem to mean that they are apathetic or indifferent to community concerns, I argue that the venue and researcher's approach may inhibit participants. Often when participants think that researchers are not listening to them, they will simply give up and remain silent. Researchers, therefore, must design culturally appropriate venues and interpersonal approaches to encourage participants to engage in the process.[79] Writing, celebrating, and storytelling are examples of these types of approaches. A community-based writing project, for instance, offers a venue in which participants can write their story on their own terms in different genres, including nonfiction, poetry, short stories, and plays. Depending on their level of comfort, community members may also discuss the texts they created, if care is taken not to replicate the structures of a formal school setting, which may alienate many participants. Celebrating survival creates a space where artists, storytellers, and musicians all come together, a place that reaffirms one's identity.[80] The annual MCN Festival represents one such place. Similarly, storytelling plays a vital role not only in passing down values from one generation to the next but in building community. Hearing one another's stories builds and reaffirms the collective story that dwells in their collective memory. When the community grasps and deploys agentive processes, this is este-cate sovereignty.

Collective celebrations and storytelling offer the possibility of more comprehensive, and perhaps less censored, accounts of the issues impacting Indian country than giving testimony at a public hearing. Group tyranny, which refers to the power of a group to subsume and obscure the viewpoints of some of the group participants, creates its own dynamic as well.[81] The dynamics of group tyranny yield a skewed outcome that represents the agenda of a few rather than a diverse collective of viewpoints. For example, two factions—Christians and traditionalists—may exist in a community. In a space centered on discussion or storytelling, one of these factions may marginalize the viewpoints of the other. If two agendas conflict, then, a writing project may work better than public speaking to avoid group tyranny. A writing project may prevent viewpoints from getting drowned out. One drawback is that a writing project might be intimidating. One way to make writing less daunting is to ask the group to recommend prompts that they care about.

Participatory methods can be used as a decolonized approach to work with Indigenous communities. While the points I make in this chapter are not an exhaustive list, they are points of departure for gaining a deeper understanding of how to work respectfully and ethically with Indigenous peoples. Getting these points across to the academy is my ethical obligation to my natal community.[82] Native Hawaiian geographer Renee Louis calls the journey of learning a spiritual one.[83] It has always been vital for me to produce knowledge that emanates from the communities that comprise my tribal loyalties: my extended family; my ceremonial grounds; High Spring, which is the Indian church my family built; and my clan, the Wolf Clan.[84] Marilyn Bread, a Kiowa legislator and de facto auntie, informed me of prayer as a system of care that is bound up in my responsibility to community future and stated that my ancestors prayed for me before I was born—and not only for me, but for all those yet to be born. If I were able to see all the prayers, they would look like stars in the night sky. Praying and considering the future of one's tribe was, and I would argue still is, a natal responsibility bound up in a spiritual journey. The value of these decolonized methodologies is the way in which they align with a Mvskoke tradition of oral history that includes long sessions of visiting with relatives, sometimes for days.[85]

Current debates around participatory research include how best to carry out ethical interactions with participants and how best to protect participants and researchers from dangerous situations. These debates also problematize the lack of follow-up discussions by researchers with participants from tribal communities, to ensure they are safe or simply report next steps. Additionally, community participants engaged in a community process with researchers might have expectations that the researcher or facilitator will help them oppose violent or racist structures, or a facilitator might falsely assume that participants have the resources—material and social—to challenge power asymmetries. One example of this is convening groups of women to discuss their home situation: perhaps they feel empowered, but in reality there might be a violent power asymmetry that can create a dangerous situation if the women act in a way that opposes the prevailing power dynamic. In cases of toxic masculinity in which gender binaries are fiercely and violently guarded, a researcher or planner who convenes groups of women or sexual minorities in a patriarchal community must consider how their community-engaged work might compromise the safety of these groups.

Tool of Futurity: Community Knowledge / Mvskoke Knowledge

Community knowledge is depicted in the Southeastern-inspired symbol in figure 8. The community knowledge symbol embodies the dynamism of Mvskoke dialogue and knowledge production, which are intersecting and always in movement. This is another example of Mississippian iconography. However, it should be noted that this symbol consists of only two intersecting lines within a circle. The significance of this is that when Mvskoke people engage in dialogue with one another, their unique embodied knowledges are intersecting and intertwining. In this exchange they are creating something larger than their knowledge standing on its own. Likewise, this symbol is greater than simply two lines—it is swirling, in movement, representing the beauty of dialogue and knowledge production. This is my particular reading of this symbol in the context of discussing Mvskoke futurity. I have taken the liberty of imbuing it with value, and my version is only one among many; however, I do so with the best of intentions in an attempt to use and convey Mvskoke ways of knowing and operating in the world.

FIGURE 8 *Community Knowledge*, relief print, Laura Harjo.

This graphic represents the many ways in which knowledge is produced in community—through practicing, experiencing, feeling, sensing, and joking, to name a few. Furthermore, the symbol can be interpreted as an intersection of a long legacy of Mvskoke knowledge that individuals carry with the kinship required to engage in dialogue with one another to project community-created knowledge. Community knowledge production without kinship yields a highly filtered knowledge; for example, in my experience with the Indigenous

Design and Planning Institute, when we have performed planning work with an entirely Indigenous team that understands Indigenous epistemologies, the community opens up more than it does with a non-Indigenous planner. There is some measure of kinship and trust, which is necessary in creating a fuller understanding of the community's perceived reality. In summary, Mvskoke knowledge production yields and reimagines kinship connections, empowers and recuperates community, connects us to and reveals the embodiment of many kin-space-time envelopes, and places the community in a process of futurity— living, activating, and speculating on possibilities. We make kinship connections over the course of a knowledge production process that places us in dialogue with one another. In one example, a workshop I was involved with in Ecuador included Indigenous community members and Indigenous students from both Ecuador and the United States. Over the course of the session, both the workshop participants and the Indigenous facilitators bonded with one another. The participatory workshop functioned to produce kinship where there was none before, and the common denominator in the knowledge production process was related to este-cate sovereignty and the allegiances and love the Indigenous peoples have for the community, the land, and all that inhabits the land—even the metaphysical, or spirit, world.

Further, from the kinship making and sharing, empowerment of the collective is generated—people feel energized and edified in part because they are strengthened by a community network of support. Participants in knowledge production power a collectively felt knowledge. There are intentional activities through which this might be carried out—for example, Prouds/Sorries, of which I share a case study in the closing chapter to examine how the tools of futurity are revealed in the process of knowledge production. Participation in a process yields community empowerment and the making and strengthening of kinship, which function to help the community recuperate from the impacts of settler colonialism, local racist practices against the community, and perhaps long-standing grudges within it as well.

Because a participatory process brings many people together to share their knowledge and produce collective knowledge together, there is a connection to many kin-space-time envelopes that are placed in dialogue and collective action. For example, in one community workshop that I conducted related to one's sense of place, workshop participants were prompted to remember where they grew up and what sort of activities they engaged in then. These sense-of-place discussions pulled in several kin-space-time envelopes that were indicative of the longer legacy of knowledge transferred from previous relatives to inform and shape participants' present-day actions and memories of their homes. Indeed, the participants held the knowledge of their relatives. To argue our relationship to knowledge further, we as individuals access kin-space-time envelopes that are our relatives and ancestors, and we also embody kin-space-time envelopes. Thus, we can (re)imagine our support systems and kinship connections through an understanding that, at the scale of the body, we have a kin-space-time envelope that enacts a constellation of memories and experiences; our ancestors carry constellations, and we too carry our own unique constellation.

Finally, speculation enables a community to contemplate and draw upon their knowledge to carefully examine their current conditions and reconstitute and extend their communities in ways that they care about now and in the future. Knowledge production and speculation provide the space for the community to create a new map, shaped by them and intended for them, to get them to the next world on their own terms. Consequently, knowledge production fully ensconces the community in futurity—living, surmising, and enacting Mvskoke futurity.

Summary: Community Knowledge

In this chapter, I have pointed out that community knowledge is known and practiced by the community in a variety of ways—it's embodied, it's felt, it's realized in daydreams and interstices. All these examples are ways of practicing knowledge in which energy is transferred. Furthermore, these ways of knowing and producing knowledge empower the community to recognize the settler colonial practices and knowledges that subjugate it. This enactment of Mvskoke knowledge production, then, is decolonial work that resists the politics of recognition—especially actions that place zero value on Mvskoke ways of knowing and valuing place, as exemplified by the current court case between MCN and PBCI, where PBCI is seeking a favorable ruling on their exhumation of Mvskoke bodies from the original Hickory Ground site in order to construct a casino in its place. Recognizing the ways in which community can be convened with dignity and ethics is important in knowledge production; however, from these dialogues, not only do new speculative imaginaries emerge, but they also reinvest our knowledge with value.

Community knowledge is a way-finding tool back to the things we know and hold as valuable. I posit that in not recognizing our community knowledge, we continue to reproduce settler colonial practices and ways of being in the world. Recognizing Mvskoke community knowledge has a far-reaching impact on the community—it can mean that bigger things are at stake. Community knowledge means that communities determine futurities for themselves and draw upon what they know and practice as resources.

Community knowledge builds upon este-cate sovereignty, kinship, relationality, and energy. These are all important elements of community dialogue. Community knowledge builds upon these to collectively produce and analyze knowledge. In the next chapter I will introduce collective power, which builds upon the futurity tools of este-cate sovereignty and community knowledge. Collective power puts a community's self-determination, kinship network, and socially produced knowledge into action in ways that can transform community.

CHAPTER 3

Breathing Mvskoke Power into Green Country

Powerscape of Mvskoke Collectivity

The basis of power in the part of Oklahoma known as Green Country has many dimensions; within this chapter I discuss collective, authoritative, and oppressive power and the role that collective power has in protecting and transforming Mvskoke community. Mvskoke people and other Indigenous nations in Oklahoma are situated within a constellation of power geometries, and within the politics of recognition they must contend with authoritative and oppressive power relations. However, for Mvskoke people and other Indigenous groups, there is a collective powerscape operating as well that provides a notion of community empowerment, an Indigenous lens for seeing and taking back control of Mvskoke experiences and their authorship and narration. This is a mode of futurity because collective practices that happen in everyday spaces inform Mvskoke theory and ways of knowing and being in the world, which can become the framework for articulating the Mvskoke experience. Interstitial thinking—related to Mvskoke spaces that cannot be categorized and explained using the taxonomies of rational science and knowledge—structures everyday Mvskoke spaces. Taking back control in order to practice, name, and explain Mvskoke experiences with Mvskoke thinking is este-cate sovereignty, it is community knowledge operationalized, and it is power. It is the kind of power that fills spaces with decolonial love and Mvskoke epistemologies, yet it also recognizes the prevailing normative power that structures the conditions of the Mvskoke community.

A community (de)centered from the locus of normative governance is freed from the requirements of the politics of recognition and grievance claims. A freedom or power to dream, create, and write from Indigenous perspectives is opened when we turn away from social justice frameworks that are concerned with strategic maneuvers and (re)forming relationships with settler structures centrally bound up in whiteness and white supremacy, and thus uninterested in (re)forming equitable relationships. Because these structures entrench Indigenous erasure, to rely on them makes us complicit in our own erasure.[1] This locus is bound up in Mvskoke people appealing to and coexisting with a state that has no concern for the perpetuation of Mvskoke communities or epistemologies. However, this chapter argues for using collective power to recognize the ways in which our communities sustain and edify us, and a residual effect of this (re-) centering on the community is resistance to the settler state. Enacting our epistemologies and community practices and making meaning from them has the power to change and reshape the ways in which we value este-cate sovereignty and source power from our everyday collective practices. In this chapter, I first demonstrate modes of collective power that are realized at the site of stompdance; I then move on to discuss the landscape of power in Oklahoma; and in the final part of the chapter I move into a discussion of an award-winning quilt created by the women of the Sapulpa Creek Indian Community. I use this case study to further illustrate collective power. But first I wish to discuss stompdance as a source of felt knowledge and collective power.

Stompdance as Collective Power

Mvskoke cultural workers produce narratives of our collective power governed by Mvskoke cosmology. The bracelet pictured in figure 9 is Mvskoke-Seminole silversmith Kenneth Johnson's rendering of Mvskoke cosmology, song, and dance. Johnson shares the meaning he gives to the symbolic elements: the turtle is used by the women who shake shells in the stompdance, the braided pattern that runs horizontally across the bracelet is the music created by the dance, the crescents represent the moon, and the central cross is the fire.[2] The focal point is a turtle, which points to the turtle's centrality in creating rhythm in the stompdance.

FIGURE 9 Turtle cuff, silverwork, Kenneth Johnson.

Stompdance is a fundamental collective practice for Mvskoke people. Mvskoke cosmology informs stompdance: the song, rhythm, and dance breathe life into a dynamic spiral, and the Mvskoke practices of interstitial thinking and dialogue with stars, animals, and the metaphysical are the cosmological foundations on which collective and dynamic practices such as stompdance are based. In the dance, the women each wear six to eight turtle shells filled with small smooth river rocks and mounted on a piece of leather; often the leather tops are crafted from old cowboy boots. The leather is punched with metal grommets to accommodate nylon, cotton, or leather laces so that the turtle shells can be tied to the women's legs; their legs are wrapped in folded towels or covered with foam pads for comfort. When the shellshaker moves forward in the dance circle, the turtle shells make a rhythmic sound as she strikes the ground with each heel in double time. The dance starts in a tight spiral formation with a tail—a line of dancers that looks like the number 9. In the center is a fire with large logs that point in four directions. Singers and shellshakers alternate in the dance line. To begin, a male singer leads the songs in a call-and-response pattern, and the lead shellshaker starts and stops the rhythm in conjunction with the song. As more people join the line of dancers, the collective energy creates a large, expanding, dynamic counterclockwise spiral. During the dance, the Milky Way is simultaneously in motion, another massive dynamic spiral that participants can witness, a huge spray of stars trailing across the summer night sky.

Looking more closely at Johnson's bracelet, the horizontal braided lines that run across the middle of the cuff represent the sonic power of Mvskoke language, songs, and turtle shells cutting through the night, the rising and falling of harmonic voices urging dancers and beckoning listeners into the spiral. On either side of the bracelet are two crescent shapes representing the waxing and waning moon, whose phases determine when the stompdance is held. At the perimeter of the circle in the center of the bracelet, adjacent to the moons, are four stars, which are a nod to another kind of energy in the galaxy. The central circle itself represents people dancing; precisely in the center of the bracelet, the four-directional symbol on the turtle represents the fire.

The bracelet is a map of the interconnections between the sky and the moon that guide the stompdance activities. Energy moves through these interconnections: the energy of each person, the collective of dancers, the movement of the songs, the sound of the turtle shells in the night air, and the energy of the central fire. The dance is an optimal balance of energy, a utopian place to step into and experience community. The social relations that create ceremonial grounds and stompdance, as well as the grounds themselves, have existed and will exist as long as the dance is practiced. The stars and constellations present during our dance season can be read as a text, and our ancestors and future relatives have read or will read these same dynamic star maps.

Concepts related to the stars, the songs, the dance, the cardinal directions, and the turtle, all embodied in this bracelet, are a source of long-existing Mvskoke power and decolonial love (vnokeckv). Mvskoke people continue to draw upon these elements, enacting power on a personal and community scale, and marshaling power during collective moments of ceremony, dance, and informal gathering. Often, as Indigenous people, we take for granted this kind of power that we already possess—that which is indomitable. Further, this power is fed by the wisdom of ancestors and our responsibility to our kin. Serving community and kin is a humble but potent form of power, and its potency is rooted in kindness and care—in vnokeckv, a form of decolonial love. Often power is discussed in hierarchical terms, such as where power presides or how it rules over something or someone. The kind of power that is predicated on a Mvskoke notion of love is instead bound up in a type of freedom—not the type of freedom that the state "gives" to people within the politics of recognition, but the kind of freedom that enacts care for one another. I begin to unpack this notion of emancipation by sharing my love for Mvskoke stompdance.

Transformational Power and Mvskoke Felt Knowledge

It is early Sunday morning, and I am driving home from Pakan Tallahassee's (Peach Grounds) Green Corn Dance. The earth is on the cusp of its change from night to day. The summer air is still and feels fresh, and I am traveling north on an unpaved road toward home. It's quiet, with no other cars in sight.

To my left, the western sky is dark blue and sprinkled with stars, while the eastern sky has a touch of sunlight at the horizon line. I take note that I am in an interstice, a space that is not delineated, marked, and understood within a conventional framework of time. The morning after Green Corn, I try to make sense of the interstice within which I have found myself, and I puzzle over the ways in which I've been edified.

Holding interstices in stasis and grappling with them, even in transient moments, reveals a decolonial Mvskoke-centric framework, which places the inadequacy of Western knowledge frameworks in sharp relief. At the dance, I sit on the south side and watch one group after another of twentysomethings walk briskly and assuredly to the fire, in a line of dancers alternating male and female, to lead a dance round. Creek young people lead the dance with confidence and power; their confidence holds the promise that our dances and songs will continue. They are part of a continuous spiral of dancers that includes their grandparents and hopefully their grandchildren. The stompdance spiral and all that it encompasses can provide access to our relatives, past, present, and future. The stars in the summer night sky have borne witness to this dance, and we have borne witness to the summer constellations and will continue to do so. That is Mvskoke futurity.

Leaving the dance, I feel light in my chest, throat, and head. I have had a release of grief, which, unknown to me, was tightly gripping me; it has been replaced by peace and satisfaction that wash over my spirit. As I continue to reflect on Dian Million's work on felt theory and felt, embodied knowledge—that which we remember and carry in our bodies—this feeling of release becomes clearer to me.[3] At once I feel an interconnectedness between the stompdance songs sung in the present and the realization that our Mvskoke relatives sang on the earth before those of us who sing today were materially present, demonstrating and teaching a deep gratitude, singing when *vce* (corn) ripened. As far back as can be remembered, we celebrated our corn harvest as a new year, joyful in knowing we would make it to the next year.

After a long nap, later in the day, I tell my mom she missed good singing. She shares with me something her mother—my grandmother, Julia Hardridge—always said: "When the [stompdance] leader is happy when he's singing, it makes everybody else happy, everyone dancing is happy." My mother reveals to me more of the edification I am puzzling over—an edification that is about collective happiness and the stompdance spiral as the accumulation of love, happiness, and energy, which is power. After she points out that everyone dancing is happy when the leader is happy, my mind flashes to many stompdance moments—yes, everyone dancing does feel good. Several memories also flash through my mind: being a child tearing through the woods with my cousins during *posketv* (Green Corn), in kindred relationality with the reddish-brown soil! We knew in which spaces it was permissible to run amok—not on the dance ground, not through the camp, and not near food preparation. In the dance, we had our own space. In particular, during the friendship dance and snake dance everyone held hands; the dance spiral would be moving from place to place, and usually the kids were toward the end of the line in their own microcosm. When the spiral would unfurl and snake to a different quadrant on the dance ground, we would swing each other hard, leveraging centrifugal force at the tail end of the spiral. Sometimes someone might fall, but everyone was laughing and happy, and we would quickly pick the fallen person up and keep on with the dance. Even if you fell and wanted to cry, you shook it off—there was simply too much positive, happy energy. These memories illustrate collective energy, happiness, and power: all this collectiveness is realized through the experience of dancing and socializing, and through the transmission and production of felt knowledge and experience.

Through this dance and ceremonial practice, the ancestors who are not present in material form are in fact present. Through Mvskoke community practice we embody our ancestors and relatives, and for their part they sustain us no matter where we are. These memories embody the Mvskoke tenet of energy transfer and propagate within a practice of social relationality as collective energy to make decolonial love, recuperation, and kinship possible. I offer up these moments to elucidate the manifestations of Mvskoke power that are present through the experience and transmission of felt knowledge at the site of Mvskoke community. Despite repeated attempts by nation-states to vanquish the life force of Mvskoke people—our songs, our language, our dances, and our relations to one another—stompdance and ceremonial grounds remain autonomous and persist. And although I travel by myself to Pakan Tallahassee (Peach Grounds) and sit by myself, I am not alone. I know this place and have kinship memories here. There is an energy, power, and life force in the songs, the dancing, and the Mvskoke people who gather to dance and be grateful and generous. It is lovely to my heart; in the entire ceremony, I can feel the embodiment of all my relatives, who inform us in many places and on many scales—the songs, the array of other ceremonial grounds represented, the stars. While the ancestors are not present in material form today, their life force is embodied in our cosmology, our language, our songs, and the values that guide us in how to interact and treat others. By "ancestors," I simply mean those whose life force and energy existed here in material form prior to the present temporality. All of this is a form of felt knowledge experienced at the site of stompdance, where many interconnections are known and felt.

Power in Rethinking the Indigenous Community

There is power in reconceiving what the Mvskoke collective can look like; we can refuse to solely rely upon U.S. census ideas that render a community as something fixed in place. Generative refusal can serve as an intervention in the way that U.S. census statistics structure thinking about Indigenous geographies and the populations that inhabit them, and the Indigenous community can generate more complex and polyvalent spatialities. Because when we subscribe solely to the geopolitical units that the U.S. census uses to organize Indigenous communities, we authorize Western truth categories and geospatial containers including race, ethnicity, and areal units such as country, Oklahoma Tribal Statistical Area (OTSA), census block, or census tract. Further, because the Indigenous population is often a small percentage of the population, especially in fine-grained areal units like block or tract, the data are suppressed to protect individuals and household identities. It can be difficult to calculate dependable data.

There are narratives that then propagate based on these data, and within community work these statistics—population, income, and labor force statistics—are used over and over again as markers to construct a story about the people that inhabit an areal unit. These delineated geographies operate as the spaces within which Mvskoke social relations are produced. I propose the idea of (un)delineating the community—whereby its locus is not a function of its legibility to the nation-state.

The term *community* is adaptable to particular uses, practices, places, and aspirations, and it is emancipatory because it does not have to be based on political boundaries but can instead be predicated on how people, plant and animal nations, and other nonhumans coalesce and relate in space. While there are many ways of understanding geography, such as according to scale or region, and I find the associated analytical framework useful, I choose to examine "the community" as the unit of examination and meaning-making analysis.

Community is useful because it is polyvalent and does not need to be fixed in place. Community functions as a rubber-band geography that is pliable and can be reformed to accommodate the many manifestations and understandings of Mvskoke imaginaries and spaces.

Mvskoke people can be found in many places; however, the commonly received way of understanding Mvskoke place is as a nation, which is a jurisdictional area encompassing eleven counties in northeastern Oklahoma. Tribal members living within this area are "home" and are residing within the Mvskoke lands. The idea of difference can sometimes be premised in relation to the geopolitical ordering of MCN: inside/outside a tribal boundary. Alternatively, difference can be predicated on regional orderings of tribes, such as the difference between western Oklahoma, which has several Plains tribes, and eastern Oklahoma, which has tribes relocated from the Southeast—stompdance tribes. There are ways in which difference moves people to deem an Indigenous person to not be of the right tribe, the right skin shade, or the right way of speaking. All of these perspectives operate to alienate Indigenous people from community and also function to preserve settler futurity.[4]

In reflecting on Mvskoke place and community from my subject position as a Mvskoke female, I already possess an embodied Mvskoke belief system, which may not look like that of other Mvskoke females; however, no one, no entity, and no law can alienate me from my Mvskoke sense of self—and as such, neither can other Mvskoke people be alienated from their senses of self and who they are. I do not need a tribal government to indicate whether I am a citizen. I do not need my community to accept me, embrace me, or recognize me; I carry a Mvskoke belief system wherever I go, and that is why it makes no difference to me who recognizes me as Indigenous. Both the strength of my ancestors and my own refusal to allow others to impose settler colonial and genocidal values as a mode of erasure are embodied forms of power that are activated by felt knowledge. Remembering the relatives and their sacrifices is another pivot point of power and agency. A powerful form of felt knowledge that we often hear Indigenous groups draw upon is the urge to remember the sacrifices of our relatives so that we carry ourselves with gratitude and build upon what they have left us. Conversely, our relatives did not solely make sacrifices, but loved and cared for one another, creating another generation of Mvskoke people. Everyone has had their journey, and we should honor and recognize our ancestors' journeys as a model of strength and as a sojourners' narrative still operating in the spiritual and celestial realms.

The Landscape of Political Power

Mvskoke collective power operates in tension with authoritative and oppressive power in Oklahoma. Within Oklahoma, political power can be conceived of in several ways, and in this section I articulate the landscape of power in the state and the particulars of a tribe's access (or lack of access) to power within the state.[5] The landscape of power gets complicated very quickly because of the geopolitical status of tribes and corresponding federal Indian policy that mediates tribes' power. In order to move on an issue, often a tribal member, a community, or the tribal nation must contend with several decision-makers, in both formal and informal structures. Examples of formal structures include the federal government and associated institutions: Congress (the Senate, the House, and relevant congressional committees), the judicial system (federal district courts and the Supreme Court), and the executive branch (the Bureau of Indian Affairs, the Department of Housing and Urban Development, and the Indian Health Service). Formal structures also include governance systems within Oklahoma—the state legislature, state agencies, county governments, and municipal governments. Internally, MCN has both formal and informal structures—for example, formal structures include the tribal council, the judicial branch, and the executive branch, while an informal structure might include decision-makers who are respected elders in the community, within the Indian churches, and within the ceremonial grounds. Although power is a broad topic, I have honed my focus to three areas of interest here: the transformative power of the Mvskoke collective, which I start and end the chapter with, and the oppressive power and authoritative power that communities must contend with in Oklahoma. My discussion of the landscape of power in Oklahoma will be focused primarily on MCN's relationship to formal governance structures and organized opposition.

Authoritative Power

Mvskoke people and MCN have endured a legacy of subjugation and authoritative power imposed by the nation-state. Authoritative power can be carried out by the state or by a tribe; it can be carried out in ways that serve communities or it can control them to serve the interests of decision-makers. I am focused on authoritative power that is formed by settler colonial ideologies and practices regarding land and territory that have structured how Mvskoke land is organized today. A large degree of MCN's efforts have been to survive the terror of the nation-state while deploying a form of este-cate sovereignty to stay alive and maintain Mvskoke lifeways. In this section, I provide a context for authoritative power in Oklahoma. Authoritative power operates as oversight and control; it has decision-makers or de facto leaders that apply laws, rules, and norms to citizens or subjects.

Political Economy of Mvskoke Land

Federal Indian policy is an example of authoritative power; it has iteratively tethered and untethered MCN to specific territories, and federal land imperatives are driven by U.S. narratives that paint Indigenous people as inferior. The relationship of federal Indian policy to Indigenous land dispossession is the point of departure for understanding power relations in Oklahoma. During the early nineteenth century, President Jackson, Congressman Wilson Lumpkin, and Secretary of War Lewis Cass staunchly argued for Indian removal.[6] Proponents of Indian removal made the following arguments: "The rights of citizens and states of the US should overrule the rights held by Indian communities . . . US states' rights, and colonial custom nullified contracted obligations and pledges to Indian nations . . . Indians were inferior people," and, in sum, the "rights of civilized, Christian, settled, agricultural and industrious states of the United States should overrule and nullify the rights of savage, barbarian, heathen, wandering Indian communities."[7] As discussed in chapter 1, this resulted in MCN being dispossessed of its aboriginal homelands in the southeastern United States through removal.

Mvskoke people were displaced to the southern plains; today they live among Plains, Southeastern, California, Midwestern, and Northeastern tribes that the federal government eventually tethered in place with jurisdictional boundaries, all of which has complicated the ownership patterns of Indian land in Oklahoma. After the Indian Removal Act, MCN was situated in a region already populated by Plains tribes—the Osage, Caddo, and Comanche, to name a few.[8] During this time the land was communally held by the tribe, and individuals did not hold title to individual parcels of land. The initial boundary of MCN in Indian Territory had already been reduced when the General Allotment (Dawes) Act of 1887 resulted in MCN's communal land being sectioned into parcels and given to tribal members.[9] Federal actions on Indigenous land during the allotment period produced a complicated checkerboard land status that creates hurdles in developing land. *Checkerboard* is a word often used in Indian country; it refers to the way that Indian land is often noncontiguous, with ownership in a pattern that alternates between Indians and non-Indians.[10]

Mvskoke people were subjected to the process of allotment, by which their families were enumerated and they shifted from collectively owned land to individually owned parcels—owning private property was a marker of assimilation. After participating tribal members were enumerated, each family received a 160-acre land parcel. These allotments were placed in a twenty-five-year trust period with the United States, during which the land could not be bought or sold.[11] The U.S. government then opened the balance of the territory for sale to white settlers, deeming it surplus property.[12] With the transformation of Mvskoke land into individually owned land, as well as the generation of so-called surplus, immense private land ownership commenced in Indian Territory. In practice, however, individually owned Mvskoke allotment land is not fully private: transactions (leases, sales) were and still are mediated through the federal government because the land is held in trust by the federal government.

This land is defined today as restricted land or individual Indian land within the practice of tribal realty. In Oklahoma, restrictions were placed on the land and ownership was limited only to tribal members who were at least half-Indian.[13] Tribal members holding restricted Indian land could not be taxed for the land; however, they could not broker or collect on their own land dealings, such as oil and gas leases or grazing leases.[14] Then and today, the government still intervenes and serves as a middleman, with any royalties placed in the Individual Indian Money (IIM) account. IIM accounts have been a contentious area, and most recently the United States government has agreed to settle over mismanaged IIM accounts.[15] The federal government's failure to uphold its trust responsibility is the reason for the *Cobell v. Salazar* victory, which ruled that IIM account holders would be compensated for mismanagement of their assets—this resulted in a $3 billion–plus settlement award. What has become problematic with regard to this land today is fractionated ownership of land, or undivided ownership interest; when there is no will, it becomes further fractionated upon one's death because it is passed on to one's heirs, and American Indian Probate Reform Act of 2004 (AIPRA) regulations eventually revert ownership of fractionated land to the tribe. In the case of land fractionation, the land parcel does not get parceled into smaller units, but the interest that the land owners have in the property becomes fractionated. Thus ownership devolves from families to the tribal government because of failure to maintain a legal instrument within the politics of recognition.

MCN has actively rebuilt its land base by purchasing land in an effort to reconsolidate; this land has a mix of statuses, and the complicated land nomenclature can create a disparate checkerboard across the tribe's jurisdiction and make adjudicating major crimes difficult. The three primary statuses that affect MCN and its tribal members are tribal trust land, restricted land, and fee simple land. Trust land is land purchased by the tribe and placed in trust with the United States government. The development of casinos must be conducted on land that is held in trust by the federal government.[16] One of the implications of trust land and restricted land is that they carry a federal status, which complicates legal matters. For example, the Major Crimes Act deems that if a crime such as capital murder or rape is committed in Indian country—in MCN's case, either tribal trust land or individual restricted land—it falls under federal jurisdiction.[17] Thus the Federal Bureau of Investigation presides over the investigation, and a U.S. attorney is responsible for adjudicating these cases. Conversely, fee simple lands are treated just like any other privately held land would be treated; these lands are taxed and fall entirely under nontribal authority.

The tribe's status as a domestic dependent sovereign, although an impaired version of sovereignty, enables a level of autonomy and protection within Oklahoma despite dramatic shifts in land holdings and land status. The tribe's land base has changed dramatically over the last two centuries; however, the tribe's status as a domestic dependent sovereign has persisted since Supreme Court Justice John Marshall provided a legal opinion regarding tribes' relationship to the federal government in *Worcester v. Georgia* in 1832. This enables some level of protection against explicit annihilation by nontribal entities, but it is still an injured form of sovereignty. I am not necessarily celebrating MCN's legitimacy in a settler colonial state; I am simply addressing this because in a settler colonial power relationship, the state legitimacy of tribes provides some protection at the scale of the subnational state. In Oklahoma, the tribe's status as a domestic dependent sovereign complicates the ability of subnational states to exert power over tribes, except where federal power has devolved to the state scale.

Located within a matrix of federal and state power, MCN has become entangled in the process of the devolution of power, by which tribes cede power and authority to the state of Oklahoma when entering gaming and tobacco compacts. Corntassel and Witmer argue in *Forced Federalism: Contemporary*

MUSCOGEE (CREEK) NATION CASINOS

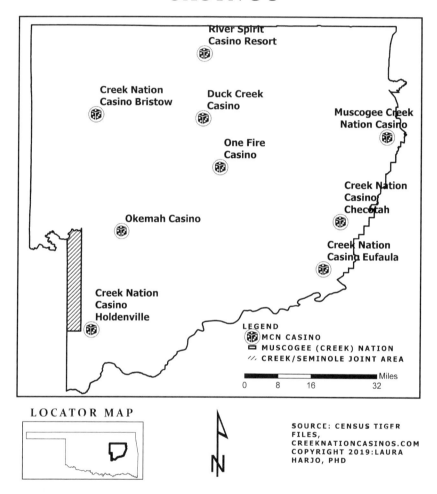

MAP 1 Map of casinos in Muscogee (Creek) Nation. Map by Laura Harjo.

Challenges to Indigenous Nationhood that the federal government has devolved significant power to the state and trace how the Indian Gaming Regulatory Act (IGRA) has done this in particular.[18] Devolution of tribal power is evidenced by the tribe's entanglement in local state-tribe negotiations around gaming compacts. First, it should be noted that, as stated above, casino developments are only allowed on federal land held in trust for a tribe.[19]

The Indian Gaming Regulatory Act is a federal policy that lays out a hierarchy of gaming, and as tribes move to a higher class of gaming, they are required to negotiate and enter into gaming compacts with the state, thus devolving their power to that state. IGRA's three classes of gaming are defined as follows: **Class I** is related to traditional tribal gaming, such as peon games (bone games) among the Southern California tribes or hand games among the Plains tribes (these are still practiced in Oklahoma). **Class II** includes bingo, pull tabs, and electronic bingo games. **Class III** includes games of chance that one would find in Las Vegas, such as slots and table games (blackjack, poker, etc.).[20] If a tribe wishes to offer Class III gaming, then the tribe is required by IGRA to negotiate a gaming compact with the state.[21] The relationship of the class of gaming to the requirement that tribes negotiate with the state government is problematic because, as set out by federal Indian policy, the tribe's government-to-government relations should be with the federal government and not the state government. These changes in how land is owned and controlled are key to understanding power relations between MCN and various scales of the state, and they have implications for how the MCN came to take its current form. This example is yet another instance of the federal government qualifying and devolving tribal sovereignty.

Oppressive Power

Indigenous peoples in Oklahoma have been subjected to oppressive power, which I define as any sort of enactment of control that suppresses Indigenous people and communities. Not all authoritative power is oppressive, and some types of authoritative power, such as environmental regulations, can protect communities from harmful situations such as polluted waterways. Oppressive power can take many forms: it can come from geopolitical units or from everyday folks in the public sphere. Local discourse is one powerful example. Discourse shapes and (re)enacts the Indigenous subject as rich, as dumb, as childlike, as a freeloader, as a relic; these ideas get mobilized in local discourse, by the media, in blog posts and comments, and by local non-Indigenous citizens. This kind of power works to maintain hierarchies in the region at the expense of Indigenous peoples and their governments.

At different moments in MCN's tribal history, the tribe has been the subject of federal Indian policy. U.S. ideologies, philosophies, power, domination, and authority are mediated via federal policy and via federal government structures. MCN has been dispossessed of its lands, had its population transferred during the Trail of Tears, and faced assimilation at the height of the boarding school era and during the Indian relocation era—these are settler colonial tactics for denationalizing a people.[22] On a local scale, the state of Oklahoma introduced legislation proposing English as the official language of the state, forgetting about the thirty-eight or more tribal languages that were spoken before the settlers arrived, some of which are still spoken, while others have fallen silent.

Based on the evidence, one might hypothesize that both the local and federal governments continually enact political practices that foreclose the tribe's expansion in material and discursive ways. At every step in the process of tribal nation-building and development, the state government is right in stride with some sort of policy, law, or institution that mediates its power, thus reducing the possibilities and vision of tribal peoples. Discursive foreclosures are the meanings produced and informed by and through the media about a people or place that are predicated on difference, concretized in an individual's mind and system of thoughts, and practiced to the detriment of communities of difference, such as Indigenous people, reducing their conditions of possibility.[23] Community vision is curtailed as small local battles are fought at the expense of realizing larger visions for self-determination.

How do MCN's possibilities and visions get scaled down and foreclosed? Tribes might construe Oklahoma's policies and legislation as hostile gestures toward Indian populations.[24] With bills such as the one aimed at making English the official language of the state of Oklahoma, the Oklahoma legislature suggests that the narrative of the state commenced when white settlers arrived. This is a dominant discourse that is embedded at the local scale and can prove tenacious in Indian/non-Indian relations in Oklahoma. Much to the chagrin of Native parents, every year in Oklahoma schools around the state celebrate the Oklahoma land rush, where children choose to be either an "Indian" or a "Sooner" in reenactments.

The local discourse about MCN has primarily centered on taxation issues, tribal/state tobacco and gaming compacts, and economic development, with a host of attached issues such as land disputes and jurisdictional issues. IGRA enmeshed tribal governments with state governments and devolved some of the federal powers to the state, by forcing tribes to negotiate tribal/state gaming compacts. The reasoning behind the gaming compact is that it is a means for the state to accumulate capital that theoretically will be used for infrastructure improvements.

Barrow offers a critical view of the state and its façade of serving the greater good while actually serving the accumulation of capital: "The state's ideological mechanisms convey the image that its power is organized to pursue the general interests of society, even though it functions in a specific relationship to capitalist accumulation."[25] This is problematic for MCN in many aspects: first, the state's ideology is so deeply embedded that it is considered common sense; second, because the state claims to serve the interests of society, this induces the general population to believe that the state's discourse and approaches are in their best interests; third, the political discourse about Oklahoma-based tribes generates racialized policies and sentiments toward tribes—that is, discursive foreclosures.

The state's ideology of capitalist accumulation is deeply entrenched and is reproduced and carried out in its position regarding the taxation of MCN; the state's attitude toward MCN and other tribes is predicated on them paying tribute to the state.[26] The state wants and expects tribal nations to pay taxes to the state—but which scale of the state (nation, state, county, municipality) gets to collect and how this surplus is redistributed is often in flux. This is the premise of a tribal-state gaming compact. A primary argument of the state is that tribes benefit from the infrastructure that the state builds. However, the same point could be argued by MCN: that the state and its citizens benefit from tribally based infrastructure projects—for example, the building of roads and water lines. The state of Oklahoma and its towns benefit when the tribe develops regional infrastructure. However, while the state frames these issues in terms of tax justice, thus inflaming public discourse and opinions about the tribe, the real issue here is that the state believes that it has jurisdiction over tribes while ignoring MCN's direct and indirect economic impact on the region. In 2014, the Oklahoma Indian Gaming Association (OIGA) reported that the annual direct impact of Oklahoma Indian gaming was $4.2 billion; the indirect impact, taking into account the multiplier effect, was $6.9 billion, which includes related sectors such as construction. Tribes' economic impact in Oklahoma is over $11 billion annually. Further, 60 percent of tribal gaming employees are non-Indian.

While tribes understand their relationship to the federal government, the state of Oklahoma is either not adept at understanding or refuses to understand tribes' unique trust relationship to the federal government. This further confounds politics, relationships, and discourse at the regional scale (between MCN and the state of Oklahoma). Parallels can be drawn to Clyde Woods's work and the ways in which he argues that capitalist regimes inter- and intraregionally inform racialized policies and discourse at the expense of groups of color.

Local Opposition to MCN Development

During the fall of 2009, a locally based community group, South Tulsa Citizens Coalition, called for the City of Tulsa to condemn property that MCN was considering for future development. At the same time, Tulsa city councilor Bill Christiansen expressed opposition to a potential MCN development.[27] The development plans were conceptual, proprietary, and unreleased. However, Councilor Christiansen did not discuss the plans with the tribe but rather voiced his opposition to the press and at the city council meeting. In a 2009 article in the *Tulsa World* entitled "Councilors Resist Land Action," Christiansen argues, "It's scary to think that the tribe could go up and down the river and buy great, developable land and take it off the city's rolls. . . . We cannot afford that as a city. We're already making service cuts and furloughing our employees."[28] Discourses of fairness and tax justice are operationalized to limit and problematize MCN land purchases. It must be underscored: this was an MCN development project that was internal and nascent; many projects unfold in the same way, as concepts that are entertained in order to assess plausibility. However, in this case, Christiansen and others frame the issue as if MCN is a burgeoning problem that must be mitigated. The press's coverage of this development plan detailed the arguments of the opposition—a city councilor, a community group, and a local developer. Each has different arguments for their opposition: the city councilor cites loss of sales tax; the community group cites an influx of more cars with no planned infrastructure development to accompany it; and the local developer cites lack of tax justice. At the heart of the controversy is the fact that the city's political jurisdiction does not reign over MCN. From MCN's point of view, it has the right to self-govern in perpetuity and has a large revenue-generating development in the area—River Spirit Casino. However, MCN is looking to diversify its financial portfolio away from tobacco and gaming. In more recent news, former Arkansas River Infrastructure Task Force member and Tulsa city councilor G. T. Bynum, currently the mayor of Tulsa, is working on a 2025 plan that involves seeking MCN's assistance in financing the upkeep of a low-water dam. This is difficult to grasp, and the relations are inconsistent, with city, county, and state seeking money from the tribe to finance local development, yet quashing the tribe's efforts to carry out the development of their own that will create a financial portfolio enabling them to support nontribal development. This is further evidence that, despite the tribe's status as a major economic contributor in Oklahoma, when tribes want to undertake development, it is critiqued and combed over more closely than other types of development (city, county, private—anything but Indigenous).

Rich Indian Racism

Jeff Corntassel and Richard Witmer discuss the concept of rich Indian racism as the targeting of tribal people by state and local policy because they are perceived as having the means to steer their own economic destiny.[29] Local, state, and federal discourse, as well as the media, frame tribal members as people who do not pay taxes. Thus there is a notion of tax injustice, of Indians getting a free ride and free use of public services. This public opinion all too easily becomes commonly received knowledge. It then becomes the norm, an ideology produced at many political scales, starting with the individual next-door neighbor, coworker, or schoolmate. The state no longer has to do the heavy lifting in subjugating a people when tribal members' next-door neighbors look at them "sideways" or suspiciously. Further, there is often an assumption that tribal governments are rich and can provide for every need, or that tribal governments squander their money, when in reality what might seem like a huge budget is offering tribal members an array of community development, health, and human services. What this means for tribal members is that people think they have money because of the rich Indian myth, when only a tiny segment of tribal folks in the United States receive large per-capita payments from gaming. In addition, Oklahoma legislators have been known to publicly express racist comments about Indigenous nations in Oklahoma—for example, the statement by former U.S. senator Tom Coburn (R) that Cherokees are not real Indians.

Tax Justice

The state's payoff for the subjugation of MCN is taxation to continue funding the central functions of the state. The fundamental functions of the state are framed in a manner that implies they are serving the common good; however, it could be argued that these functions serve one class within the state—the capitalist class.[30] In Oklahoma, the capitalist class and opponents of tribal sovereignty include the oil and gas industry, the convenience store chain QuikTrip, and One Nation United, a national anti-Indian organization.[31] The general argument within the state is that tribes are draining the state by receiving federal funding or support. Another commonly expressed argument is that if tribes aren't paying their fair share of taxes on their economic development, then they are depriving the state or another geopolitical entity such as the city of Tulsa.[32] Thus, tribes are targeted as contenders against the state. They are subverting the central function of the state, which is to funnel money to support capitalist accumulation.[33]

Shut Your Mouth, Child

To draw from American Indian studies and critical race theory, keeping Indigenous people in a box or treating them as nice little figurines in a cupboard relegates them to the status of safe, childlike entities and makes it easier to deal with them. When they are confined to the category of childlike primitives, they are not threats to the state.[34] The moment they say something that is not quaint or childlike, they then become contenders against the state. In Corntassel and Witmers's terms, Indigenous nations that have resources and financial means and resist the state are "contenders," while smaller tribes lacking the resources to resist the state are "militants."[35] When Indigenous nations are perceived either as contenders or militants, an environment of win/lose is established. In terms of contenders, it behooves the state to conquer this contender. When they are considered militants, they become criminalized, and their social justice movement is reduced to criminal activity that must be quashed. The trope of militant or contender is then articulated through the media—newspapers and television— until it becomes the norm.[36] The next-door neighbor will perceive people who are rightfully resisting oppression as militants or criminals. This then advances the state's agenda of extinguishing any threats to its central government, for a threat means less money to continue reproducing its ideology in the form of a neoliberal polity.

Are You Even Indian??

Another delegitimizing form of discourse is the attempt to debase tribal identity through the manipulation of stereotypical images of Native Americans for political purposes—noble, savage, primitive, childlike.[37] A problem that is unique to Indigenous peoples located in industrialized nations is the way they are perceived by non–tribal members and the way they advance legal claims. Regarding how they are perceived, often there is a romanticized notion of Indigenous peoples that is informed by popular culture. Within popular culture, the idyllic Indian, "the White man's Indian," wears a headdress, lives in a teepee, rides a horse, and hunts buffalo.[38] When tribal members must deal with non-Indians who are not familiar with specific tribal groupings, they find that non-Indians often do not realize that there is not one monolithic Indigenous identity (or one Muscogee identity, for that matter). This misconception leads nontribal individuals to bring issues of authenticity into the dynamic. Being Indian is evaluated according to the criteria of "the White man's Indian"; non-Indians say things like, "Oh, they do not look Indian," when a person does not have long black hair or high cheekbones.[39] This same question of authenticity enters the conversation when local policy makers question and problematize the authenticity of tribal members. The ultimate measure of legitimacy for an Indigenous people in the United States is federal recognition. Thus, even though Indigenous nations may have gone through the nation-state's defined procedures to ensure legitimacy, this very state-sanctioned legitimacy is still called into question by state actors such as state and federal legislators. Corntassel argues that the question of legitimacy or lack thereof is opened and reopened depending on how much an Indigenous nation seems to pose a threat to the state.[40] In the case of the neoliberal state, the threat in question is the perceived threat to its stream of revenue collected through taxation.[41]

The reality of the delegitimizing discourse that I've discussed is that this is the context that Mvskoke people and other Indigenous groups in Oklahoma must contend with. It is a discourse deeply ingrained into and normalized by non-Indians in Oklahoma; I would venture to say that Indigenous groups in Oklahoma are nonplussed by the current state of the nation in which white supremacy is unabashedly and publicly valorized and practiced. I have examined material and discursive power relations between MCN and local, regional, and federal scales of the settler nation in a wide variety of ways, and I will now turn to a discussion of collective and transformative power.

Tool of Futurity: Collective Power

The graphic pictured in figure 10 is inspired by Southeastern designs, and again we see the repeating lines that are the hallmark of Mississippian iconography.

FIGURE 10 *Collective Power*, relief print, Laura Harjo.

I use this particular symbol to represent collective power: it represents the dance of four etvlwas connected to one another. Stompgrounds members welcome visitors from other grounds to theirs, to participate in their dances; there is an interconnectedness among ceremonial grounds. Each of the bends in the symbol marks the center of a tribal town, where a sacred fire would burn during a stompdance. The three lines represent the number of rings a dance might have. In this symbol there are four metaphoric fires that are tied to four dances, all happening simultaneously. Each of these grounds or towns is connected to the others in lines that continually flow. This is a view of several communities and of the connectedness of all Mvskoke communities, which is a form of collective power.

Mvskoke communities in their many iterations—stompgrounds, etvlwas, chartered communities, churches—are empowered by felt knowledge and alter-Native ways of engaging to transform, envision, and enact Mvskoke futurity. I begin to unpack this further with a case study from Sapulpa Creek Indian Community.

In the summer of 2017, the women of Sapulpa Creek Indian Community created a quilt together; each person constructed her own quilt square. In general, the community is often involved in art-based learning and projects, such as sewing Seminole patchwork, pucker-toe moccasins, and aprons, weaving reed and river cane baskets, and beading. This time, however, instead of working on individual projects, they decided to take on a sizeable collective project to create a quilt, and the chartered community supported this effort by supplying the necessary resources—the space and the sewing materials. Vicki Potts was the primary coordinator, and she provided sewing instruction, as did other women.

Creating this quilt was a process that involved making decisions about what the women would create together and what they wanted the quilt to look like. There were decisions to be made about the pattern and fabric. All of the women went to the fabric store together to pick the fabric for the chosen sewing pattern, in which each woman would create a hand-sewn appliqué depicting an Indigenous woman. Thus each quilt square was unique. The women met at the

Sapulpa Creek Indian Community Center and constructed their quilt squares together. There were varying degrees of sewing skills and abilities. However, the women persisted regardless. They were engaged in an iterative process of teaching and learning together; each woman might be a teacher in some moments and a learner in others. They worked on the quilt over a period of three months, all the way up to the night before the Creek Festival Quilt Show in June. They pulled an all-nighter because many in the quilting entourage wanted to go to the Friday night stompdance in Okmulgee, about a thirty-minute drive away from Sapulpa. However, the women prevailed in finishing the last stitch and delivered the finished product to the art show on Saturday.

The project was intergenerational, with women from a range of generations involved in creating it, making it an act of dialogue and collective power. Each of the women who took part in creating the quilt demonstrated a degree of responsibility to the collective, especially with regard to completing this significant project. While one group of women went to the stompdance, there was a small group that stayed behind and worked on stitching the quilt, and when the women returned from the dance, they stayed up late finishing the quilt: the relationship between both groups, the teamwork involved in the trading of shifts, is what is illustrative of collective power. The relationship is forged from a responsibility to each other. This uninterrupted and fluid effort requires a high degree of dialogue; the women had this with each other, and they had been working on it for several months as they constructed the quilt. Thus they were able to create a community quilt collectively.

The community quilt is a material manifestation of collective power because it is a piece that would have been more difficult for one person to complete on their own without dividing the labor among many individuals. This division of labor enables the burden to be shifted from one individual and taken up by many. Together, the community can create something much more extensive and vibrant than one person could create on their own. When we look more closely at the quilt, we see a plurality to the women depicted on the quilt squares because each woman created her own quilt square. In the appliqué figures they sewed, some of the women have long straight hair, or hair tied in a braid or ponytail, or short curly permed hair; some have black hair, and some have salt-and-pepper hair. These representations are compelling because they are inclusive of many versions of what an Indigenous woman or girl can look like. The quilt is a map of the interiority of each of the women who participated in its construction. Thus it is also a form of knowledge production. However,

FIGURE 11 Sapulpa Community quilt and two of its creators. L to R: Edna Berryhill, Ellen Harjo. Photograph by Laura Harjo.

in this process of collective power, what is also operating is Million's felt theory: the women are producing social relations with one another, strengthening their social networks and support systems. One participant reported that they enjoyed themselves and laughed together, and on some nights when they were not able to meet their desired progress, they visited, and this was just as valuable to her. They were able to get to know each other better, and the quilt has since garnered two first-place blue ribbons at two events—the Creek Festival Quilt Show and the Creek County Fair.

Transformative power as a tool of futurity enables Indigenous communities to understand the ways in which they already possess the capacity to change their community, a capacity that is located in their collective and felt knowledges. This is a different kind of power: it is not power that is located in place or in a center, as the Western model of governance suggests; it is not top-down or bottom-up, but rather horizontal. It interconnects kinship relationships (human and more-than-human) and mobilizes them as actions that benefit the community. Within Indigenous communities there is an interconnectedness that defies Western geopolitical orderings—for example, there is a spiritual realm that does not adhere to human-conceived boundaries, as well as plant and animal nations that are not contained by political borders or urban development.

Collective Power and Collective Economy

Mvskoke people work mutually to achieve livelihoods that ensure the maintenance of their households.[42] This transpires across kinship connections among extended family, nonblood kin, and households that draw upon these relationships in ways that are mutually beneficial—for example, if someone has a car and can give someone else a ride to the grocery store, the second person can give them gas money or prepare and share a meal with them.

Although demographic indicators paint a picture of struggle, there are ways in which Mvskoke people rely on one another to maintain their households that are rooted in Mvskoke values of generosity and reciprocity. There is an element of sharing, and a belief that what you can share is more valuable than what you can accumulate for yourself. Providing means for a household to reproduce itself—food, transportation, a place to do laundry—helps that household to persist, and the household members remember these generous acts and reciprocate in other ways when they are able. To an outsider, the reciprocal gift might seem to outweigh the generous acts, but people reciprocate what the act was worth to them. This too is bound up in Mvskoke traditions of visiting a *heles-hayv* (medicine man) or doing a favor in the form of manual labor, like cleaning gutters—you reciprocate in kind according to the worth you perceive. In this way, the act is not commodified with a market value, but instead has a value rooted in Indigenous futurity: you have tended to my spirit or my family, opening a new possibility for my household. A family might be a family of artists and reciprocate with a gift that would be worth a fair amount in the prevailing market economy.

Furthermore, this activates este-cate sovereignty, in which relationships are paramount, as well as Jacob's concept of a community making its own power with everyday acts.[43] Thus, alterNative economy is a subversive power that persists despite the state apparatus. When using this term, I capitalize the letter *N* to put emphasis on the Indigenous aspect of the word, *Native*. Communities persist, enacting a type of mutual help in which the individual who fixes your car might trade his services for wild onions and a set of shells for a female stompdancer in his family. AlterNative economy is a way of operating and persisting that flies under the radar of the market economy; many communities have enacted this and thrived in this way. I don't see this economy of mutual aid as a reaction to the capitalist settler economy: it is something that existed long before. We know this, we live this. However, Indigenous communities are framed as broken from the standpoint of a market economy. AlterNative economy was "the economy" in Mvskoke territory, and it predates the U.S. capitalist economy; in reality, a capitalist economy should be the alternative, not the Indigenous economy. There is power in reframing who we are and how we are represented by shifting our thinking about economy and the Indigenous community—we move away from the narrative of an underperforming community.

The material consequences of uneven power dynamics can be seen most starkly in the premature deaths in Mvskoke communities that lack access to needed resources. However, according to Linda Tuhiwai Smith, we should heed and represent the communities' counternarrative: while communities may not have access to formal development, I think that the label of "underdeveloped community" can be refused because they are deploying their own alterNative economies. When these alterNative economies are recognized, we must credit local knowledge and ingenuity. These alterNative economies function despite the structural racism and settler colonial logic we see at many important sites— the educational system, access to fair lending practices, and protection from predatory credit practices. Predatory lending practices rob communities now and dispossess them of their futures. Can a future lush with possibilities be imagined when everything you earn is directed toward paying off a high-interest loan, with no wiggle room for replacing a blown-out tire or a dead car battery, or even getting an oil change? In Arigon Starr's comic *Super Indian Vol. 1*, Mega Bear—the faithful sidekick to Super Indian—has his mother sew his purple superhero outfit. This is an example of alterNative economy: sewing your own clothes, catching rides with family and friends, and sharing a relative's washer and dryer.

So a scavenging economy develops, based on actions like collecting soda pop bottles and turning them in for change to buy an ice cream cone, as well as a mutual aid economy, in which someone who knows how to make a Mvskoke dress makes one for someone's daughter or granddaughter in exchange for auto mechanic work or grass cutting. This alterNative economy is an exchange of services, a barter economy instead of the market economy that exchanges capital (money) for goods and services. In an alterNative economy, the ontology of the object or good may shift with its use; it transforms from individual property into collective property. Responsibility for the object might rest in the hands of a primary steward who oversees its care and maintenance, but I have also witnessed collective effort toward the upkeep and care of such community goods that shows the mutual responsibility of community members and family members to one another.

For example, I have a 1985 Chevrolet truck in Oklahoma that my dad and I co-owned. We named it Tenetke Hvtke (White Thunder)—it is massive, imposing, and loud. It has character. A white truck with a red hood, it has an army sharpshooter rifle sticker and a United States Army sticker with large declarative letters in the back window, as well as an interior roof sticker that proclaims, "NO PARTY TOO BIG, NO BEER TOO TALL." Tenetke Hvtke remains just as I inherited it from my male relatives who possessed it: from one uncle who passed away it gained the courageous party sticker, and from my youngest uncle, a Vietnam War veteran, it gained the sharpshooter and U.S. Army stickers. Indigenous communities understand the utility and practicality of a truck: for those engaged in the alterNative economies that involve automobile parts in junkyards, dressers and bed frames at garage sales, and bicycles and tools at auctions and flea markets, it is crucial to have a truck to transport such goods. Tenetke Hvtke is more-than-human kin to the extended Harjo family; our family both used the truck and played a role in repairs.[44] Other examples might include a car owned by one family member that is used to haul other family members to town to buy supplies, or an individually owned washing machine that functions as a collective asset.

Through my work on this project, I have witnessed many burned-out buildings destroyed by arson in the space of MCN, especially in the rural towns of Hanna, Dustin, and Okmulgee. Narratives of Detroit and New Orleans similarly point to blighted physical and built environments. What some might consider blight is only on the surface; beyond these are narratives of place and kinship that remain invisible and uncredited. The stories of the "blighted" rural spaces of MCN likewise give way to a vibrant social fabric that includes ceremonial grounds like Pakan Tallahassee and Indian churches. Within these communities are dances, songs, prayers, and laughter—always laughter, which has sustained Mvskoke people for millennia. The cultural landscape for Mvskoke people in Oklahoma serves as a type of power. This is a power that often remains invisible to outsiders, and possibly invisible to community insiders too: when one is a fully ensconced community member, it is hard to be aware of the power of what you have. Thus, to undertake a deep reading of landscape, of space, of place, reveals yet another type of power and another tool of futurity. Chapter 6 includes exercises for community members to assess power and to realize the power that is bound up in felt knowledge and memory.

The implications of enacting Mvskoke practices of power are that we understand the power of the collective to create, transform, and function as a system of care. While this creating and transforming can serve our ways of thinking about and practicing este-cate sovereignty and knowledge production, others may argue, "Well, how is it going to serve grievance claims?" This book is not an exercise in how to navigate normative governance systems; it is an exercise in how to recognize the power of what we are already doing and see value in that. The implications, then, are that alterNative economies, power, and systems of care are not situated in the politics of recognition but instead within the community. Community is more than community by proximity.

Summary: Collective Power

Collective power is evidenced in many ways—in particular, I point out the ways in which it is produced at a stompdance, through quilt making, and in alterNative economies of sharing and exchange. All of these examples enable a community to continue reproducing and sustaining itself. Community dancing, creating, and sharing is transformational power; it carries the capacity to change, shape, and reimagine communities in ways that Mvskoke people value. Collective power is an alterNative way of decolonizing thinking about community power. The reality of the power landscape in Oklahoma is such that Mvskoke collective power must operate in tension with hegemonic types of power. However, despite this, Mvskoke people enact a decolonial collective power that embodies vnokeckv, rather than recreating hegemonic power imposed on them in forms such as the authoritative power and oppressive power that are carried out by local political institutions and local discourse about Mvskoke and other Indigenous people in Oklahoma.[45] A Mvskoke counter to this is illustrated by the quilt made by the women of Sapulpa Creek Indian Community.

Collective power is a way-finding tool back to the practices that Mvskoke people perform together; it provides a map to the next world by pointing to the practices that bring us together and invoke us to talk and share, in service to social relations. It is also a way-finding tool back to the idea that the collective working together can accomplish more than one person. There is potential and skill in our everyday practices. At face value, when we are fully ensconced in everyday practices, practicing them may seem insignificant, but they hold a great capacity to move, transform, and change communities and social relations. It is important because everyday collective actions hold power; pausing for a moment and making connections between ancestor relatives, future relatives, and ourselves is instructive. It is from this position that we realize a type of power that is unobstructed by space and time. Collective activities produce collective power; when people practice activities like creating a quilt together, dancing at the stompgrounds, cooking a community meal together, or playing in Indigenous softball tournaments, it brings them closer together, strengthening community networks of support. Collective power builds on the previous tools by spiraling self-determination, knowledge, practices, kinship, and energy together. Emergence geographies are the spatialities produced by these Mvskoke social relations, and I will discuss them in the next chapter.

CHAPTER 4

Emergence Geographies

Clearing the Fog

In one of our emergence stories, there was a great fog that obscured everything; it blocked the people from finding one another. Then a huge bird swooped in, flapping its large wings. This powerful wind rippled the earth into the present-day mountains in the southeastern United States.[1] This cleared the way for Mvskokvlke to move from darkness and fog and to be able to see one another. Mvskoke people emerged from the fog to find their kin and form groups that would become known as clans. Clans are passed down matrilineally and have persisted, connecting one through one's mother to the emergence of Mvskoke people.[2] There are many iterations of being Mvskoke, and there are probably just as many different iterations of the Mvskoke story of emergence.

One's clan is traced to the Mvskoke emergence story, and it situates one across time and space. While working for Cherokee Nation, I sat in on a Cherokee history course, and at one moment the instructor firmly declared to the class that there is absolutely no reason to know your clan today, insisting that the prevailing conditions no longer necessitate clans. While I am not Cherokee, their political, economic, and cultural structures are like those of Mvskoke people. Thus I was confused by her declaration, and I vehemently disputed this disavowal of clan identity with her. Knowledge of one's clan also places one in direct connection to and relationship with a Mvskoke social fabric and Mvskoke knowledge system that persist and (re)emerge across time. Even if our clans no longer function in the same way they used to, time does not stand still, nor does the way in which we relate to time, place, and culture. Mvskoke people are responsive in many ways to the contemporary moment, as I argue in this book—culture is not static. That does not mean that clans become evacuated of meaning or significance.

The story of Mvskoke people is the narrative of movement: movement into clans, the movement of energy from entity to entity, the movement of stomp-dance, the movement of the songs and language from generation to generation. In many ways we are just like the flowing bodies of water we have always lived near. Mvskoke people are always emerging, moving into formation—the clan, the tribal town, the community—and finding one another, whether in Los Angeles or Alabama. Mvskoke people have continually asserted who they are; in old geographies and newer geographies, they continually seek to gather strength and (re)form communities, whether in places like Indian Territory or in twenty-first-century Oklahoma. We still tell our creation story, and the community speaks its collective knowledge. Mvskoke removal to Indian Territory is one such movement. The politics of recognition produced routes of genocide over land and water, but the Mvskokvlke produced ephemeral spaces during removal along the route for our relatives who died and moved between the material and spiritual realms during this traumatic flow of people from east to west. These ephemeral spaces are Mvskoke responses to settler-enacted geographies and routes.

The journey to Indian Territory is a spatial narrative about (1) displacing people from natal community to Indian Territory, and (2) displacing them from human form to spirit form. This spatial narrative is a metanarrative generated by federal Indian policy and punctuated by numerous ephemeral Mvskoke productions of space, which I illustrate through Mvskoke burial practices on the Trail of Tears. This movement of Mvskokvlke is a route, a flow—genocidal and forced, but a flow nevertheless—over land and water from the southeastern homelands to current-day Oklahoma. A series of burial places invoked the homelands of Alabama and Georgia and the spirit world in ways that sustained Mvskoke psyches and bodies subjected to intolerable conditions, even as they tended to their deceased kin.

Mvskokvlke were clothed in attire not appropriate for winter storms and cold; in some cases, their footwear was worn down, and a bloody trail was left in the snow. Overhead hundreds of buzzards followed, hovering, waiting, and inherently knowing how death moves.[3] Mvskoke people were not afforded the time or permission to bury their dead; the most they could do was take their relative to the side of the trail and cover them with rocks and a blanket. But by taking care of their kin who died along the trail in this way, Mvskokvlke created sacred places along the route to present-day Oklahoma, and along the way produced ephemeral spaces. Energy moved across many scales and many forms: as the "deceased" relatives transitioned to another form, moving across the material and spiritual realms, perhaps their energy or presence was pulled to a different place, or perhaps their life force ushered the group on the journey to Indian Territory, or perhaps they traveled to the source of all energy—the Milky Way.[4]

In these moments, scale and place are instantiated in ways that are not readily tangible but are apparent to those with a honed consciousness. Prior to removal, there was already a church tradition established among Mvskoke people—to what degree, I cannot say. However, the current community contends that Mvskoke people sang Mvskoke hymns to sustain themselves through this traumatic event. Mvskoke people drew upon what they valued, and what nourished their spirits and bodies, to stay alive under indisputably fatal conditions.

Mvskoke people made places and held space for their relatives to transition to the next place among the stars, and burial traditions from the Trail of Tears are still narrated and practiced in the contemporary moment. Today, when a Mvskoke person dies, often this practice is still invoked: a blanket is placed on them—a Pendleton or a quilt, the person's favorite blanket or one gifted by someone—as part of the individual's spirit journey, and the soulful Mvskoke hymns are sung for them. The narration of the blanket story at funerals is a form in which the community speaks; in the retelling of the origins of this practice, we are urged to remember that the relative is joined with the larger Mvskoke collective. Spiritual leaders and pastors presiding over the interment of the deceased remind funeral attendees of their responsibility to Mvskoke people and of their duty not to squander their gifts but to recognize them and use them for the benefit of Mvskokvlke.

After this traumatic journey, Mvskoke people reemerged from grief and trauma and consecrated the land for future ceremonial and etvlwa uses. Within Indian Territory was another emergence story and a new iteration of the etvlwa; Mvskoke people ceremonially lit the western council fire, which was their first ceremonial fire in Indian Territory.

When the Upper Creeks started on their long trail from Alabama to the new
Indian Territory, a pot of ashes and a burning brand were taken from the council
fires at Tulwa. Each day along the trail, a brand would be taken from the previous
night's fire to light the fire at the close of a day's march. In this manner, from
day to day throughout the entire trip, the camp fires were lighted along the route
from the embers of the last camping place. Upon their arrival in the Creek Nation,
they selected a site on the crest of a hill overlooking the Arkansas River on which
grew a mighty oak tree. The site was high enough that they could view the plains
to the south and east. With much ceremony, they scattered the ashes over the
ground surrounding the tree. This meant to them that their western council fire
was actually burning from the flames of their Alabama homeland.[5]

Lighting the fire of Locvpokv tribal town emplaced their etvlwa, and this
functioned as a (re)emergence.[6] Figure 12 shows the Creek Nation Council
Oak. There space was appropriated for the first western etvlwa, and fire instantiated a new scale and a new place, and maybe even emplaced the Mvskoke people
within the original bloc of Mississippian people that spanned the Southeast,
Midwest, Great Lakes, and lower plains of what is now called the United States.
The etvlwa fire at the Council Oak tree is arguably one of the first sites of political governance for Mvskoke people in their present-day jurisdiction. Tracing
some examples of Mvskoke movement since emergence demonstrates how (re)
emergence and place making happen in many moments, places, and ways—this
is an area rich for further examination and conceptualization. Regardless, place
making is central to Mvskoke survivance and futurity.

Mvskoke people continue to craft emergence stories out of stories of subjugation, rising out of a dark time and the impact of a forced removal. Stories
recount the U.S. Army officials' horses being fed better than Mvskoke people
at Fort Gibson in Oklahoma, with Mvskoke people scratching through the
horses' scraps to survive.[7] Mvskoke people emerged from this time to establish
their own settlements and ceremonial grounds. The Dawes Severalty Act of 1887
fractured lands, changing land from communal to individually owned, and the
subsequent Curtis Act ensured the wholesale dismantling of all Mvskoke lands
and the Mvskoke tribal government and court system—this was the federal
government's approach to assimilating Mvskoke people, along with others. The
list goes on and on—and in its face, Mvskoke people, the object of repeated
federal policy meant to manage Indigenous peoples, continually craft their own
emergence stories.

FIGURE 12 Creek Nation Council Oak in Tulsa, Oklahoma. Photograph by Hot-vlkuce Harjo.

Prior to becoming a chartered community with its own community center and Head Start buildings, my own community, Sapulpa Creek Indian Community, as my mother informed me, met in a Jiffy laundromat in town and at a now-defunct mall: this was the space that was available to rent for meetings. When Mvskoke people continue to appropriate space, this is a contemporary emergence story. (Re)emergence shows up in many ways. There are many pivot points for Mvskoke people. Sharing and discussing these critical junctures of a community's continued (re)emergence provides an opportunity to convene community and craft a participatory timeline. Consequently, a community can (re)collect the critical parts of their story and the community memories most important to the members. A community-created timeline can articulate the values and principles Mvskoke people hold fast to in these (re)emergence stories. These are guiding principles or tenets of being Mvskoke, which transcend geographic place and are rooted in embodied Mvskoke ways of being in the world.

A twenty-first-century notion of emergence appears in both the analog and the virtual community, the former being actual sites where people come together physically and the latter being internet-based communities. This reemergence of analog and virtual Mvskoke relationality collapses the time-space continuum. It is not necessary to journey far to go home: one can Skype, FaceTime, or Facebook message one's kin.

We know that it is important for people to determine for themselves the choices that they feel are best for them and their respective communities—this is self-determination. However, another important concept in this work is to understand what matters the most to people, what they value—be it aspects of tribal government, their community, or Mvskoke lifeways. Therefore I chose to conduct a survey, which I called the "Creek Community Survey," to ask Mvskokvlke what they care about and what they thought the long-range outlook was for MCN, Mvskokvlke, and our lifeways. This survey can be analyzed in diverse ways, the first being as a map to knowing which policy and program areas tribal members explicitly want MCN to work on. However, other ways to read the survey results include grasping a sense of prevailing community values and understanding at which geographic scales people feel they have the most agency and connection. In this chapter, the narrative of Mvskokvlke picks up in the early twenty-first century, in which there is a virtual emergence of the Creek community found within online sites and groups where Mvskokvlke find fellowship or rant about the current state of affairs of MCN. Because of these active virtual Creek communities, I chose to make the Creek Community Survey accessible online as well as available in a hard copy to fill out.

Autonomous Creek Towns Prior to Removal

The development trajectory of the Creek community originates in the aboriginal homelands in the southeastern United States and is informed today by a tribal charter that outlines how chartered communities can develop. Prior to removal, Creek communities were autonomous tribal towns that governed themselves; many had their own dialects of Mvskoke, while Euchees have their own linguistic stock that is different from Muskogean.[8] However, tribal town autonomy shifted, and during the eighteenth and nineteenth centuries the towns organized into a larger nation in response to the influx of European settlers and their encroachment on Muscogee territory. This confederacy is known today as the Muscogee (Creek) Nation.[9] Negotiations with settler nations—France, England, and then the United States—also played a role in the development of a more formal "Creek Nation." These countries negotiated with other sovereign entities by means of exchanges or agreements between the supreme ruler of one territory and that of another. Coalescing the tribal towns into a nation did not quite conform with how the Mvskoke people organized themselves politically; however, negotiating with these other countries required a supreme leader. MCN came from the act of coalescing many tribes within the southeastern region, as a response to settler colonialism and for the sake of survival. Over time, however, tribal towns have been subordinated as subnational polities, save for the three federally recognized Mvskoke tribal towns.

Cultural Geography

Traditionally the tribal towns had a center where political and cultural activities took place, and at the perimeter were dwellings.[10] After removal, the same sort of town morphology (layout and design) was articulated in the ceremonial grounds or stompgrounds, as well as in the Indian churches. The ceremonial grounds took on the names of their pre-removal sites—for example, Arbeka or Weagoftee. Some gained new names, such as Pole Cat or Duck Creek, based on local place names. There is a fire at the center of the grounds where all dance, and arbors where the men sit.[11] At the perimeter of the grounds are camps where participants eat, sleep, and visit.

MUSCOGEE (CREEK) NATION CHARTERED COMMUNITIES

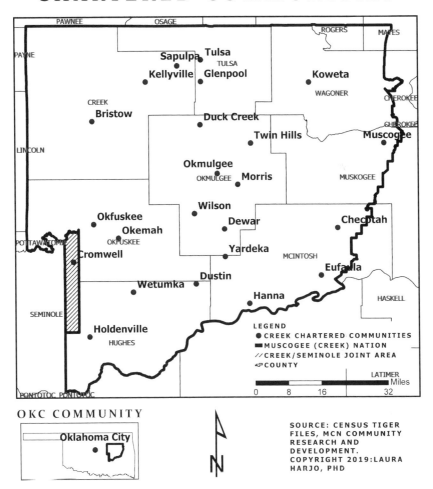

MAP 2 Map of MCN chartered communities. Map by Laura Harjo.

While the chartered communities (see map 2) have developed primarily in incorporated areas, several subcommunities existed before the chartered community. The development trajectory of the community from precontact times up to now has consisted of tribal towns, ceremonial grounds, Indian Baptist or Methodist churches, and chartered communities. Tribal members still identify with precontact tribal towns, ceremonial grounds, and Indian churches. MCN took a turn toward normative governance structures for the etvlwa through the creation of chartered communities; the chartered community structure requires technical skills of community members such as knowledge of bookkeeping and allowable expenditures, facilities management, and community planning. The chartered communities are required to maintain bylaws and a leadership board. Consequently, not all communities have the time or ambition to operate a chartered community. A normative form of organizing and governing themselves might actually hamper them from fully creating the kind of community they desire.

These various communities work actively to improve the quality of life or standard of living. Three sovereign tribal towns within MCN have constitutional governments. At the scale of the federally recognized tribal town, tribal government members have triple nationalities—MCN, the USA, and one of the three federally recognized tribal towns: Alabama-Quassarte Tribal Town, Kialegee Tribal Town, and Thlopthlocco Tribal Town. Thlopthlocco and Alabama-Quassarte Tribal Towns both have casinos: Thlopthlocco's is located adjacent to Interstate 40, a major transportation corridor, while Alabama-Quassarte's is located in the small town of Wetumka. This town has a population of approximately 1,400 and is one of the larger towns in the region. Thus, Thlopthlocco has been able to build a larger government in comparison to the other two tribal towns.[12]

Stompgrounds is the vernacular term for ceremonial grounds.[13] This site and the accompanying ceremonial practices are the origin of Mvskoke epistemology. Green Corn, or *posketv*, is the new year for Mvskoke people; it is a time of personal renewal, and the past year's transgressions are forgiven at this time.[14] Traditionally, houses would be cleaned, old pots would be thrown out, and all ill feelings toward others would be released so as not to be carried on into a new year. The stompgrounds assist or heal one's psyche.[15] The stompgrounds have typically been sustained by their own members, who build and repair the semipermanent camps and outhouses with their own means. The members also personally cover the costs of purchasing and preparing food for hundreds of visitors coming to their stompgrounds, although some stompgrounds organize fundraising during the winter months, such as indoor stompdances with food sales and bingo. The stompgrounds have typically been kept separate from the tribal government, except for an annual monetary gift that the tribe now gives to the various stompgrounds. The Indian churches within MCN's jurisdiction are highly organized and part of larger establishments—the Southern Baptist

Convention and United Methodist Church. Tribal towns, stompgrounds, and Indian churches are separate, but all are transmitters of daily lived practices of being Muscogee, which is the base of MCN.

Based on the ways in which Mvskoke geographies emerge, I posit that there are four types of emergence geography: (1) concrete, (2) ephemeral, (3) metaphysical, and (4) virtual. I offer these provisionally. In the first instance, concrete geographies relate to material places, such as towns, communities, and the built environment. We might see an MCN chartered community, a ceremonial grounds, an Indian church, or an area of settlement as examples of concrete emergence geographies. Areas of settlement can take the form of allotments where extended kin live; another example might be the tribal housing subdivisions across MCN. The second type is ephemeral geographies—these can be an event that occurs seasonally or intermittently, such as the Creek Festival, wild onion dinners, or a family softball game. Ephemeral geographies are not tied to a particular place and can remain in movement. Other examples of such geographies might be impromptu meetings of a group of Mvskoke people; in cases where Mvskoke groups do not have a formal meeting place, meeting places can take form wherever Mvskoke people decide to convene. A sports tournament might function as an ephemeral geography in that it convenes for a weekend and then dissipates. In the case of Indian removal from the Southeast, when Mvskoke people died along the way, a series of impermanent burials were created to pay respects to the deceased; these sites marked and memorialized the individuals' transition to and journey through interstitial spaces. The third type of emergence geography is metaphysical, which can consist of spaces and places that connect to a spiritual realm. In the previous example, the impermanence of the burial site is an ephemeral geography, but an individual's energy presence and journey are part of a metaphysical geography. An example of this is the Hickory Ground site and the cemetery located in Alabama in current-day Poarch Band Creek jurisdiction. MCN considers this to be a sacred space. However, Poarch Band of Creek Indians exhumed Mvskoke bodies from their burial sites to construct their casino expansion. While the case is pending in the settler colonial court system, MCN is arguing that the site's sacredness has been diminished by the actions of Poarch Band of Creek Indians. The exhumation conflicts with Mvskoke beliefs and practices related to disturbing the burial places of deceased ancestors. Moreover, metaphysical spaces reemerge, as in the story of reestablishing a Mvskoke town site in present-day Tulsa.

The fourth type of emergence geography is virtual geographies, which are shaped in the current moment by information and communications technologies (ICT) and technologies such as virtual reality and interactive mapping that combines ICT, virtual representations, and drone imagery. This type of emergence geography is not fixed in place and inhabits virtual space. As information and communications technologies continue to develop and reform, so does the use of these spaces by Mvskoke communities that find utility in convening within virtual spaces on the Internet and in social media and maintaining social relations there. These four emergence geographies that I suggest are predicated on contemporary Mvskoke practices, notwithstanding new formations of the ways in which Mvskoke communities convene and reemerge; emergence geographies are open to further development and reconstitution.

Survey Design and Emergence Geographies

In 2009, I conducted the Creek Community Survey. Emergence geographies shaped the design and administration of the survey instrument and its questions and provided a framework for grappling with the complexity of Mvskoke spatialities. The entire survey instrument that was used can be found in the appendix. It is important to understand the legacy of many spatialities of Mvskokvlke in order to ask comprehensively where Mvskokvlke perform their social relations. The survey sought to understand three Mvskoke-produced scales—MCN, community, and personal participation in the futurity of Mvskoke lifeways. From these three scales, Mvskokvlke shared what concerned them most and provided insight into their relationship to tribal government and community and their wish to extend Mvskoke lifeways. As I embarked on this, I continually returned to community folks, checking in with them about the research approaches. Using this method, I built upon a research justice framework in which I was not the sole producer of the questions. The goal of the community survey was to create information about the Mvskoke community at three geographic scales—the nation, the community, and the Mvskoke tribal member—that was generated by the community. It was also meant as a site for community members to share their struggles and their wishes. As I began the initial survey design, I was in conversation with various community members, asking for their feedback on survey questions, checking if the questions sounded off-base, and requesting help in shaping the linguistic cadence of the questions. I eventually posed these questions through a survey instrument administered to 326 participants, which was at times a delicate and tense conversation. The analysis was equally delicate, as there are explicit and implicit ways in which the community chooses to draw attention to and ask for recognition of their concerns, their assessment of current political and cultural conditions, and their aspirations to move these conditions to a better place. If one were to solely examine the literal meaning of the question and the literal meaning of their responses, this would only capture one facet. There is a deeper context, and in some ways there is a Mvskoke way of being in the world that is a dance. I perform this dance even when I ask my questions, because it is too rude, too imposing, to ask someone straight-up questions that are considered standard social science questions: How much money do you make? Rude. What do you do for a living? Rude. Are you married? Rude. So there is a dance involved in the questions I generated: they pass muster in academia, but they are truly structured to resonate with Mvskoke ways of being in the world, to ensure that we can perceive what the community is saying in several different dimensions. These are questions that in some moments do a lot of heavy lifting, meaning that they take a lot of thinking and sometimes might do triple or quadruple duty in terms of what the response reveals—wants, needs, voids, sense of agency, values, and geographies, to name a few things. A survey cannot capture all of the depth and context of participants' felt knowledge, though, which resulted in extended conversations with participants after completing their survey.

Many took time to stay and visit with me and discuss their concerns about the tribe and what their wishes were for the future. And as we work through the survey results, we find that there are implicit ways in which the community is expressing its concern. In summary, this is sacred work that embodies wishes, concerns, and visions for Mvskoke people expressed by Mvskoke people. In the end, the survey proved to be lengthy and was a bit of a time investment, requiring ten to fifteen minutes to take it. For this reason, I am grateful for the participants' gift of time and input. I am also grateful that it meant enough to over three hundred people to respond and express their needs and their desires for the tribe, their respective communities, and Mvskoke lifeways.

Community Survey Design

The survey drills down deeply with primary data, without having to rely on secondary data to understand the dimensions of the community. For example, tribes often must rely on census data to ascertain the prevailing conditions of the community. Initially, the survey set out to cover several dimensions that shape MCN. The survey primarily focused on tribal policies and community values that MCN needed to heed and maintain over the next seven generations. The survey design was initially influenced by the Nation Building school of thought, which included the work of D. H. Smith, Steven Cornell, and Joseph Kalt, focused on tribal policies and community values within the politics of recognition.[16] Although my scholarship has pivoted away from this particular knowledge stream and embraced critical Indigenous studies and Indigenous feminisms, the survey information is still valuable because it articulates the areas that community folks deemed most important. As an act of reciprocity, it remains important to share the feedback that the community provided, and in a stompdance call-and-response of data and analysis, futurity can be imagined. Sharing the community feedback can serve as a call to the tribe and communities to respond with a plurality of imaginaries that are not solely located in tribal policy and development. Perhaps community can respond by enacting este-cate sovereignty and community knowledge—this might look like a community-crafted quilt, a Mvskoke film festival, or a digital game.

Community values embody what Mvskoke communities believe is important. What is important here, and very unique to Indigenous planning, is that community planning does not solely address where a community should place a building, what it should look like, how we will get the financing, or how we will sustain this community asset. It is those things, but my focus here is not on that. My focus is on the way in which community values are interrelated and informed across time and space. While there are many types of plans, ranging from short-term strategic plans to plans that geopolitical regions refer to as "visions"—for example, Tulsa County's Vision 2025—often the focus in planning is on the present or some proximate time juncture; it focuses on the place we are in now and is often related to the physical design and development of a place.[17] There is an impulse to address the current most demanding issues of concrete geographies, and this consumes energy and resources that are necessary to put into Indigenous community futurity and concomitant lifeways that occur in other settings such as ephemeral and metaphysical geographies. Indigenous communities have much to grapple with in challenging the status quo of local public discourse. Tribal policies and community values provide a foundation for tribal planning: MCN's tribal policies are what the tribe has chosen to focus on and invest resources in, and community values can inform MCN about how to carry out its policies and where its policy focus should be. The survey elicits members' views of the effectiveness of the current tribal government, the issues members perceive as most important for improving their quality of life, and the importance of practicing and sustaining MCN's culture and lifeways.

Two previous surveys performed by Cherokee Nation and Seminole Nation informed my decision to use a convenience sample for my research. Both nations have performed language surveys, and both have documented the issues with using a tribal random sample, which led them to use a convenience sample.[18] Based on my experience at Cherokee Nation with a needs assessment survey and a Cherokee language survey, I was aware of the downfalls and difficulties involved in conducting a random sample of a tribal government and its citizens. The central issue when conducting a tribal nation random sample is that it is often developed based on a tribe's citizenship database. There are inherent problems with using a database in this way. Often registration rolls are not updated very often unless the updating is done proactively by the tribal member. There is scant benefit to mailing in a signed request or traveling to the citizenship office to personally update one's address, for tribes that are small enough may have intimate knowledge of the location of their members. Still further, some tribes maintain a well-functioning relational database in which tribal members making contact for services are updated in a master table. In my previous work with citizenship databases, I found that deceased citizens were still listed as active members. The lack of address updates and the failure to purge deceased citizens from the databases result in returned surveys. It is a waste of money to invest in mailing out a random survey if the majority of the sample is returned undeliverable. The crux of this matter is what is referred to as dirty data; it takes a commitment to investing time and resources in the continual upkeep of such a database. In a similar vein, in the Geographic Information Systems (GIS) field, the more accurate the data that is needed, the more expenses are incurred.

I needed to choose an approach that I could carry out with limited resources. I was able to use the online survey service Survey Monkey to both administer and store the survey. Working with MCN, I was allowed to include an article in the *Muscogee Nation News* and information about the survey and a link on the front page of the MCN website; they also sent out an email with a URL link to the survey to all their employees. I also printed over three hundred surveys and handed them out at the Creek Festival, at tribal council meetings, and in the corridors of tribal government buildings. I obtained a list of chartered community addresses from MCN's Community Research and Development Department and mailed surveys with self-addressed envelopes. Although this approach was not as effective as I would have liked, I received surveys from two communities. I had community mail-outs returned as undeliverable, which again points to the accuracy of the addresses the tribe maintains.

Geographic Concerns

The spatialities produced as a result of Mvskoke social relations and epistemologies require specific attention in the function of tribal planning. Hegemonic planning approaches fail to capture or understand Indigenous experiences and spaces. Geography plays a central role in tribal planning, because it can reveal lived Mvskoke experiences by helping understand how nongeopolitical spaces are produced. Further, geopolitical spaces carry with them particular jurisdictional complexities related to MCN's eleven-county area. MCN regional and jurisdictional issues pose complex problems for tribal planning because MCN members do not live in one concentrated area, but rather in multiple sites throughout Oklahoma and other states—a result of the MCN diaspora. Hawtin and Percy-Smith as well as Christakopoulou et al. define community in terms of an area that performs particular functions: a place to live or to socialize, an economic community, a personal space, or part of a city.[19] However, I would define it to include many spaces and places including virtual communities and ephemeral communities such as skate crews or language groups. As I initially embarked on this work, my unit of analysis was and remains the community. I started with a more limited definition of community and had to expand to accommodate the many ways of being Mvskoke and the many kinship relations we have to various aspects of the world—the animals, plants, wind, sky, and stars, to name a few.

The spatial differentiation of Mvskoke communities is predicated on the availability of resources—water, jobs, capital. Furthermore, communities might operate differently depending on whether members remain in their Oklahoma etvlwas or if they migrate to a larger city like Tulsa to engage in the wage economy. In Oklahoma, the northern and southern parts of the jurisdiction may create different experiences for tribal members. For example, communities in the northern region of MCN are adjacent to many more services, such as a major hospital and places to purchase durable goods, while in the southern region there is a larger concentration of ceremonial grounds but less access to services, with it being a very long commute either west to Oklahoma City or north to Tulsa. Mvskoke planning, therefore, must consider regional influences as well as jurisdictional issues.

Jurisdictional issues affect how tribes prioritize and carry out policies, negotiating federal and state laws. As a "domestic sovereign," MCN must negotiate with the federal government which laws can be enacted and enforced. Although MCN is not bound to municipal, county, or state laws, it faces continuing challenges from these jurisdictions, which attempt to wrest away MCN's sovereign power—challenges that will presumably extend into the future.

Survey Site

Creek Festival, held initially at Nichols Park in Henryetta as a softball tournament, is now a huge festival that has grown in its number of participants, its activities, and its duration over the past three decades.[20] This festival was organized by a handful of MCN employees who raised money through activities like bingo, started a gift shop at the main complex, and carried out the festival annually. The tribe now appropriates half a million dollars for the festival, and it has moved away from its humble roots to become an enormous event. In 2009, when I conducted my survey, it was the thirty-fifth anniversary; this festival now attracts thousands and calls people back to MCN for an event akin to a large community reunion.[21] The 2009 festival theme was "From the Same Fire," informed by the belief that Hesaketvmese (Maker of Breath) gave the Muscogee people fire when the earth was new.[22] The logo for the festival represents some essential elements of MCN—the animals represent the clans, the fire represents the ceremonial grounds, and the Mississippian symbol represents the fire, the sun, and the four directions.

The softball tournament is front and center stage and fills up two weekends. One weekend is fast-pitch softball and another weekend is slow-pitch softball, with separate men's and women's brackets. While this has been and continues to be the anchor event, there are many other events: sports (basketball, volleyball, golf, horseshoes); cultural events (a parade, stompdance, Creek hymn singing, a living legends ceremony); an International Professional Rodeo Association (IPRA) rodeo; concerts featuring Brandy, Joe Diffie, and James Otto; children's activities; and senior events (jacks tournament, bingo, horseshoes).

My Okmulgee ("Mug Town") Harjo cousins graciously agreed to help me with setting up and breaking down my survey booth, assisting with handing out surveys and drawing people in to the booth. I bought a small folding table at Walmart and clipboards and pens from the dollar store. My cousin Connie made sure to inscribe "Harjo" in permanent marker on all the clipboards. Even though my cousin Terrence was in charge of clipboard management, some of them came up missing, which became a constant source of jokes. Involving family was fundamental: just as I dialogued with community and relatives about shaping the questions, I was with a kinship collective in carrying out the survey. My uncle Lil, who despite his nickname is old enough to be my father, was visiting at another booth, and when he got too carried away in the fun, targeting our research team with a water gun, I had to shoo him away to prevent him from disrupting the administration of the survey.

It is not conventional academic practice to involve your relatives, but it is conventional practice to involve relatives in the community. Thus involving kin enacts a tool of futurity—collective power—in the form of an alterNative research action. The process of the research deepened social relations with the community and with the family—another tool of futurity, este-cate sovereignty. In reflecting on this, I see an importance to having an all-Mvskoke research team; drawing upon my experience with working on all-Indigenous community engagement teams, there is less difficulty establishing a rapport and trust than there would be if we were a group of non-Indians. Solely being Indigenous does not equate to a free pass, though—there is still distance if you are not of the same tribe. In the case of the Creek Community Survey, having an all-Mvskoke research team went far with people. There was a kinship connection on two different levels. First, there was a shared Mvskoke experience, which created relatability and made energy transactions much more fluid—we were our own community liaisons. Second, these were our actual kin—if we were not related through blood, then we established connections through the kinship-making process of asking where someone is from and who their relatives are. Another aspect of an all-Mvskoke research team is involving local community members in the community engagement process. My cousins grew up in Okmulgee, the site of Creek Festival, and have a longer community relationship with folks in Okmulgee—although not everyone attending the festival was from Okmulgee.

The first day of the survey coincided with the first day of the Creek Festival, and it commenced at the Muscogee (Creek) Nation Senior Housing Community located on Polose Circle in Okmulgee. In a grassy area next to Polose

Circle, there was a huge tent set up that housed an art market, and local folks were selling beadwork, art, chips, and soda. Other booths were distributing health information. Elders came streaming through the art market, groups of them in matching T-shirts to represent their local communities. Folks stopped because they were curious about what I was doing. I explained to them why I was there and showed them the survey. Elders declined to participate in the survey—I sensed that the survey just looked too long and they were not convinced that their investment of time would provide any benefit. I respect that assessment.

The rejections were informative because they instructed me to reconsider the survey length: a survey instrument that is too long will lose people's interest quickly. Also, I could consider a more engaging participatory method with elders. In hindsight, I would edit the survey down to fewer questions and make the remaining questions more crisp and concise. I would systematically have it reviewed by segments of the population representing different ages, genders, and sexualities. When I was developing the questions and iteratively obtaining feedback, it never dawned on me or anyone else to consider its length. As well, when Cherokee Nation conducted a needs assessment survey and a Cherokee language survey, I cannot recall this arising as an issue. However, because I administered every aspect of the Creek Community Survey firsthand and did not delegate it out, this exposed me to the survey respondents' reactions to its length. A prime example was when one of my cousins was filling out a survey: his brow was furrowed, and he rubbed his head and proclaimed, "Damn, I feel like I am taking an SRA reading test." We laughed at his throwback to his grade-school days during the '80s, but I took this to heart and made a mental note to heed it should I participate in future survey designs.

The scorching summer heat prompted me to adapt the survey administration at the last minute. I purchased bags of ice, bottles of water, and a large bin, and as a reciprocal gesture, I provided ice-cold bottles of water to survey participants. The weather that weekend was around 95 degrees with 77 percent humidity—it was hot! The survey participants were delighted to quench the heat with a bottle of water and to have a venue in which to vent. Some stayed and lingered to share the changes that they thought needed to happen in the tribe. I feel that this is one of the most important things that this research yielded, giving people space and a venue in which to vent, share, and think. It was producing dialogue! As the day progressed from morning to evening, there was an obvious change in the composition of the crowd. During the morning there were elder events, and midday had the staunchest of athletes and spectators, then the evening time included wider ranges of ages. A larger crowd was present after the sun went down and the area cooled off.

The nighttime attendance included an enormous crowd of teenagers participating in the spectator sport of watching one another. I still provided water, but with the change of temperature and crowd, I also gave University of Southern California (USC) pens, biscotti, and candy to participants. It was a strange and random collection of items, but these were items that I was able to obtain with my meager resources as a graduate student. My youngest cousin, Connie, went out into the nighttime crowd with these items to administer the survey and my cousin Terrence and I remained at the booth.

The survey booth had a stream of people all through the day, and when I would explain to them what I was working on—understanding what people cared about and how to integrate that into community-building—it was rare that they would turn down completing a survey (except for the elders). Surprisingly, even individuals who were not Mvskoke wanted to help because they believed in the mission of the project. I reconnected with family and friends who passed by and urged them to send their family and friends to the booth to fill out a survey. I was armed with a map of the Creek communities and my Institutional Review Board disclosure statement.[23] What was interesting is that after some folks looked at the community map, which depicted only chartered communities—a narrow definition of community—they told me that their community was missing. Participants' perception of community and of the fact that their community was missing from the map, rendering it invisible, is another important finding. The chartered Creek community is visible and imbued with agency and its own geography; however, how do we account for communities that are not chartered communities, but communities nonetheless?

Later in the evening, the recording artist Brandy was on the outdoor stage about fifty yards away, it was dark, and I had no lighting at my booth. Despite this, I still had a survey participant, an elder, adamant about taking the survey. His reading glasses were failing him, so I read each question and each possible answer to him, and together we completed the survey—in the dark while listening to an R&B concert. With most people I conversed with, I was able to find close connections, and I found that often I was only one or two degrees of separation from them and their family. For example, in the case of the individual I read the survey to, I knew his daughter and my father knew him. Also, the gentleman's sister was a neighbor and helper of my late grandfather in Dustin,

Oklahoma. In many ways, administering the survey was like having a conversation with family, and this aligns with the Mvskoke tenet that we are all connected.[24]

Survey Findings

The survey findings reveal what tribal members find important at three different geographic scales or cuts—the tribal nation, the community, and the body. The findings provide insight into tribal members' views of MCN's effectiveness, concerns they perceive as fundamental to improving their quality of life, and dimensions of MCN culture and lifeways that they believe are important to practice and sustain. It can be a struggle for community members to be heard, and many had plenty to share. Therefore, I am taking the space to report back on all the questions because the community deserves to have its community knowledge explicated and conveyed. The survey questions address how today's tribal government effectively prioritizes policy issues and negotiates with federal and state entities. To meet these challenges, MCN must clearly define its community's current and future identity—a community comprised of a heterogeneous blend of urban and rural members, members who practice and embrace traditional values, members who may not practice these values but identify themselves as Mvskoke, clan members who may have distinct practices, and members with varying priorities.

The report on the findings is structured in the following way: First, I provide a profile of the survey respondents. I report the survey findings at the scales of intertribal nation (Indigenous nation), community, and tribal member (physical body). I purposefully chose to embed several geographic markers in the survey, such as zip code and community, and this survey will continue to speak spatially as long as people want to dialogue with it.

The youngest survey participant was eighteen years old, and the oldest was seventy-eight years old. Three hundred and fifteen participants responded to the age question, with the average age of respondents being forty-two years old. Eighteen percent of the participants were less than thirty years old, while 21 percent were fifty-five years and older. Out of 326 who responded to the question about what zip code they currently reside in, 13 percent lived outside of Oklahoma, and 77 percent lived in Oklahoma. I also asked what zip code participants were raised in—310 individuals responded, and 7 percent of them grew up outside of Oklahoma. This tells us that there is some out-migration from Oklahoma. The gender composition of survey participants was overwhelmingly female (69 percent).

National Scale

INTERTRIBAL

Respondents were asked, "Compared to other tribes, how well of a job does Muscogee (Creek) Nation perform?"[25] There were three areas—political (running its government), economic (creating profitable businesses), and cultural (preserving the Creek language and culture)—in which to compare MCN's performance to that of other tribes. They were asked to rate the performances based on a Likert scale of poor, fair, not sure, good, or excellent.

In the first area, *running its government*, respondents gave the following answers: poor (25 percent), fair (28 percent), not sure (19 percent), good (24 percent), and excellent (4 percent). In the second area, *creating profitable businesses*, respondents gave the following answers: poor (26 percent), fair (25 percent), not sure (22 percent), good (24 percent), and excellent (3 percent). In the third, *preserving the Creek language and culture*, respondents gave the following answers: poor (19 percent), fair (27 percent), not sure (16 percent), good (30 percent), and excellent (7 percent).

MCN

MCN values can be understood in terms of how tribal members value the political, economic, and cultural aspects of the tribe. MCN values are comprised of what Muscogee people believe is important. Further work with this survey could include cross-tabulating survey data by gender, age, and community.

Policy Areas

Respondents were asked how they would prioritize the following seven policy areas if they were in the position of being chief for one day: (1) community development, (2) job development, (3) health care, (4) affordable housing, (5) business development, (6) cultural preservation, and (7) education. Participants were asked to appraise each of the seven areas using a three-category scale of low priority, moderate priority, or high priority. Of the seven areas, 50 percent or more of participants provided a high-priority assessment to six of the seven areas. Of the participants who answered the question, the proportion that provided a high-priority assessment in each area was the following: education (89 percent), health care (87 percent), job development (71 percent), cultural preservation (66 percent), affordable housing (55 percent), business development (50 percent), and community development (44 percent). In summary, four of the priority areas are concerned with the individual, ensuring that individuals are healthy, educated, employed, and living in adequate shelter. The majority of participants felt that nearly all the areas are vitally important.

Present and Future: Providing Services to Tribal Members
The function of the question "How well do you think Muscogee (Creek) Nation does in providing the following services?" is to gain an understanding of participants' perceptions of how the tribe is currently performing in existing tribal policy areas. Most of these services are restricted to the MCN eleven-county area. The ten areas participants were asked to assess are either policy areas or funded departments within MCN. The areas are: (1) affordable housing options, (2) art and cultural opportunities, (3) community development, (4) elder services, (5) health care, (6) job development, (7) preservation and maintenance of Creek songs, dances, and stories, (8) the teaching of the Creek language, (9) tribal business development, and (10) youth services. Participants are asked to rate the areas on a five-category scale as poor, fair, neutral, good, or excellent. Participants assessed the ten areas at time points of the present, 20 years in the future, and 150 years in the future (seven generations).

If we turn to the present time-point assessment, participants gave all ten areas an average rating of fair to okay, which tells us that overall they believe MCN is doing an okay job, with opportunities to improve in all areas. Next the community was asked to speculate on the future; the first query about the future focused on twenty years from the time of the survey and the next query focused on seven generations from the time of the survey, asking them to assess the same ten policy areas listed in the previous paragraph. They were asked the following questions: "What condition do you think the following will be in within 20 years?" and "What condition do you think the following will be in within 7 generations? (The year will be around 2150)." In the next twenty years, participants believed that the best-performing policy areas will include improved tribal business development, community development, youth services, culture, and the Creek language. Conversely, tribal members believe that the lower-performing policy areas in twenty years will be affordable housing, art and cultural opportunities, job development, and health care. In seven generations, the policy areas in the best condition will be tribal business development, arts and cultural opportunities, youth services, job development, affordable housing, elder services, and health care. In seven generations, the policy areas in the poorest condition will include teaching the Creek language and preserving and maintaining Creek songs, dances, and stories. Respondents were less optimistic about the condition of their language, songs, dances, and stories at a seven-generation mark. Regarding MCN's political, economic, and cultural condition in seven generations, the majority of participants believed that each of these three areas would remain about the same.

This question asks participants to speculate about the long-term conditions of the tribe's policies in different areas. Participants echo the same sentiments as in the previous question—that the tribe will be in okay condition in twenty years. Participants were also asked to consider the condition of tribal policy areas in seven generations. Tribal members rated that the tribe will be in okay condition in all areas in seven generations. When asked to consider these policy areas at two temporal junctures—twenty years and seven generations—the responses were mostly optimistic.

Community Scale

In another question, participants were asked: "Are you an active participant in a Creek Community?" Three hundred and ten people answered this question. The majority of participants (61 percent) indicated that they are not active in their community; 39 percent indicated that they are active members of their communities. This question deserves attention in defining what we mean in everyday discourse when we say "Creek community." The answers suggest that participants may view community participation in a very specific way, such as attending community governance meetings; consequently, the number of people who indicate that they are active is lower than expected. The number of affirmative answers regarding participation in a Creek community is probably more reflective of survey participants who are active in MCN chartered communities. In addition, defining Creek community can warrant further inquiry in order to gain a better understanding of what Mvskoke people imagine active participation looks like, given that it can present itself in a number of ways, such as teaching another person to sew or teaching another person language. Those activities which are pursued through formal organizations are not the only ways in which community is functioning. Thus, broadening the possibilities of how we define and imagine community will make it more apparent to survey participants how Muscogee people or Indigenous communities are enacting different modes of futurity that can still be distinguished as forms of community.

Respondents were asked in what ways they think their community is succeeding. The items surveyed in this list were developed with community members before the survey was conducted: I asked them what the qualities of a successful community were and what the qualities of a failing community were. The top areas of success were reported as follows: people attend community events and gatherings (62.7 percent), people help one another (51.5 percent), has a casino (50.4 percent), revitalizing language (43.3 percent), and revitalizing culture (40.3 percent). These areas align with the Muscogee belief, shared in chapter 1, that we are all interconnected and related. The survey provides data regarding which elements of success were said to be present in their communities; the markers of successful communities that occurred with highest frequency were those focused on the community gathering and helping one another. Because these ideas of success operate at a less formal scale than that of the tribal government, I posit that this is collective power at work, and the idea of people helping one another is tied to este-cate sovereignty, which consists of placing positive energy and intentions toward our kin—human and more-than-human—and assuming the idea of responsibility to kin. Further, these aspects of relationality are performed with decolonial love—the intention to create and assist one another in realizing and living a full life.[26] A little over half of respondents chose "has a casino" as a way their community is succeeding; tribal members view this as a revenue stream that will provide direct support to community members. The last two major areas that tribal members viewed as successful were revitalizing language and revitalizing culture—these areas are directly related to Mvskoke lifeways that are performed collectively as well as forms of knowledge production. These are the dimensions of Mvskoke people that make us unique; however, they also tie us to a larger complex of Southeastern tribes that stompdance and play stickball, and whose medicinal plants grow in a temperate climate.

When participants were asked in what ways they think their community is failing, responses were high in many areas, but the top areas were alcohol abuse (63.7 percent), drug abuse (58.1 percent), fighting among community members, which can be either physical or verbal altercations (58.9 percent), no jobs (52.6 percent), and community members not involved in the community (51.9 percent). I argue that the top three dimensions mentioned—substance abuse, fighting, and nonparticipation—work against the futurity concepts of este-cate sovereignty and collective power. If community members are wrapped up in alcohol and drug addictions, it might make it difficult to perform their responsibility to kin or to reach out to their kin with vnokeckv. Substance abuse disrupts the edifying flow of energy from being to being. Moreover, substance abuse, fighting, and nonparticipation in community are merely symptoms; they emanate from something more deeply rooted, such as trauma related to epistemic violence, or the education of our children in a school system where they are misunderstood and the knowledge of their people is never valorized as truth. Also, there is the struggle of searching for work in either a rural context or an urban context where you know that as an Indigenous person you will probably get passed over for a job. The dimensions that survey participants chose most frequently here demonstrate that Mvskoke people have deep concerns related to that which disrupts energy, relationality, decolonial love, kinship, and collective power.

Returning to the Mvskoke belief that we are all connected and all related, it also makes sense that a failing community is indicated by lack of community involvement and a low degree of cooperation between individuals.[27] The option "no central meeting place" received the fewest responses in the question about ways in which communities are failing. This is probably because most Mvskoke communities have community buildings that MCN has constructed. This means that most Mvskoke communities already have some resources to use in conceiving of and operationalizing modes of futurity of their choosing.

Body Scale

INDIVIDUAL PARTICIPATION IN MVSKOKE FUTURITY
At the scale of the individual, participants were asked if they wanted to engage actively in community-based activities. This section of the survey showed the most affirming attitudes on the part of Muscogee people. People were interested in participating in the spiritual, intellectual, and aesthetic aspects of MCN.

MVSKOKE IDENTITY MARKERS
Tribe
Respondents were asked what tribe they identify with: Muscogee (Creek), Alabama-Quassarte, Thlopthlocco, Kialegee, and/or Yuchi. Of the 323 participants, there was a small group of respondents who identified with more than

one tribe. Overall percentages of tribal identification were the following: 93 percent identified as Muscogee (Creek), 6 percent identified as Yuchi, 5 percent identified with Thlopthlocco Tribal Town, 3 percent identified with Alabama-Quassarte Tribal Town, and 2 percent identified with Kialegee Tribal Town. This question had a 98 percent response rate.

Clan

Participants were asked to identify their Muscogee clan, prompted with: "If you know your Muscogee clan, please write it in. For example, Bear clan, Wolf clan, Wind clan, etc." This is a societal grouping that predates European contact. These clans have archetypes, attributes, and functions within the community—they provide guiding principles for one's life. For instance, the Wolf Clan is a grandfather clan and is supposed to take care of the people. Anecdotally, it is thought that people are not as aware of their clan membership as they once were. However, among the 330 survey participants, 78 percent reported their clan membership, contradicting the stereotype of dying clan membership and knowledge. Tribal clan is passed down through families from the mother. This question was open-ended and participants were provided the opportunity to write in their answer. Clan groups represented include Wind, Alligator, Bird, Turtle, Tiger, Wolf, Bear, Deer, Fox, Raccoon, Fish, Possum, Sweet Potato, Potato, River Sand, Panther, and Sand Creek.

Tribal Town

Tribal towns, as indicated in earlier chapters, are a Mvskoke geopolitical organizing unit that predates European contact. The tribal towns numbered over fifty in the Mvskoke aboriginal homelands, and today there are three federally recognized tribal towns that reorganized as nations. However, many people still affiliate with their pre-removal tribal town. These tribal towns and ceremonial grounds can have different Muscogee dialects and cultural practices. Respondents were asked if they knew their tribal town. This question was open-ended, and participants could write in their response; 213 participants answered, yielding a response rate of 65 percent. Respondents listed the following tribal towns, spelled in the form that participants provided: Thlopthlocco, New Tulsa, Nuyaka, Arbeka, Muddy Waters (Weogufkee), Eufaula, Polecat, Cussetah, Alabama-Quassarte, Kialegee, Hickory Ground, Peach Ground, Greenleaf, Tulsa, Fish Pond, Concharty, Coweta, Muscogee, Hillibi, Wetumpka, Duck Creek, Okfuskee, Lokvpokv, and Tuskegee.

Stompgrounds / Ceremonial Grounds and Mvskoke Churches

During pre-contact times, stompgrounds were part of the Mvskoke tribal town; after the federal government removed Mvskoke people to Indian Territory, as discussed earlier in the chapter, this dimension of the tribal town splintered. Today ceremonial grounds are in rural areas. Although the tribal town does not operate in a wholly intact way in one discrete location, as it did in the original homelands, with the functions of kinship, ceremonial life, collective activities, and maintenance of households fixed in place and operating from a tribal town settlement, I posit that the etvlwa happens in any number of ways and is connected to community, clan, tribal town, ceremonial grounds, and Mvskoke church. Participants were asked, "If you identify with a stomp ground (ceremonial ground), which one?" Fifty-two percent of survey participants indicated that they identify with a stompgrounds. This tells us that over half of participants are participating in traditional cultural practices. Church identification represented an even larger proportion of the participants. When asked, "If you identify with a church, which one?" 65 percent of participants indicated that they identify with a church. Many of the churches in MCN are Mvskoke churches that are central to the community. Within these churches, the Muscogee language is spoken in some cases, and hymns are sung in the Muscogee language as well. Affirmative answers to the stompgrounds and church questions tell us that among the survey participants there is an elevated level of participation in Muscogee cultural practices.

MVSKOKE LIFEWAYS, KNOWLEDGE, AND PRACTICES

The following questions give us a more intimate profile of the survey participants and their interest in Mvskoke practices. This illustrates that people are feeding the notion of este-cate sovereignty and collective power, and that they are finding energy, kinship, knowledge, and some degree of freedom from settler colonialism. They are finding ways to enjoy the collective power of Mvskoke energy, kinship, and vnokeckv, which strengthens relationality and responsibility to other entities outside of oneself.

Questions about participating in "Creek ways of life" asked participants to weigh in on five areas that provide insight into knowledge and collective practices. These questions gauge the importance of cultural practices that distinguish the Muscogee people. Overall, tribal members rated all areas as high in importance, especially Creek language, Creek worldview, community gather-

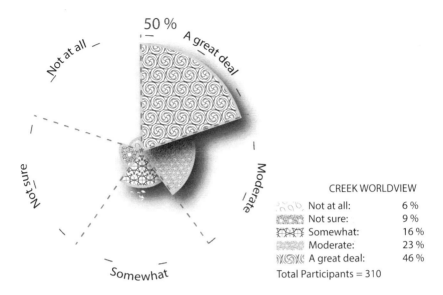

50 %

Not at all

A great deal

Not sure

Moderate

Somewhat

CREEK WORLDVIEW

Not at all: 6 %
Not sure: 9 %
Somewhat: 16 %
Moderate: 23 %
A great deal: 46 %
Total Participants = 310

FIGURE 13 Graph: How important to you is participating in a Creek worldview? Illustration by Pablo Lituma.

ings, Indian churches, and stompdance. This indicates that most of the practices in this section are highly valued by MCN tribal members.

Creek (Mvskoke) worldview is open to interpretation by the participants; however, when asked about its level of importance to them, 46 percent of respondents assigned it a great deal of importance. Combining the categories of "a great deal" and "moderate," 69 percent of the survey participants responded affirmatively. This response implies that folks are not devaluing Mvskoke worldviews and ways of knowing; it provides evidence that Mvskoke people are committed to perpetuating and practicing Mvskoke worldviews. This is another dimension that warrants deeper investigation so as to understand specific ways in which they imagine Mvskoke worldviews—this is the work of creating a Mvskoke imaginary.

The responses here are a little puzzling, because in a previous question, 52 percent of participants reported an affiliation to a stompgrounds / ceremonial grounds; however, only 32 percent of respondents said they placed a great deal of importance on participating in stompdance. The two affirmative categories combined—"moderate importance" and "a great deal of importance"— tell us that 54 percent of survey participants claim an affirmative interest in

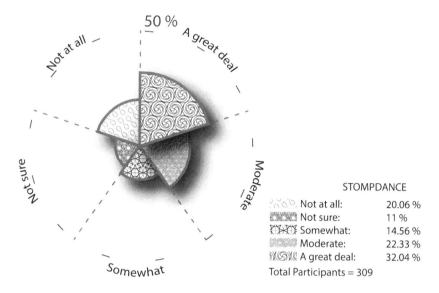

FIGURE 14 Graph: How important to you is participating in stompdance? Illustration by Pablo Lituma.

stompdance. Surmising some factors related to lower interest, it might be that perhaps people are not sure where to go, when to go, where to park, or where to sit when they get there. Many of the dances are word-of-mouth, and the grounds are in current-day MCN territory. People might not have the resources to travel if they live far from a stompgrounds. The dances take place at night. Therefore, people and families might not have the time commitment to travel and stay at a dance all night if they have other weekend commitments. A couple of summers ago I was en route to a stompdance, and I ran into some childhood friends at the gas station and invited them. They were apprehensive and said: "No, our mom said if you go to church you are not supposed to go to stomp-dances." To which I replied, "It will be okay, come on!" This exchange is not only illustrative of unsureness in participating in Mvskoke lifeways, but also of the power of a family matriarch to inculcate values in her offspring.

Survey participants attached high levels of importance to participation in Indian churches: 41 percent placed a great deal of importance on this. Combining the two affirmative categories again of "a great deal" and "moderate" yields 67.85 percent—nearly 70 percent of survey participants assign higher levels of importance to participation in Indian churches. The Indian churches could prove to be much easier to participate in because they meet throughout the

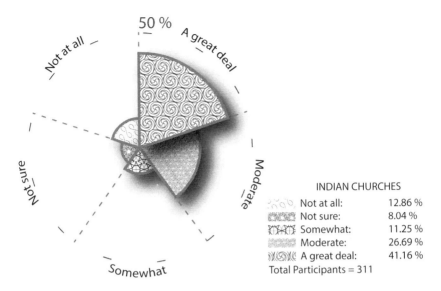

FIGURE 15 Graph: How important to you is participating in Indian churches? Illustration by Pablo Lituma.

year and are located both in town and in rural areas. The primary religions for Mvskoke people in northeastern Oklahoma are Southern Baptist and United Methodist, which plugs local rural communities into larger institutionalized religion—these relationships scale up to gatherings such as Indian Falls Creek Baptist Assembly, larger conventions, and international and North American evangelizing missions. However, at a more local scale, the churches function as a Creek community, with associational and devotional aspects to the gatherings.

Creek language is another area of traction among the survey participants, and 75.19 percent reported affirmatively, including responses of "a great deal" and "moderately," that it was important to them to participate in Creek language. This Mvskoke lifeway received the highest and most affirmative number of responses, which distinguishes it as one of the most valued dimensions for Mvskoke people.

Nearly 40 percent of participants placed a great deal of importance on traditional medicine; combined with those that denoted a moderate level of importance, this yields 58.92 percent of respondents who affirm the importance of participating in traditional medicine.

Twenty-eight percent of participants placed a great deal of importance on participating in stickball. The two categories of affirmative importance total

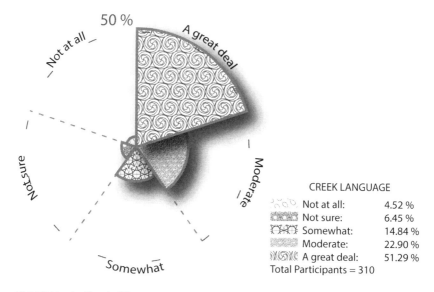

CREEK LANGUAGE

	Not at all:	4.52 %
	Not sure:	6.45 %
	Somewhat:	14.84 %
	Moderate:	22.90 %
	A great deal:	51.29 %
Total Participants = 310		

FIGURE 16 Graph: How important to you is participating in Creek language? Illustration by Pablo Lituma.

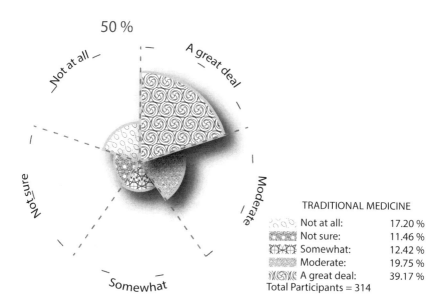

TRADITIONAL MEDICINE

	Not at all:	17.20 %
	Not sure:	11.46 %
	Somewhat:	12.42 %
	Moderate:	19.75 %
	A great deal:	39.17 %
Total Participants = 314		

FIGURE 17 Graph: How important to you is participating in traditional medicine? Illustration by Pablo Lituma.

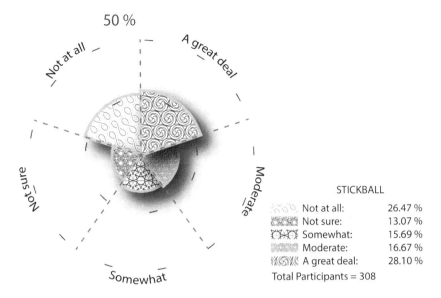

50 %

Not at all

A great deal

Not sure

Moderate

Somewhat

STICKBALL

Not at all: 26.47 %
Not sure: 13.07 %
Somewhat: 15.69 %
Moderate: 16.67 %
A great deal: 28.10 %
Total Participants = 308

FIGURE 18 Graph: How important to you is participating in stickball? Illustration by Pablo Lituma.

44.77 percent of participants. One aspect of this question to note is that the majority of survey participants were females, and at the stompgrounds, stickball is played primarily as an all-male game. At some grounds they also have more social co-ed games, and stickball games outside of ceremonial space, such as inter- and intratribal competitions, have included women as of late. However, stickball has functioned as primarily a male sport, which may explain survey participants' lower degree of interest in participating in stickball.

Survey participants had high levels of interest in participating in community gatherings. When asked about its level of importance to them, 39.6 percent said it had a great deal of importance. The combined categories of "a great deal" and "moderate" show that 70 percent of survey participants responded affirmatively to wanting to participate in community gatherings. This too is demonstrative of Mvskoke people's interest in participating with other Mvskokvlke, which relates back to the tools of futurity. The aspect of relationality is connected to este-cate sovereignty; the aspect of performing community connects to collective power.

In the final question related to Mvskoke knowledge practices, participants were asked about their ability to read, write, and speak the Creek language. The majority of participants (84 percent) can speak some amount of the Creek

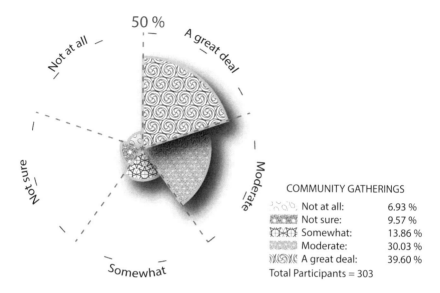

50 %

Not at all

A great deal

Not sure

Moderate

Somewhat

COMMUNITY GATHERINGS

Not at all: 6.93 %
Not sure: 9.57 %
Somewhat: 13.86 %
Moderate: 30.03 %
A great deal: 39.60 %
Total Participants = 303

FIGURE 19 Graph: How important to you is participating in community gatherings? Illustration by Pablo Lituma.

language; only 16 percent responded that they cannot speak the Creek language. Participants reported low levels of literacy, with 30 percent unable to read Muscogee and 47 percent unable to write the language, yet most participants can speak some degree of the language, even if only a few words.

ECONOMICS: PERSONAL

To understand the economic context of the survey participants, they were asked to what degree they were experiencing difficulties related to the current economic recession. There are six areas they were asked about: food, shelter, utilities, medicine, employment, and gasoline. Four major areas stood out in which participants had the greatest amounts of difficulty: these were buying gasoline, paying utilities, buying food, and housing costs. Respondents reported that they were not feeling the effects of the economic recession at all in terms of employment issues, such as layoffs, finding jobs, and buying medicine.

In the areas of day-to-day survival, tribal members assigned the most importance to the need to buy food; the need for fuel to transport themselves and their family, because there is very little public transportation; and the need to pay their utilities so that they can have electricity and gas to warm their homes and cook their food.

Discussion of Findings

Community knowledge is a tool of futurity—a means of finding our way to the lush promise. If we do not have community knowledge, then there is a gaping void of guidance. The overarching findings of this survey and its three scalar cuts—tribal nation, community, body—provide insight into the ways that futurity operates at three different levels. However, based on the types of responses participants provide, I argue that the degree of certainty with which they answer, whether positive or negative, can be indicative of the degree to which they feel able to enact este-cate sovereignty, in order to create the lush promise for themselves and their communities, at the level of each of the three scalar cuts. Providing spaces for communities to make their knowledge known was one of the original intentions of the survey, and although MCN has conducted surveys in the past, they could consider providing more participatory opportunities for the communities to share their knowledge and expertise in MCN's decision-making processes. Hence, I will now share a summary of the survey findings, as well as provide an analysis and a suggested futurity-based response: emergence geographies.

When MCN was compared to other tribes, survey participants believed that the nation was doing good in terms of culture, while politically it was rated as fair and economically it was rated as poor.[28] Therefore, politically and economically there was room for improvement. When generally asked about how well MCN addresses various policy areas, respondents gave mostly neutral answers. When asked to consider different time frames of futurity—twenty years and seven generations—participants provided mostly neutral answers. Ostensibly, the further folks are removed from having an impact on the decision-making process, the less definitive their answers are about the outcomes, and, perhaps, the further into the future they are asked to speculate, the more challenging it is to imagine the tribal government. When asked to consider their communities, survey participants provided explicit feedback about community success and failure. The success or failure of a community was largely related to communal aspects of peoplehood, which are connected to living near and associating with other Mvskoke people and to enacting relationality and kinship—crucial elements of este-cate sovereignty. Participants placed a great deal of importance on participating in cultural elements such as the Creek language, a Mvskoke worldview, and traditional healing practices. The cultural areas had the most affirmative and highest response rates.

Survey respondents perceived that the tribe had room for improvement in the three major focus areas related to the tribal nation in the survey—political, cultural, and economic. Furthermore, tribal members signaled that the economic and political aspects of MCN had further to go than the cultural. Thus, future efforts for engaging tribal members and developing the tribe could focus more deeply on their perceptions of the political and economic spheres of MCN— more specifically, ensuring that the tribal government is highly functioning.

The major takeaways were that people think the tribe is doing okay and will continue to be okay over the next seven generations, with slightly lower ratings in the political and economic areas, which rank below the cultural aspect. A large percentage of respondents noted that they were struggling economically and that if they were chief for a day they would focus on health care, education, and job development. However, in my one-on-one interviews and in comments about the survey, one area of concern reiterated was that they felt that there was a lot of fighting among the branches of government. In this respect, it almost seemed that they felt they were a third party watching all of this transpire within the tribal government.

On the other hand, the response pattern about their individual interest in Mvskoke lifeways was much more varied. When survey participants were asked if they felt it was important to them to participate in Mvskoke lifeways such as worldview, Mvskoke churches, stompdance, stickball, traditional medicine practices, community gatherings, and language, these survey questions received the highest degree of fluctuation and variation. Participants placed importance on different dimensions. If I order the dimensions that received the highest proportion of survey respondents who chose "a great deal of importance" in participating in them, it is as follows: Mvskoke language (51 percent), Mvskoke worldview (46 percent), Indian churches (41 percent), community gatherings (40 percent), traditional medicine (39 percent), stompdance (32 percent), and stickball (28 percent). This reveals that although participants were not as certain about the tribal government's performance now and in the future, they had clear positions about Mvskoke lifeways.

Call for Emergence Geographies

To return to the subject of geographic scales, the scales that I focus on are based on my holding particular processes and conditions in stasis to examine Mvskoke ways of being in the world; however, the scales produced when this survey was administered are not the same spatialities from fifty or one hundred years ago. Scale allows for flexible geographies that can be renegotiated and reconfigured as necessary.

The scalar dimensions of the survey stand out. As mentioned earlier, the survey was structured to aid in understanding Mvskoke people's view of the tribal government, their own community, and their personal commitments to participating in and maintaining Mvskoke lifeways. People appeared to have more pronounced positions when the questions related to their personal commitments, while in remarkable contrast, the average answer to the tribal government questions was almost neutral across the board. This urges us to examine this phenomenon more closely. Survey participants were incrementally queried about various forms of Mvskoke social relations—their relationship to the tribal government, to community, and to their own participation in Mvskoke lifeways.

Agency is the ability to act, and when we examine the arc of the responses, we find that community members were more responsive at the scales of their community and their personal commitment to the practice of Mvskoke lifeways. The data suggest that there is a scalar notion of agency, and with an entity as large as MCN, tribal members feel that it is such a large structure that they do not have any impact. However, at the scale of the community, there may be a couple hundred people, or even just a small few, participating. The community, the household, and the body might be sites where Indigenous people feel that they have more autonomy. Where there is a breakdown in autonomy, part of the community work lies in building personal and collective power of self-determination, respect, love, and consent—relative to relative, household to household, and community to community. Conversely, given a traumatic history of racism and violence, community, household, and body might carry a legacy of Foucauldian self-regulation.

Community members had the most to say at the scale of the body—questions that inquired about the scale of the body relate to their personal commitments and agency. Consequently, they have the ability to enact este-cate sovereignty at smaller scales at which the politics of recognition do not operate or where they can have more control over refusing the politics of recognition. The findings from my survey tell an interesting story about participants' views on the tribe's national and community governance structures, and on their own participation in MCN peoplehood. This translates concretely to the survey participants' relationship to formal tribal government: the larger the governance structure, the less agency they felt they had, and the less affirmative their responses about the tribe. There were generally neutral responses when they were asked about the condition and performance of MCN's government. Ultimately, it appeared that the closer they were to a scale where they could enact a Mvskoke worldview, the more affirmative their responses were. The actions community members take at the individual scale co-create a community scale, which is collective power. Based on these findings, I conclude that community-based methods would provide the conditions in which Mvskoke people can find their way to a community scale, whereby they might enact tools of futurity that make and connect us to kin and draw upon the community's knowledge to collectively take action, whether action related to the culture or to connecting community to needed resources. Further, a community scale can produce space for enacting Mvskoke worldviews and values. This leads to the final tool of futurity proposed in this project: emergence geographies.

The actions of este-cate sovereignty, community knowledge production, and joining together to act collectively do not require the formal MCN but can be staged within emergence geographies of the types that I introduced at the outset of the chapter. These are the sites, spaces, and places where everyday Mvskoke people enact these activities of futurity. Emergence geographies are both produced and reshaped according to the needs of the community because Mvskoke people do not stand still. Mvskoke people have always deployed emergence geographies, and today is no different. The ways in which emergence geographies get deployed today actually have produced new types of spatialities.

Mvskoke emergence narratives commence with a tribal emergence story in which the people come out of the fog and form into clans. Indian removal resulted in Mvskoke land cessions and flows of Mvskoke people to Oklahoma, which required a renegotiation of burial rituals invoking material and metaphysical geographies. At the site of the Creek Nation Council Oak in Tulsa, a ceremonial appropriation of the material emergence geography took place, and fires from the eastern homelands were relit.

Tribal town settlements in Alabama and Georgia operated as dwelling space, ceremonial space, political space, and social space. However, Indian removal was a traumatic upheaval of the way tribal towns operated. Presently, functions of the pre-removal tribal town are splintered and scattered across the land. Ceremonial grounds and churches now take up the spiritual components of the once-holistic operation of the tribal town. The political functions of autonomous tribal towns are simultaneously coalesced and splintered, with MCN taking up the governance work of the bulk of the former confederacy of tribal towns. The three federally recognized tribal towns continue to carry out the political work of the pre-removal tribal towns. The social relations aspect of the Mvskoke tribal town is also taken up in a variety of ways—through the chartered communities, at sports tournaments, and at Mvskoke churches, stompgrounds, and MCN-sponsored events. These are just a few sites in which this aspect of the tribal town is carried out. Dwelling space is scattered too, with Mvskoke people living in a variety of places; perhaps the most communal forms of housing are those that were constructed by MCN, including housing subdivisions and elderly housing in Okmulgee, Oklahoma. Notwithstanding the splintering and dispersal of functions that operated in a holistic manner within the pre-removal tribal town, Mvskoke people continue to reemerge in ways that renegotiate knowledge, community practices, and space to carve out the geographies that they need to maintain themselves as a people. Today, Mvskoke people are carving out the spaces that they need, and they are not waiting on anyone or anything to create the lush promise or the futurities they wish to both envision and enact. It is within these spaces that the tools of futurity operate: este-cate sovereignty, community knowledge, and collective power. Just as Mvskoke people have continually reemerged and reformed settlements, spatialities morph and move; in the same ways, in a contemporary moment, Mvskoke people are not waiting on the tribal government to conceive of and create the possibilities that they need for their communities. They are emerging in a multitude of ways and producing their own emergence geographies. There are a number of ways in which this presents itself: the formation of community groups not tied to a fixed place, artist collectives, language immersion programs, sports and leadership programs, and food sovereignty projects. Examples of this include groups within MCN territory but outside the reach of MCN's governance: 4 Love of the Game (a Muscogee youth development organization focused on sports), Mvskoke Food Sovereignty Initiative, Puetake Vcake Foundation (a Muscogee language immersion school), and Mvskoke ceremonial grounds.[29] These projects are formed at the nexus of este-cate sovereignty, community knowledge, and collective power, at sites of emergence geographies.

Mvskoke Food Sovereignty Initiative (MFSI) is illustrative of emergence geography; the intent of MFSI is to teach individuals and communities how to grow their food. They create community-based food-growing projects to provide fresh produce to their community and neighbors. Rita and Barton Williams are instrumental in teaching others to grow and can their food: in figure 20,

FIGURE 20 Mvskoke Food Sovereignty Initiative: Kristie Ann Sewall preparing okra for canning. Photograph by Rita Williams.

Kristie Sewall is learning to can okra in Rita's canning shed. Teaching through experiential learning, Rita has taught Mvskoke women to fry their chunks of pumpkin in agave instead of sugar in response to the impacts of diabetes.[30] MFSI imagines the processing of traditional game meat and is assessing this possibility, but must grapple with the different scales of policy to bring the processing to fruition. In the meantime, they are growing and harvesting native possum grapes for wine and jelly, among many other traditional crops.[31] They are not waiting for anyone to give them permission to imagine and create futurity— they are enacting and marshaling all their resources and abilities to do so.

MFSI provides us an example of a crucial emergence geography that punctures the capitalist landscape.[32] MCN encompasses primarily rural areas that lack the tools necessary (tariffs, taxes, price and wage controls) to fully regulate and/or invoke the flow of capital. On top of this, development of tribal trust land happens under the watchful eye of the federal government, meaning that capitalist development on MCN land is often out of MCN's control and operates on a different scale.[33] While the survey results seem to valorize the individual, in fact they provide evidence of how the individual and the community scales are coproduced.

Emergence geographies become a critical component of futurity, especially with the depopulation of rural areas that are witnessing Indigenous migration to cities. It becomes important to conceive of ways in which people can articulate their communities and appropriate the spaces required to carry out the other three prongs of futurity—este-cate sovereignty, community knowledge, and collective power. In this way, emergence geographies are a pivot away from settler colonial geographies that seek to keep Indigenous people tethered to containers of space. And as Indigenous peoples inhabit these containers of space they are then marked by their fellow tribal members, as well as others, as living either in Indigenous space or, if they are living in the city, outside Indigenous space. Emergence geographies have the power to collapse this particularly exclusionary binary. Thus, emergence geographies make Indigenous spaces and places possible anywhere Mvskoke people exist because the people carry their embodied knowledge and practices with them wherever they go. Mvskoke individuals have the power to instantiate Indigenous spaces, places, and community.

Tool of Futurity: Emergence Geographies

The symbol in figure 21 represents emergence geographies; this graphic is based on a Southeastern symbol. I use this icon to represent the ways that Mvskokvlke and our communities have continually (re)emerged across time and space. This icon is typically noted as a sun symbol, and it often appears in works by Mvskoke artists and in Euchee tribal lore. The center of the symbol resembles a cross; however, this is a four-directional symbol that represents sacred fire, including the council fire, which is an important element of Mvskoke tribal towns. The earth lodge located at the Ocmulgee National Monument is an example of a council fire that functioned as a decision-making space and not as a stompdance space. In addition, this symbol represents the four directions, the four stages of life, the four seasons, and four types of life, a Mvskoke knowledge imparted to me by the *heles-hayv* Tommy Lewis. This symbol can be

FIGURE 21 *Emergence Geography*, relief print, Laura Harjo.

understood as a site of emergence or the act of mapping sites of emergence, which I explain next.

I have chosen to draw this symbol to depict movement and emergence as breaking through mainstream spatial representations of Indigenous space, place, and community. Movement is central to the idea of ever-emerging geographies, and the serrated edges are a geography that is bursting or breaking through to insist that Mvskoke space, place, and community be recognized. However, on closer look, the serrated edges are similar to the points in a Lakota morning star design, representative of the planet Venus; it also bears a resemblance to Indigenous Andean terrestrial observations of planetary alignment measurements at the equator.[34]

This chapter has set forth a theory of reemergence for Mvskoke people that is reflective of their experiences of coming out of fog to create the necessary spaces and places to sustain themselves. The geographies of Mvskoke communities have shifted and reemerged over many millennia. For example, the Creek Festival was born out of the work of a committed group that chose to carve out transformational spaces, and it functions today as a de facto homecoming for MCN regardless of stompdance or church allegiances. As a tool of futurity, diasporic communities such as those Mvskoke communities in major U.S. cities are carving out their own reemergence geographies. Dedicated Mvskoke people are creating transformational space; without waiting on the tribal government or any other government to step in, they are taking action in the form of nonprofits, grassroots organizations, and the teaching of language, food sovereignty, and leadership coupled with sports.

Emergence geographies are where all of the tools of futurity operate together—they are the spaces and places where the tools are staged and operationalized for realizing futurity and the lush promise of the Mvskoke imaginary. I posit that emergence geographies are exhibited in four unique ways: (1) concrete, (2) ephemeral, (3) metaphysical, and (4) virtual. However, these geographies are subject to revision, as conditions, technologies, and the ways in which Mvskoke people assemble will change over time. Concrete spatialities are those that are bounded in or fixed to a particular place. MCN's eleven-county jurisdictional area is an illustration of such a concrete, delineated geographic area. However, a concrete geography can be a reservation, a legal description of a community, or a community building or complex—such as MCN's tribal complex, or their omniplex, which has permanent softball fields and courts, vendor arbors, a stage, a water splash pad, and a multipurpose building. Next are ephemeral geographies: these are community convenings that assemble and disassemble in certain moments. For example, a community group that convenes in a variety of places functions as an ephemeral geography. An ephemeral geography is exhibited in a flash mob in a city to protest MMIWG.[35]

Next are metaphysical geographies, which manifest in a number of ways, such as staying in communication with ancestors and relatives. One such example is connected to MMIWG: they are no longer present in material form, but their energy is unstoppable, and they invoke us to action—with flash mobs in protest or with the community-generated beadwork that is part of the WWOS installation. Our ancestors invoke us to action when we visit their graves or draw upon memories—their legacies and lives inform us of the orginal instructions. Metaphysical geographies are simultaneously heady and sobering because within them we connect to more-than-human entities, instantiating a scale that eclipses human social relations but places us in connection with ancestors, stars, and the stories and instructions they hold. This is a spiral to the stars that moves us between human and more-than-human entities, while invoking a spatiality across time and space. Finally, virtual geographies emerge from information and communications technology, largely the Internet; however, phones have served a similar function. These produce virtual spaces in which to stage assemblages of Mvskoke people and community—through ICT such as video chat and conferencing, social media, listservs, online groups, and websites that serve out resources to communities. This can also include the use of technologies such as drones and virtual reality (VR) to imagine old and new geographies. Although Linda Tuhiwai Smith problematizes VR that is used by non-Indigenous technocrats to appropriate and gaze at Indigenous spaces, we see how drones were used for digital activism and counter-storytelling at Standing Rock to document and advocate for the #NoDAPL movement.[36] To close, I will share a story about frequent visits to the pawn shop to reflect emergence geographies.

Fred Moten shares that "the everyday is beautiful, what is in the everyday in the cracks of the sidewalk are the interstices that hold something beautiful."[37] That which is invisible is situated in the banal experiences of the everyday, or in things that seem broken. Moten's "cracks of the sidewalk," then, is a metaphor for the everyday, lived experience. For example, at first glance, a trip to the pawn shop may resemble "a crack in the sidewalk." For me, however, a trip to the pawn shop was a delightful experience, not a visit to a shopping outlet for the destitute. A trip to the pawn shop was heavily layered with family wants, needs, and memory. A family foray into Tulsa included stops at newish and orderly pawn shops, like EZ Pawn and Cash America, as well as older pawn shops. During one visit to an old-school pawn shop, the Second Hand Rose Pawn Shop, the place smelled like it was saturated with grease, dirt, metal, and rust. This smelt knowledge immediately evoked decades-old deep memories of being four or five years old in my grandfather's cinderblock garage behind his house in Weleetka with my father, grandfather, and uncles, while they worked on cars and laughed. My olfactory knowledge connected me with a particular kin-space-time envelope that was a metaphysical geography.

I snap out of the metaphysical geography of Weleetka and back to my pawn shop visit when my daughter points at a tattered handwritten paper sign that reads, "No Playing Stairway to Heaven," posted high on the wall near the guitar section. We look at each other and laugh. My father tells my daughter to go pick a movie and he will buy it, and she intently peruses a hundred movies, making sure to select the right one—she cannot squander this opportunity! Sometimes we walk out of a pawn shop with what we need, like a computer monitor; sometimes we get what we want, such as an iPod classic or a 35mm camera; and sometimes we encounter the unexpected, such as a Black Hills gold ring, coveted jewelry in Indian country. Even today the siren song of a missed opportunity, like that of getting a bike or an opal ring, still calls to me. Within this story, relationality is concretized—not because we "consumed" together, but because we found humor and memories together, building relationality and shifting the pawn shop into an alterNative economy.

The pawn shop is the impetus for my own dreams and futurity. I liquidated all of my valuables at Big John's Pawn Shop in Sapulpa, Oklahoma, and used the proceeds to purchase a bus ticket and pay book fees to attend what was then Haskell Indian Junior College. I still feel a twinge of remorse for pawning the items. During the last summer that I spent with my father, I told him that I wanted to go back to the pawn shop and look for those items, even though at least twenty-five years had passed since I had pawned them. In his gentle, nonjudgmental, caring way, he said, "Yeah, we can do that." My relationship and my kinship network's relationship to the pawn shop produce ephemeral and metaphysical geographies, alterNative economy, a connection to family and place, and the gateway to other possible worlds.

The pawn shop, then, is the interstice of the economy and the community. Fred Moten's observation that the "cracks of the sidewalk" are filled with visions, dreams, and concerns of daily life inspires work related to Mvskoke futurity. My family experiences at the pawn shop carry all these ideas, even if the storefront belies the depth of place—you do not realize the futurity waiting for you in the pawn shop.

Summary: Emergence Geographies

Emergence geographies materialize from the Mvskoke emergence story, which moves us out of the fog and into our clan grouping; if one traces our origin story, our migration story, our emergence story, our changing needs, and the crises that have impacted our tribal towns, Mvskoke people have always been in movement. We have always moved and we are not fixed in place, thus a static geography does not fully represent the ways we take up, make up, and produce space. However, emergence geographies that represent the concrete, ephemeral, metaphysical, and virtual ways in which we make community can help understand the places where MCN and Mvskoke communities manifest. The Mvskoke community survey speaks to the ways in which people ponder, speculate, and conceive of three geographies of MCN: the tribal nation, the Mvskoke community, and the level of the person. An analysis of this survey reveals the geographies in which Mvskoke people feel that they have the most agency. Subsequently, I argue for emergence geographies as spaces that community members have always carved out, and for the ways in which they show up today as grassroots movements and nonprofits.

Emergence geographies are a way-finding tool back to the realization that we do not need to buy land to reclaim our communities—while this is important, there are many ways in which we are producing our own community spaces and negotiating those spaces. There is a belief that people need to be in their community of origin or their tribal community to be a "real Indigenous person." Emergence geographies provide a framework for moving beyond prevailing settler geographies that enforce particular types of spatialities. Emergence geographies are important because identifying the ways in which Mvskoke communities are producing space and community outside of the explicitly delineated geographies of the official chartered community or MCN political jurisdiction opens up other spatial possibilities for the community beyond these geographic containers. Emergence geographies empower communities to create and build community without the encumbrance of the politics of recognition and its concomitant geographies. They provide a set of geographies that facilitate the tools of futurity. Emergence geographies are the spaces and places where the map to the next world is written and performed. All of the tools spiral together in movement, each of them a way-finding tool: Este-cate sovereignty is a way-finding tool to our energy, kinship connections, relationality, agency, and power to act without permission. Community knowledge places our energy, kinship, and different ways of knowing in dialogue. Collective power operationalizes our power, knowledge, and relationality. Finally, emergence geographies are the space and place produced in the performance of este-cate sovereignty, community knowledge, and collective power. Mvskoke futurity, then, consists of este-cate sovereignty, community knowledge, collective power, and emergence geographies. These symbols function as symbolic language and embody the multilayered meanings of Mvskoke futurity.[38]

Mvskoke/Indigenous Futurity Praxis

> *When the moon has stomp-danced with us from one horizon to the next,*
> *such a soft awakening. Our souls imitate lights in the Milky Way. We've*
> *always known where to go to become ourselves again in the human com-*
> *edy. It's the how that baffles.*
>
> —Joy Harjo, "The Place the Musician Became a Bear"

Placing your body in a stompdance is in and of itself an act of futurity; it is a political act of resistance. Putting your body in the dance means more than dancing: it is a dialogue between the singers and shellshakers, between the dancers and the relatives outside the circle, and there is dialogue among those not physically dancing. People have different abilities, and just because they are not dancing does not mean they are only passively there—they are still participating. For example, as a teenager I drove Grandpa to stompdances and softball games; I carried his lawn chair for him, gently held onto his arm, found a spot for him to sit, and guided him to it. He had lost most of his vision to glaucoma. However, it never entered my mind to ask ableist questions like, Why do you want to go to a softball game or stompdance that you cannot see? Mvskoke knowledge is accessed through all the senses, and Mvskoke practices are experienced through all the senses. While Grandpa was listening to the stompdance, I was in the spiral dancing. People would stop by and sit by Grandpa and visit with him. Grandpa was carving out his version of futurity from his lawn chair. The stompdance spiral provides several modes of futurity: listening to the dance connects the listener to kin-space-time envelopes of our ancestor relatives, dancing produces a collective celebratory practice, and visiting with one another provides for kinship-building moments. The stompdance spiral instructs us with way-finding tools to futurity—to the lush promise.

Tools of futurity integrate a larger number of people into community action based on their abilities. Some types of community action are not inclusive of everybody: people may not have the ability to be present at a protest, for example, because of physical mobility issues, social anxiety, or family commitments. However, conceiving of many modes of futurity opens the possibility for more to participate based on their abilities.

The fact that we are having a fine-grained dialogue about when and where to have stompdances is an indicator that people want to dance.[1] Stompdance continues to emerge in a variety of places and is resurging in many ways. The dances have never been vanquished, which is demonstrative of Mvskoke resistance. Mvskoke resistance consists of practices that provide a theory or way of understanding the world that is lived, experienced, performed, and embodied; these community-generated theories are formed and enacted at the stompgrounds and other locations of community—for example, homes, MCN Elderly Nutrition Centers, or basketball games—to sustain Mvskoke communities.

In the stompdance, each dance throughout the night is called a round, and each round is a new iteration of the spiral with a new configuration of dancers. Each dance round is led by a new leader, and support is provided by singers, shellshakers, and dancers who often belong to the leader's household, community, ceremonial grounds, and extended kinship network. You can sense the reach of a stompdance leader's collective and social relations as the dance commences. The spiral collects dancers, with the inner rings often consisting of household and ceremonial grounds associates. The ever-morphing collection of dancers into a spiral is an emergence geography, representing and populated by different communities on any given round as the line fills with people based on networks of stompgrounds or the singer. However, the dances are comprised of people from other ceremonial grounds too, who help a ceremonial grounds to have a big, full dance.[2] Kinship is bound up in helping people out. My mom would always say, "Oh look, there's so-and-so from such and such stompgrounds—go help them out, go dance." In another related example, maybe one of our community members did not have a large kinship network, and my mom would suggest that we help them out by going to dance while they were leading.

The configuration of the spiral is also predicated on the decision to jump in and dance. The spiral does not happen without movement, people, singers, and shellshakers—without them, the spiral disappears. However, Mvskoke people are renegotiating the practice of stompdance; it no longer solely occurs at the ceremonial grounds. Stompdance is practiced at indoor dances during the cold months, with food sales featuring hamburgers, corn soup, stew, and fry bread. Winter and fundraising dances have been taking place for decades at locations like Okemah Community Center, Glenpool Community Center, and Sapulpa Armory, to name a few. There is a public dance at Mvskoke Festival with vendors selling their wares that began in the late twentieth century. These versions of stompdance happen in the open under lights, or inside a building with dimmed lights. These too are modes of futurity; the stompdance spiral is not disappearing but rather appearing in new emergence geographies.

These dances are always in movement, shifting and reemerging from round to round, from dance to dance, comprised of new iterations in which people with their own experiences populate the spiral. The spiral is always in flux, always in movement, and many of our Southeastern cultural symbolic languages with their repeating and curvilinear patterns, which are forms of communicating ideas, have a sensibility of movement embedded in them.[3]

As I move into this discussion of the spiral in flux, I use the tools of futurity to read how Mvskoke and Indigenous communities already perform and can potentially continue to perform futurity. The futurity spiral is in flux because these are only provisional ideas, and thinking related to this will continue to include other actors over time. It is all up for renegotiation as conditions change, understandings of community processes deepen, or different tools are used to understand the community and its context. Furthermore, there are many other paths, ideas, and knowledges in the project of Indigenous futurity. Finding our way to Indigenous futurity and enacting it involves a plurality of ideas and people. I invite others to join this conversation by dialoguing about, renovating, and retooling the ideas presented in this book, because ultimately the impetus is vnokeckv for our community, kin, and lifeways, and the wish that they continue to perpetuate and thrive.

For the purposes of explicating Mvskoke and Indigenous futurity praxes and the set of theses generated from understanding a futurity praxis, I discuss praxis and the theses as two distinct maps to the next world, and I represent them as spirals. The first spiral involves recognizing, recuperating, and remembering our Mvskoke connections to one another; it deepens the desires indicated by Mvskoke survey participants—their commitments to Mvskoke lifeways. It is the making of a map of sand that shifts and moves in response to the people and their vernacular practices. Thus, this spiral can be practiced by other Indigenous peoples when they recognize commonality between Mvskoke ways of knowing the world and their own, such as recognizing human and more-than-human kin. The second spiral is comprised of the theses that this project has prompted. These are questions for the future; they are an invitation to a conversation. This map is still coming into being, and in flux, because all of its elements, uses, and destinations change. The more the Indigenous community is understood and the more we valorize different forms of knowledge production, the more the map changes—thus, how we get to the next world is predicated on how we understand our desires and the power of all community knowledge.

Futurity Spiral: Map of Sand to the Next World

A map made of sand is ephemeral. The map being comprised of sand implies that it can be made by anyone who desires to; it doesn't require expensive resources but rather Mvskoke practices and ways of knowing. The map to the next world is created and enacted by Mvskokvlke and their communities. It shifts and is reconstituted in relation to community contexts and challenges and in relation to how we Mvskokvlke understand and practice Mvskoke lifeways such as language, stompdance, faith-based practices, and vnokeckv.

One version of the map to the next world is a futurity spiral that gathers together este-cate sovereignty, community knowledge, collective power, and emergence geographies—each of these concepts is rife with emancipatory and transformational possibilities. When the concepts are placed in rotation with one another, they are in movement and charged with power, like the stomp-dance spiral—but in this case, a spiral of futurity. I propose that these elements of futurity overlap and operate on many registers to make possible modes of futurity that a community can and does carry out. Moreover, these elements operate in the present moment in ways that enact our relatives' unactivated possibilities, allow us to speculate on future temporalities, and place in motion actions that will bring these imagined possibilities to fruition. The following case study is an example of moving across time and space to enact the unactivated possibilities of a Mvskoke woman who had egregious violence done to her.

Beading Case Study

In the cool fall Oklahoma evenings, at the interstice of day and nightfall—twilight—a young Mvskoke woman named Jeannie Coffey or Ms. Coffey, a mother, counselor, and nurturer of young Mvskoke people, would drive to the houses of Mvskoke youth. Stopping at each of our houses and either honking or running to the door and knocking, she would pick us up to work on beading projects that she mentored us in in a classroom at the local school. She chose to do this on her own time; my dad made sure that I was prepared to walk out the door when she arrived so as to respect her time. I was always ready and excited to participate in this evening activity with my peers. We looked forward to these evenings. Each of us worked on a chosen project: mine was beading on a loom, creating a set of beaded barrettes. I still have the beadwork, but I did not place it on barrettes; it is incomplete because the mentoring was incomplete. In the spring of my sixth-grade year, Ms. Coffey's ex-husband purchased a gun at a sporting goods store, came to her office at the school administration building, and shot and killed her. This man took my cousin's mother from him. He took our beautiful teacher from us. However, he did not take the social fabric she co-created with the youth, nor did he take away her example of vnokeckv, nor her futurity. The seeds that she planted live on.

A closer reading of this experience provides more insight than simply a bunch of Creek kids beading. We can see decolonization of a truth regime through the centering, learning, and practicing of local knowledge in the form of beadwork. Within the prevailing truth regime, Indigenous people are rendered hypervisible—in this case, the bodies of Mvskoke students in a predominantly white school are flagged as different and deviant, thus necessitating surveillance—and simultaneously invisible, not the right body for the space, thus overlooked. However, our beading teacher created a transformational space for us, a safe space—a Mvskoke space. Through beading and the transformational space it produces, the participants experienced a bubble of freedom, which is a mode of futurity that does not require a formal bureaucracy. Activities in Indigenous communities often occur outside of conventional modes of planning and development; outsiders do not get to define what proper planning looks like in this transformational space, or what futurity is for my community. Planning and futurity are embodied and practiced in this mode of futurity, not written on paper.

Here, (re)emergence is bound up in the reappropriation of the space of the junior high science room and its use as a site to enact local knowledge praxis and decolonized relationality to one another. In this transformational geography, a protective community space is produced in which youth embrace their peers and forge kinship bonds to one another and a trusted adult. Young participants grow their communication skills by sharing beading techniques, designs, and color combinations, and by troubleshooting together; these actions provide reliable support that fosters the practice of community knowledge, Mvskoke values, and kinship relations with their generational cohort and someone from an inter-generational cohort—the teacher. These actions provide and build confidence for Indigenous youth and plug them into the community—today this type of community is called an artist collective. These treasured experiences enable the formation of an emergence geography that is intergenerational, because as Mvskoke youth we coproduced our actions with Ms. Coffey.

The shared beading experience is demonstrative of este-cate sovereignty, which in this case is a demonstration of autonomy (freedom from state impo-sition and bureaucracy) and self-determination at the scale of the body and of the beading collective. Radical sovereignty is the possession of power and authority over oneself to act, and such agentive action functions as a form of resisting erasure. Youth who practice beading are building a social fabric with their generational cohort to enact forms of este-cate sovereignty in others. The Mvskoke youth's generational cohort sustains their social fabric in other ways outside of the beading collective too, in a range of activities at the neighborhood and regional scale. On the local scale, these might be playing softball, kickball, and shadow tag in the streets, running through the woods, and swimming in the local creek. Regionally, the social fabric might be maintained through sports tournaments, stompdances, and Mvskoke church activities like Indian Falls Creek and other church camps. Youth are enacting este-cate sovereignty when they gather and agentively choose to participate in activities together, and this too is resistance to the settler colonial logics of elimination. Their collective action of playing and creating is a form of resistance to systems, entities, com-munities, and individuals that would prefer to see Indigenous peoples invisible, assimilated, and disappeared.

The shared beading practice builds upon already rich teachings; through beading we concretized Mvskoke values that extend across time and genera-tions. We learned patience, aesthetics, and the reward of delayed gratification in a completed piece of beadwork. We learned the elements needed to play "the long game" in building community. Local knowledge is both valorized and practiced in the teaching and learning of beading. Beading instruction transfers the skills involved in beading: threading your needle; waxing and knotting the thread; placing bead colors into patterns reminiscent of a fire, a bright sunrise, a deep pink sunset, a sparkling night sky, or a brilliant rainbow; and placing a bead at a time on the needle to slowly and carefully create a representation of important elements of the land, cycles of the day, or seasons.[4] Then, after a new piece of beadwork is created, the beader is equipped with a new set of experiences, and as the beader spirals back through the process, each iteration of the practice improves.

Each interaction with any part of the process of beading imparts values and wisdom, providing small challenges and subsequent solutions. One beaded piece can have hundreds or thousands of beads, depending on the size of the beads and the size of the project, and beads range in size from roughly 1.5 millimeters (a size 15 bead) to 2.2 millimeters (a size 11 bead). Beading is an interactive process and it can take weeks, months, or years to complete a project; through this process a beader gains skills, aesthetic sensibilities, and patience. For example, when the challenge of a broken needle occurs, you learn not to shove your needle through a small bead, and not to try to shove it through leather without using an awl. The difficult task of unknotting unwaxed thread: wax your thread and it will not tangle. A broken bead: pick beads uniform in circumference. A bleeding finger pricked by a needle: do not rush and jerk your needle through a tough spot. A bead stuck on a needle: pick your beads carefully as you work. Dark brown beads that ended up placed where dark blue beads belong: sit in a well-lit area. The rhythm of time must change with these practices; it is like trying to run in water. Beadwork is created patiently and slowly. Being engrossed in the piece makes long stretches of time pass quickly: something that took twelve hours might feel like it only took two hours. This is the bending of time, and also a Mvskoke reckoning of time. An Indigenous reckoning of time is shaped in many ways, through actions such as the production of felt knowledge and ceremony, that do not adhere to a clock. Engaging in ceremony is a time-bending experience, and beading is ceremony.[5]

Admittedly, there are nimble bead workers who are highly gifted, who can feel their designs and bead them calmly and with ease. There are other bead workers who bead at lightning speed to make their family's regalia, or for a living. Particularly in a capitalist economy, time speeds up because the market demands that the work of beading be carried out rapidly and productively. The pedagogy of teaching and learning community knowledge does not solely impart a particular skill; it involves a set of practices for operating in community and in the world. You learn that you must place one bead on a needle at a time, that anything that you construct takes forethought, time, skill, and patience; these are practices that are groomed and honed over time. This bundle of practices and competencies enables communities and their members to persevere in long-term endeavors, such as the time-bending involved in sitting calmly for hours in an Indian Health Service clinic or hospital waiting room, or the long game of a community conceiving its community visions and working to fulfill them.

Beading is power; it is felt knowledge, embodied knowledge, that situates the body as an archive that houses information about the arrangement of colors, patterns, and designs. The beader draws upon this archive of embodied knowledge to create the art. Beading is only one example of time and effort in the production of embodied knowledge—knowledge of some community practices takes a lifetime to acquire. While we might take for granted our embodied knowledge, it is critically important to recognize that it is powerful, takes work and patience to accumulate, and is just as valid as other kinds of knowledge. It is of paramount importance because our embodied knowledge is produced in the context of our communities—Indigenous spaces and places. Embodied knowledge is our third door of knowledge that only we as an Indigenous community can create. Thus, when outside researchers come into Indigenous communities, observe, extract embodied knowledge, and decontextualize it to answer their research questions, this is a form of epistemic violence. In summary, they do not get to take our embodied knowledge, which we collected over a lifetime, to commit violence to it and with it. Indigenous communities lament, "They already have everything else of ours, what else do they want?" I understand on a deep level community members' refusal (and my relatives' refusal) to share their embodied knowledge with outsiders.

Ms. Coffey demonstrated, through her acts of kindness and generosity, a peaceful and loving way to be in the world. Showing us an intergenerational act of decolonial love in gathering and teaching us, she was a young woman who took the initiative to carry out this activity with youth, invoking futurity together with us. Futurity means that despite the nation-state's projects to eliminate us, here we are—living! Here we are, practicing beadwork, speaking our language, which was meant to be silenced, and living a life never meant to be lived after our ancestors were genocidally removed to Oklahoma. We should have been erased. However, we are living the futurity of our ancestors in a current kin-space-time envelope, and we stage our community's futurity in a kin-space-time envelope that could be realized today, or years from now, depending on which temporality the community wishes to focus on. We are living our futurity in the current moment; we are living out the stolen lives of our ancestors and relatives and living out the futurity of our beading teacher who was murdered. Ms. Coffey's transference of Mvskoke values and practices in working with youth means that those youth carry her embodied archive as our own.

When we enact futurity, we involve community practices, knowledge, and relationships of many kin-space-time-envelopes, and all of these elements guide us. Our invocation of kin-space-time-envelopes places us in relationship to kin, including kin who are not blood kin but chosen. As a consequence of dialoguing and relating with all forms of kin, such as those residing in the metaphysical realm, futurity shifts the ontology of human life, pivoting away from simply an existence on earth bookended by birth and death toward lives conceived of as a life force. Our relatives' life force has the power to move and invoke us to action and responsibility to community.

Unactivated possibilities relate to imagining and carrying out what could have been had settler colonialism not taken root, on a range of scales—across a broad geography, or at the scale of the body. For example, one practice we perform as we travel to communities is recognizing the Indigenous peoples of the land; however, in some cases, Indigenous peoples are frozen in a settler-structured spatiality. Land recognition is an important practice to remind settlers of the presences of Indigenous peoples and to unbury Indigenous nations from a palimpsest of settler-imagined spatialities. Indigenous practices of land recognition identify our locations of belonging with earth and water at or before European contact. Land recognition is beneficial for recovering our histories; however, this is a practice in which we locate ourselves within settler time-space, giving primacy to temporal considerations. It is a practice that forecloses recognition of Indigenous movement and belonging that occur after European settlement. Unactivated possibilities mean that we can unfreeze these spatialities related to land and open them up to other ways of relating to community, water, air, and kin. Communities materialize in many forms and spaces, activating spatial possibilities.

Often communities already recognize connections beyond territory—for example, at a stompdance, the speaker might recognize other stompgrounds that are attending the dance and recognize that they have long supported the stompgrounds that is holding the dance. Additionally, if we look at kinship connections and spaces of belonging, Mvskoke people are connected to a much more ancient society, Mississippian people. The Mississippian people arguably covered a significant portion of the eastern United States; thus, as Mvskoke, we can connect our spatial imagination to a broader region of belonging, connection, and possibility.

The beading case study that I presented activates the beading teacher Jeannie Coffey's life force; we enable her embodied knowledge. Her life was cut
short, and the youth she taught activate her sacred embodied knowledge. Her
embodied knowledge becomes the youth's embodied knowledge, which makes
knowledge production and exchange a form of ceremony. Further, in her work,
she treated all as kin—an act of este-cate sovereignty, of vnokeckv, of exchanging supportive energy and creating kinship connections.

Mvskoke Futurity Praxis: Mvskoke Community

Mvskoke futurity praxis is based on concepts derived from Mvskoke practices,
but it's not restricted to Mvskoke communities—it can apply to other communities that are predicated on similar concepts of vnokeckv, kinship, and holistic
and inclusive knowledge systems. Praxis is a process of trial and error acquired
through practice. In the beading case study, the practice of beading improves
with each iteration of the process; every aspect of the beading process is reflected
on for improvement or recalibration, and over time a praxis develops and the
practitioner gains new insight and techniques. Whether they are a Mvskoke
language practitioner, an archer, a wood-carver, a shellshaker, or an athlete, their
practice improves over time, whether formed in solitude or among social relations. In a like manner, all futurity praxes develop and strengthen over time.

Mvskoke futurity praxis, in this project, is structured by este-cate sovereignty, Mvskoke knowledge, collective power, and emergence geographies. Like
a stompdance spiral, in which people who step in or out reshape the dance at any
given moment, this practice of a Mvskoke futurity praxis can contract or swell.
Notwithstanding the possibility of a community enacting a linear, sequenced
process of Mvskoke futurity, practicing any part of this process serves futurity
and resists settler logics of elimination. Further, practicing Mvskoke futurity can
continue shaping communities with the same vigor, vision, and intent of their
ancestors, and with responsibility and love for their relatives now and those that
will come into the world after them. The tools in chapter 6 can be used to (re-)
center the community and produce community-driven practices that embolden,
heal, and reinvigorate community.

There are many ways in which Mvskoke people have been or are currently
involved in community practices that demonstrate autonomy of community and

person, create emergence geographies, transfer local knowledge, produce felt knowledge, and invoke kinship relations and commitments to one another. In the following section, I provide lists of community practices that enact futurity, rooted in the elements of sovereignty, local knowledge, collective power, and emergence geographies. These lists are not exhaustive, and I encourage others to consider what is missing from them and create projects informed by their experiences and desires.

Projects of Futurity

In the lists that follow are suggestions for enacting community forms of Mvskoke futurity praxis. The suggestions are organized in a scaled manner, from the level of the individual, household, and community to a broader reach that involves many communities. Further, in examining the lists, folks can see the ways in which they are already performing futurity. To perform futurity is to refuse what Indigenous artist and hip-hop scholar Jarrett Martineau calls the trope of the dying, disappearing Indian—a trope that has been necessary for the settler to take Indigenous lands and lives.[6] Many of these projects are carried out already by communities and individuals. Each of these practices operates to enact some measure of este-cate sovereignty, community knowledge, collective power, and emergence geographies. Even at the scale of the individual, I posit that individuals are still producing Mvskoke spatialities and futurity— Mvskoke spatialities are embodied, and individuals are enacting them wherever they are, whether fixed in a particular place or in transit moving along Interstate 40.

INDIVIDUAL ACTIONS FOR FUTURITY PRAXIS
1. Speaking Muscogee
2. Singing in Muscogee
3. Making art
4. Practicing shaking shells
5. Beading
6. Sewing
7. Making ball sticks
8. Identifying medicinal plants and making medicine
9. Bow making and shooting

10. Hunting
11. Fishing
12. Delivering food, firewood, and other necessities
13. Checking on an elder or neighbor's welfare—for example, to see if they need a ride, medicine, etc.
14. Creating new Mvskoke stories
15. Creating Muscogee-language video and media
16. Growing and canning food
17. Caring for the habitat and health of more-than-human kin, such as medicinal plants, water, sacred sites, turtles, etc.
18. Creation of films and literature

ONE-ON-ONE ACTIONS FOR FUTURITY PRAXIS

1. Speaking Muscogee
2. Teaching another person to bead
3. Teaching another person an art practice
4. Teaching another person about medicinal plants and their uses
5. Teaching another person to shake shells or sing stompdance songs
6. Teaching another person to sew Mvskoke dresses, Mvskoke vests, Seminole patchwork, or quilts
7. Teaching someone to weave a stompdance belt
8. Teaching someone to handcraft a set of turtle shells or cans for shell shaking
9. Teaching another person to fish, hunt, and dress and butcher game
10. Teaching another person to grow, harvest, process, and can food

GROUP SETTINGS FOR FUTURITY PRAXIS

1. Teaching Muscogee language
2. Fiddle dance at Mvskoke Council House
3. Participating at Mvskoke stompgrounds
4. Attending Mvskoke churches
5. Participating in formal or informal community events, attending community meetings, or volunteering for community events
6. Singing and teaching Mvskoke hymns
7. Participating in community dinners and wild onion dinners
8. Painting a community-produced mural
9. Dancing in an Indigenous hip-hop dance cypher

LARGE INTRATRIBAL ACTIONS FOR FUTURITY PRAXIS IN GROUP SETTINGS

1. Playing traditional games such as Mvskoke men's stickball, co-ed stickball, and Euchee Indian football
2. Playing softball, basketball, and volleyball, locally and in tournaments
3. Participating in events at the Mvskoke Festival
4. Attending and/or camping at church meetings at places like Mvskoke-Wichita-Seminole Baptist Association Assembly Grounds, Oklahoma Indian Missionary Conference Northeast District Campgrounds, or Falls Creek Baptist Indian Assembly
5. Participating in stompdance

GLOBAL ACTIONS OF MVSKOKE FUTURITY

1. Situating Muscogee people within an international social movement, such as the United Nations Permanent Forum on Indigenous Issues
2. Convening an International Indian Treaty Council meeting in Okemah

MVSKOKE COMMUNITY "OUTSIDE" OF MCN'S ELEVEN-COUNTY JURISDICTION

1. Participating in California Creek Association
2. Participating in New Mexico Creek Association
3. Participating in Oklahoma City Chartered Community
4. Writing about other worlds via comic book and science fiction narratives

Indigenous Futurity Praxis: Indigenous Community

A Mvskoke futurity praxis is flexible because the configuration and uses of tools of futurity can shift according to a community's needs and uses. A community might have planning, research, organizing, and knowledge production needs, which are related to social justice–based issues. Moreover, the concepts of Mvskoke futurity, este-cate sovereignty, knowledge production, collective power, and emergence geographies can operate alone or in tandem to heal settler colonial–based ruptures in the community and affirm the power of energy, kinship, and decolonial love.

The flexibility of a Mvskoke futurity praxis is important because communities are endeavoring to create futurity in numerous ways, choosing numerous different paths. I respond to the plurality framework that conceives of multiple modes of futurity. I have chosen to focus on modes of futurity that do not center on the politics of recognition. However, this should not preclude other communities conceiving of modes of futurity that engage with and oppose nation-state structures to meet short- and long-term needs and goals.

I will now introduce another case study that demonstrates an Indigenous futurity practice. The case study is based on the work of the Green Corn Collective (GCC), a group of Southeastern Indigenous women who are scholars, artists, and community builders, and who use the tagline "a constellation of Indigenous feminist bosses."[7] As a collective we have a commitment to creating anti-violence actions and growing the consciousness and practice of radical sovereignty, kinship making, and collective power.

I begin first with the collective's project of zine making. There were four of us involved in producing a zine related to MMIWG (see figure 22). The zine was intended to affirm women who are working professionally to alleviate violence against Indigenous women and women who are subjected to violence in their communities and homes. Within the zine were poetry, artwork,

beading instructions, and methods of community dialogue and self-care. The collective also created beading kits to hand out with the zines. This zine has been shared in venues such as zine fests, conference roundtables, and workshops. I will discuss the presentation of this zine at two sites: the "Community-Centered Efforts to Address Violence Against Indigenous Women and Girls" roundtable at the National Indian Nations Conference: Justice for Victims of Crime, in Palm Springs, California, the territory of Agua Caliente Band of Cahuilla Indians; and a workshop at a regional gathering, Strong Hearted Native Women's

FIGURE 22 "Beading a Path to the Future" zines, created by the Green Corn Collective. Photograph by Kimberly Robertson.

Coalition's Sexual Assault Against Native Women Conference, in Temecula, California, at Pala Band of Mission Indians' facilities.[8]

In the Palm Springs and Pala workshops, with primarily Indigenous women, the methods we used were to provide zines and beaded earring kits and to conduct the Prouds/Sorries activity. The Palm Springs workshop had well over fifty participants, while the Pala group had twenty-five in a more intimate setting. Both groups consisted of community workers focused on eliminating violence against women and violence in the community. The primary intent of the workshops was to affirm community and provide tools for resilience through various mediums: poetry to give inspiration, the meditative and affective practice of beading to generate collective power, suggestions for self-care, and methods to spark community dialogue. The zine was inspired by the Indigenous women who created the moccasin exhibit *Walking with Our Sisters* and the communities that hosted and cared for the installation. Their work through affective practices such as beading circles and dialogue has prompted community grieving responses and action to stop the disappearance and murder of Indigenous women and girls.

Our collective quickly designed and created the zine, which took about two weeks through email exchanges, because we do not live in the same location. It is important to draw upon media through which communities can self-publish their narratives, their stories, and their knowledge. GCC's self-published zine enabled us to move communications containing community-based responses to MMIWG swiftly. This proved to be an important dimension of this process, and it would serve communities well to publish their own information and distribute it among themselves. Just as important are the possibilities opened when communities disseminate their knowledge, their ways of making sense of prevailing conditions, and the interventions they wish to propose for their communities. For example, the collective Indigenous Action Media published a zine containing information related to what has been named the "ally industrial complex," which problematizes noncommunity allies who co-opt a community's politics for their own benefit, exploitation, or knowledge edification, or to gain self-serving attention as saviors to the community.[9] The zine and the beading kits provided something material for the community to walk away from the workshop with, so that the convening could continue to pay it forward.

The beading kits provided a way to offer an activity to create a collective felt experience and to collectively create and recuperate community. Many in our collective are beaders, and we felt that there is individual and collective power when beading takes place as a socialized practice.[10] In the more intimate setting of twenty-five people at Pala, they were able to take out their beading kits and begin beading at their tables during our presentation and through the rest of the day—a perfect example of este-cate sovereignty within this community workshop process.

Earlier in the day we also participated in an art workshop facilitated by Indigenous scholar-artist Sarah Biscarra Dilley. We worked on collages; Biscarra Dilley provided us with magazines, encouraging us to browse through them and, if an image struck us, to cut it out. My own pile of images began to grow, and I constructed my own collage that didn't seem big enough to accommodate all the pictures. However, this is a delicious dilemma to have. Biscarra Dilley sensed our dilemmas and said, "Make two collages!" As I flipped through old *National Geographic* and *Arizona Highways* magazines, I was enchanted by images and consequently sucked into a kin-space-time vortex. I imagined multiple futurities as I cut out pictures of maps, horses, a group of women of color in an energetic dialogue, Hawaiian softball players, and an old truck. This is an example of cultural symbolic language at work: instead of grappling with ideas about futurity through written words, the group of women grappled with their interiority through images and creating artwork. It was critical that this art-making activity was sequenced prior to the GCC activities, because the collage activity was an exercise of feeling and creating, and it stimulated ideas that the group later shared during the GCC activities. This approach takes pressure off people for a number of reasons: it provides an opportunity to process your thinking on a particular topic, it is an unassuming approach to presenting ideas as cultural symbolic language, and it provides a setting for individuals who falsely believe that their knowledge is not "good" enough to be part of a formal process of knowledge production. This collaging activity lowered my own stakes in relation to the way I sometimes overformalize my thinking about knowledge production. It also assisted me in refining my theories around knowledge production: we assume knowledge production is always a hard, arduous process, when in reality we construct community knowledge every day, easily and without thought. In this respect the collage exercise was enlightening. The activity quietly tapped into unconscious constellations of kin-space-time envelopes that were roiling around in my head, envelopes that draw upon worldviews and memories that shape and direct how we see and know the world. This activity is a mode of futurity.

The last activity we carried out during our session was Prouds and Sorries; this exercise is one that I learned from Dick Winchell, within the context of planners from outside of the community who complained that community people were apathetic when the planners were the ones who didn't know how to engage Indigenous communities. The reality of the situation is that the best kind of facilitator is one who doesn't cast blame on the community when the community is not interested in participating in his exercise or meeting. A facilitator must do better by continually building a relationship with a community and continuing to reflect on the methodologies that invoke dialogue in safe spaces and in safe ways. We carried out Prouds and Sorries by posing two questions to the workshop: name five things that you're proud of that your community is doing regarding violence, and name five things that you're sorry about that your community is doing regarding violence. Workshop participants were provided two pieces of paper on which to write their answers. The first version of this activity was in a large ballroom setting with a crowd of fifty or more; we collected the participants' responses, but the participants were not required to share their answers, which allowed them to give consent on whether they wanted to provide us what they had written. We then read every single voluntarily shared response into a microphone—this was their knowledge that they had produced! Nobody who wanted his or her answers shared was left out; the collective was given the opportunity to hear what everyone else had to say. This provides an equalizing platform, because everyone's ideas are considered regardless of the power and position that is attached to them when deliberating openly. Before we began reading the Prouds and Sorries, we asked participants to listen carefully for any themes that emerged: Are you hearing some of the same Prouds and Sorries repeated? What is interesting is that this setting was a national conference, and participants identified their local conditions as well as the assets on which they could continue to build their anti-violence efforts.

Next steps for the session could be to use the information to inform a planning process—for example, identifying strong dimensions of the community to address the Sorries or the challenges, and designing programs to address violence in the community. Another step could be a research agenda that investigates community-identified issues more deeply to formulate a fuller and comprehensive response. For example, one issue that came up repeatedly was the power asymmetries that tribal councils create in communities, forming an echelon of decision-makers and causing the community to feel that they had very little access to or influence on a democratic system. Thus, a particular research program might begin to grapple with the ways in which the community might draw upon their knowledge and experiences to formulate claims within the politics of recognition, or the ways in which they might invoke concepts of este-cate sovereignty and collective power to formulate possibilities that circumvent the politics of recognition to imagine other possible worlds.

Or perhaps topics arose in the workshop that compelled participants, such as violence against youth, and they might choose to organize a campaign around a dimension of such a topic—for example, the settler logics of elimination related to the overcriminalization of Indigenous youth in the schools. Using an array of approaches with telecommunications and digital media, they can organize a campaign that formulates particular asks to target decision-makers. Further, deploying and sequencing next steps in the campaign might include a power analysis that seeks to understand those either in opposition to or in support of the overcriminalization of Indigenous youth, and to understand which actors have the ability to influence decision-makers.

I want to finish discussing this case study by reflecting on the more intimate setting of the second GCC workshop; we reflected on the first iteration of the workshop and recalibrated our practices based on what worked and what we thought needed to be improved upon. The second workshop was smaller than the first, and we benefited from rapport-building activities—which are also a form of este-cate sovereignty—that were staged before our session. Specifically, Biscarra Dilley's collage activity and both breakfast and lunch were sequenced before our session, which allowed our workshop to operate in tandem with connections made during the collage activity and meals. The GCC session took an alternate direction and created a safe space because people were not immediately thrust into a two-hour-long workshop. They were able to eat and to visit, creating relationality and connections, and they participated in activities and listened to informational speakers.

Two aspects of the workshop that changed in the second iteration were the inclusion of more dialogue and the opportunity to create a collage. Having more time for dialogue and art-making decelerated the full-throttle feel of the national workshop, which was conducted in a short amount of time, after which people moved on to the next workshop of their choosing. This more intimate setting provided more time and space for participants to reflect on their thoughts and to dialogue with one another and workshop presenters. When we facilitated the Prouds and Sorries, we provided two sets of colored index cards;

we asked them to write their Prouds on one and their Sorries on the other. We used colored cards to make it easier to sort assets and challenges visually. However, instead of reading their cards out loud, we entered into a dialogue in which we asked participants to share their Prouds and Sorries of their own volition—but we did not pressure anyone to share. There was rich dialogue, and participants were filled with energy, as in our larger national workshop. However, this was a regional workshop with Indigenous women's coalitions working against violence, and many of the women already enjoyed established relationships with one another. Consequently, there was already established traction in terms of collective power. We added a third question to this activity: What would you like to have happen in your community? In a similar fashion to the national dialogue at the Palm Springs event, at a regional scale the women had converging ideas and themes, and they quickly analyzed them and moved on to reflection and next steps of action. This context provided the conditions for a vibrant conversation that moved on to formulating actions. When we wrapped up the workshop, many of the women stated that they deeply appreciated the opportunity to engage in dialogue and wished for more opportunities to continue their conversations. Finally, we collected the cards from everyone who was willing to share and laid them out on the table by color so that others could view the collective responses, including the participants who wished to remain anonymous during the dialogue session. During this moment, participants took pictures of the cards to contemplate and analyze on their own accord. As a group, we also decided to place all our collages on the table so that we could share, admire, and ponder over one another's work.

What was derived from both the national and local workshops was an affirmation of energy, kinship, and decolonial love. All participants had immense community concerns at stake, and both workshops were full of energy and dynamism; the people were coming together in a demonstration of este-cate sovereignty, knowledge production, collective power, and emergence geography in the site of the workshop. Conversations were full and active, brimming with ideas—a show of este-cate sovereignty and community knowledge production. Everyone in the room had self-selected as a participant in the workshop, and their commitment to their respective communities illustrates a show of responsibility; these are elements of collective power. Further, it was a show of jumping scale and of an emergence geography in that it generated ideas across many communities to produce a national emergence geography related to intervening and stopping violence against women and Indigenous communities.

The GCC used zine making to publish and communicate our ideas in an informal way, while the workshops we conducted with the Prouds and Sorries exercise worked to promote the use of collective power. The tools of futurity can be sequenced however a community feels it is most appropriate. If they are sequenced in the order in which I present them in this book—este-cate sovereignty, community knowledge, collective power, emergence geographies—each of the concepts builds on the next.

The sequence of activities operates to produce many modes of futurity. Sequencing can be structured to correspond to a planning process, which involves building rapport; determining issues in the community, the community's vision and aspirations, and how to accomplish these visions and aspirations by identifying and operationalizing strategic areas of focus (e.g., language, community, health); assessing the power landscape within which a community must move its agenda; and understanding how communities produce space.

Other modes of futurity to which the tools can be sequenced are a conventional planning process, a research process, a community organizing process, or acts of way-finding. Acts of way-finding can include a deepened consciousness of este-cate sovereignty and knowledge, the invocation of both concepts to yield community power or collective power, and Mvskoke instantiation of scale, space, and place. This conceptual apparatus operates to deepen a sense of self that is informed by Indigenous epistemologies. It is the notion that one is either becoming conscious of or forming one's Mvskoke subjectivity. Each tool is meant to deepen and validate our everyday practices and provide space to make possible our yet-to-be-imagined possibilities, the unactivated possibilities of one's relatives, the possibilities that we dream for the current temporality, and the construction of ways to bring to fruition a Mvskoke imaginary within a future temporality. For example, we come to realize the way este-cate sovereignty operates in the everyday through relationality and through Mvskoke energy transfer—that it is agentive and when operationalized has immense power.

Futurity Spiral: Map to the Next World in Flux

In this concluding section, I discuss the map to the next world, which is in flux. There is much to be worked out in order to create a map or plan to the next world we wish to see, and I present a series of theses for those with an interest in building communities. Throughout this book, I weave in Indigenous community

TABLE 1 Matrix of Futurity Methodologies and Tools

FUTURITY METHODOLOGIES	FUTURITY TOOLS (CHAPTER 6)
Este-Cate Sovereignty (Radical Sovereignty)	
Mvskoke energy	Where I Am From
Mvskoke love	Connecting with Kin and Felt
Kinship/relationality	Knowledge
Not fixed in place	
Already happening in every case	
Acts agentively, not requiring permission from normative governance structures	
Mvskoke Knowledge (Community Knowledge)	
Felt knowledge	Community Timeline
Mvskoke narratives	Zine Making: Local Knowledge
Dialogue	Production
Place—material and metaphysical	
Collective Power	
Affective	Prouds/Sorries
Collective felt experiences	
Experiences and practices are power	
Accumulation of energy	
Shapes everyday experiences	
Found in vernacular spaces	
Emergence Geographies	
Concrete	Map Biography: Memory and
Ephemeral	Sense of Place
Metaphysical	Land as Kin
Virtual	

narratives and take into consideration the imperatives of sovereignty, decolonization, cosmology, and power. These imperatives are the theoretical underpin-
nings that inform any kind of community-situated work—whether it is community engagement, planning, development, or social movement work. Pausing
to reflect on what is important to our communities and what brings them peace,
joy, gratitude, and resilience provides instruction about what to honor in the
process of community planning. A map to the next world can take many forms

and shapes—this map of a Mvskoke futurity praxis is one such map. However, there are many other maps that are waiting to be told or conceived.

Mvskoke futurity praxis is composed of actions and activities that actively, whether intentionally or unintentionally, produce the concepts of este-cate sovereignty, community knowledge production, collective power, and emergence geographies. There are ways in which communities are already unintentionally enacting modes of futurity, such as building kinship networks at a softball tournament, reappropriating space for a kickball game in the street, speaking the Muscogee language at home, or participating in a regional gathering of Mvskoke churches at Indian Falls Creek.[11] While a Mvskoke futurity praxis is flexible and can be used to address the politics of recognition, I choose to answer the call to action from critical Indigenous studies in looking to our communities for the source of our validation, recognition, and knowledge.[12]

I am apprehensive about the use of the tools and their misappropriation. In using the tools, it is important to think about who is facilitating the work and to what end. As an example, one the tools of futurity, "Where I Am From," is a poem template that announces the author's social location. The author remembers and (re)connects with kinship, their personal geographies of importance, and sense- and feeling-based knowledge. The process of remembering can be a deeply emotional activity: some might grieve over the loss of these connections or reflect upon the richness of their experiences with deep gratitude. After a panel discussion about how participatory action has the potential to change or shape our lived and built environments, I was conversing with a young woman who was familiar with the "Where I Am From" poem-writing action and had conducted workshops using the poem as a creative writing activity. During our conversation, a man who was also on the panel approached us and interrupted our conversation to ask her a question. After he finished his thread of the conversation, I turned the conversation back to what we had been speaking of before we were interrupted. I asked the young woman if she would be willing to read the part of my manuscript that addresses the "Where I Am From" tool. She agreed, and the male colleague—the interrupter—proceeded to ask if I would send it to him too. He informed me that he was working with a third-party contractor on police/community dialogues (whatever all that means) in Albuquerque and wanted to read my work and send it on to the third-party contractor to use. I declined his request. Police and community relations are troubled, and the Albuquerque Police Department has been the target of a Department of Justice investigation for police brutality. Further, previous community dialogue engagements reinforced the uneven power dynamic between the police and the local community.[13] I believed that granting an entity that a community perceives as their aggressor access to a tool that makes visible their social locations and vulnerabilities is a gross misappropriation. In particular, we would need to know more about the process and purpose of knowing deeply personal information about people who feel subjugated by the police: Are the police going to extract this information as a form of further surveillance? Are the police going to reciprocate and share their own vulnerabilities and social locations?

From an intentional perspective, a community can make deliberate decisions to use the tools for building kinship and networks of relationality, and for producing and sharing knowledge. They can also be used in a deliberate manner for tactical ends, such as building a rapport among community members and stakeholders prior to convening a community planning session to identify what they care about and what their wishes are for the community. After identifying their wishes, they might analyze what they have found and make meaning out of them, then begin to conceive of concrete actions and solutions that activate these wishes. They should own the process, and these tools enable them to do so.

A Mvskoke futurity praxis is a set of methodologies and methodological tools that are theorized and strategized with aspirations of reconstituting the Mvskoke worlds and modes of futurity within which Mvskoke people wish to live. Methodologies of futurity restructure conventional thinking about sovereignty for Mvskoke community; the battle cry of "Sovereignty! Sovereignty! Sovereignty!" is structured within the community with energy, relationality, and vnokeckv. A Mvskoke futurity praxis is structured by the realization that your grandma, aunt, cousin, and uncle all carry the elements of este-cate sovereignty and activate them on a daily basis, in conversation, or in the humor involved in roasting you. These forms of everyday sovereignty articulate a futurity praxis that means community can be instantiated at a scale of one person and reconstituted in ways that instantiate a virtual collective of material places, such as #MMIWG, #INM, or #NoDAPL.

Theses for an Indigenous Futurity Praxis: Embodied Futurity

We carry the tools of futurity within us. As one illustration, Mvskoke artists such as Danielle Fixico, Buffalo Gouge, Starrhardridge (also known as Starr

Hardridge), Charlie Johnson, and Kenneth Johnson are creating work that reflects Mississippian iconography. In particular, the work of Hardridge and Fixico reflects silhouettes of figures whose interiority consists of Mississippian iconography, which is Mvskoke symbolic language.[14] Mississippian iconography operates as an ancestral gift that continues to sustain Mvskoke people, and Mvskoke people renegotiate the symbology and make meaning of it within prevailing conditions and their community contexts. Artists such as Johnson, Fixico, Hardridge, and Gouge infuse their own meaning into the iconography, which yields titles such as *Mvskoke Knot* and *Star Knot* in Kenneth Johnson's work.[15] Likewise, I renegotiate this iconography as well, creating block prints and infusing meanings into them that are related to futurity and based on the Mvskoke community research presented in this book.

Spiral to the Stars has argued for the concepts that lie behind the set of Mississippian/Mvskoke symbols that I have drawn, concepts that help us conceive of ways of realizing the freight of our daily actions and the knowledge that sustains us and our communities. Mvskoke artist Danielle Fixico has an untitled piece that depicts a woman stargazing; in the foreground, her silhouette is filled with Mississippian iconography, which represents Mvskoke concepts, values, and knowledge that she embodies while she is in dialogue with the constellations. Similarly, Mvskoke artist Starr Hardridge employs a pointillist technique that uses seed beads, thus renegotiating our way of using beads. In his piece *Renewal*, he depicts a Green Corn Dance; in the foreground are dancers and in the background is corn, a perpetual element that sustains us in myriad ways— providing physical sustenance, felt knowledge, and kinship building, among other things. It is a contemporary depiction of a stompdance leader, wearing a cowboy hat with a feather, and a shellshaker is behind him wearing a skirt. The stompdancers carry a Mvskoke interiority, as indicated by the symbolic language that their silhouettes hold. Their symbolic language travels with them wherever they go; therefore, they instantiate a scale of Mvskoke community that is embodied, thus unalienable.

Decolonizing community consists of decentering its focus from Western, settler colonial practices and re-centering on its local epistemologies and belief systems. Community knowledge production and the remembering of one another as kin operate as practices of resurgence and recuperation in communities. The action of remembering kin involves the members of a community lovingly reconfiguring their relationships to one another, to land, and to more-than-human entities. Remembering kin is also the act of seeing one another's

FIGURE 23 *Renewal*, painting by Starrhardridge.

light, which can be defined as their energy or their unique spirit.[16] Indigenous peoples grapple with multiple dimensions of making their map of futurity. In what follows, I have summarized Mvskoke futurity and its tools into sets of theses that correspond to each of the symbols. The theses are couched in ways of thinking that disrupt settler colonialization and are aligned with emancipatory community practices that run counter to land as property regime.

FUTURITY

1. Futurity is the invocation of many temporalities and spaces to form an imaginary constructed of energy, kinship, community knowledge, collective power, felt knowledge, responsibility, and emergence geographies. It is something that communities can practice now and in the future, in order to imagine unactivated possibilities, live them out, and leave their own archive of knowledge and possibilities.[17] We must recognize community's ability to assert self-determination and to conceive of, act upon, and appropriate the space necessary to realize community aspirations.

2. Futurity is a way of being in the world that recognizes the energy of all entities and their relationships to one another—that is este-cate sovereignty.

3. Futurity is a way of knowing the world and producing knowledge, and it is produced by all forms of entities, human and more-than-human. All of these entities produce community knowledge.

4. Futurity is a form of collective power, animated by responsibility to one another and to more-than-human entities, that nurtures, supports, and sustains.

5. Futurity is space and place produced via relationality and connections to humans and more-than-human entities. Some places can be mapped in a fixed way while some are unfixed, in movement, or simply unfixable—these are emergence geographies.

ESTE-CATE/RADICAL SOVEREIGNTY

1. If the tribal government is not in a place to carry out community-based work or is too dysfunctional, then futurity work can happen with a small, organized group of Mvskokvlke and should not have to be sanctioned by the tribe's larger governing structure. This approach can be used by organized groups from the smallest to the largest size—it is scalable.

2. The community's desires and wishes for the future are (re-)centered and valorized in the process of community-building.

3. Individuals and groups carrying out plans must remain cognizant of the fact that the community-building process, methodologies, and outcomes will lift everyone's boat—everyone's life will improve, not just those of an elite few. Planning should be conducted in a way that resists elevating the desires of only a privileged few or a privileged sector of the community. Furthermore, all segments of the community should be involved in shaping visions and decisions for the entire community. In the past, women have given up their rights for the "greater good" of justice for the tribe, which is one of the ways in which sexual assault on Indigenous women has been allowed to pervade communities.

4. The community already possesses self-determination, power, and agency, and enacts these elements on a daily basis.

5. Este-cate sovereignty enacts a form of human and more-than-human emancipation and relationality in ways that decenter human and anthropocentric wishes and desires and consider the needs of more-than-human entities.

KNOWLEDGE PRODUCTION

1. The community already has fine-grained knowledge, which does not always fit into coarse taxonomies, and thus community knowledge is often reduced to broad, unsubtle explanations by Western knowledge.

2. When community participatory work is carried out, the process should include specific opportunities to gain the input of elders, schoolchildren, young adults, women, other dissident or marginalized groups, tribal members living outside of the jurisdiction, disabled people, LGBTQ2S people, and other silenced communities such as domestic and sexual abuse survivors.

3. Futurity work should empower community members to recognize and disrupt settler colonialism and oppressive structures in their community through understanding the relevance of their experiences and family narratives.

4. We must recognize the diverse ways a community speaks: it produces knowledge through many untapped texts that not all are privy to—in some cases, only those who have been initiated. These texts include stories, narratives, videos, pedestrian accounts of place, ritual, and ceremony. They

may be legible only to the community itself, such as in the case of the Zuni Map Art Project. We should recognize that community knowledge is both explicit and implicit.

COLLECTIVE POWER

1. The community does not have to ask permission.
2. We must see and make visible the profound and spectacular ways in which community is doing and being (acting, performing), and we must refuse to accept outsiders' characterization of a community as apathetic—this means that we change the lens with which we view community. Understanding what a community is proud of and what it is sorry about is one way to start the conversation.
3. We must find freedom, emancipation, and empowerment in multiple spatialities, such as at the scale of the physical body, coalescing with others into a stompdance spiral that connects to the stars, or in the collectivity of social movements like Idle No More or NoDAPL.
4. We must see the ways in which alterNative economies are at work in MCN. Again, this can be considered in terms of what is legible within a market economy—the exchange of goods and services for money. However, MCN communities and households thrive in alterNative economies in many ways. In this way, they operate in the interstices of the United States, the state, or the county.
5. We must work in ways that do not require the nation-state or even the tribal government. People may say that you cannot do the work without money, which is to say without resources, but are we limiting ourselves in the ways we think of how to acquire resources and what resources look like? We must recognize that we carry our own sets of resources. We must look and see differently, for there are ways in which people are doing the work that invoke alterNative economies.
6. We must recognize that the invocation of the politics of recognition is a limitation on carrying out a full spectrum of Mvskoke ways of being in the world.
7. We must recognize that the logic of Mvskoke thought is unique to Mvskoke people and that it operationalizes and accesses felt knowledge.
8. Collective power can mean more than oppositional power or advocating a grievance to an entity that does not care. It can be transformative power, the power to live and be alive, the power to enact decolonial love—living

a life that is full. We practice collective power when we shift the notion of what a full life is away from capital and commodities to something that is filled with relationality, positive energy, safe spaces, and geographies of emergence.

EMERGENCE GEOGRAPHIES

1. We must see the ways in which alterNative notions of community are at work in Mvskoke communities, and we must see that community exists in many iterations and forms.

2. We must understand the historic legacy of how different geographies are produced—land, property jurisdiction, diaspora, boarding schools, and local intertribal networks—to see, know, and make legible the landscapes of sub-jugation and emancipation that Indigenous communities and individuals navigate, take advantage of, and create.

3. We must untether our notion of space and place from a prescribed area, because this delineation proscribes our possibilities, placing limitations on the possibilities that can manifest and where they can manifest. Many versions and kinds of space and place exist. There are some we can identify because we have the theoretical and analytic tools to do so, and some are still slippery, defying definition and taxonomic ordering. However, the common denominator is that they challenge the containerizing geographies of settler colonialism.[18]

This work requires treading a fine line: honoring Mvskoke practices while refusing to appeal to the people and institutions that do not believe in us or wish to see us thrive. In this book I have drawn upon the aspirational dimensions of critical Indigenous studies to inform how we think of Indigenous community and how we as community builders, planners, cultural workers, and dreamers (re)conceive of community aspirations. The idea of the future, while it has aspirational intentions, signals to the community "not yet," that the future is a discrete place "over there" that the community is going to have to wait for while they sit in their current moment. The future can seem unattainable and out of reach, a paradox—that is, an intangible place that the community cannot arrive at yet, while at the same time it is a discrete place on a linear timeline. Thus, futurity is the intervention for a hamstrung future. Futurity shapes Indigenous communities and grounds them in their respective ontologies and epistemologies. It is not solely speculative in imagining communities;

it also considers the present moment that is shaped and instantiated by many kin-space-time envelopes. Mvskoke places are produced by multiple layers of Mvskoke stories and experience that spiral to the stars. Both the body and the stars hold an archive of stories and felt knowledge about Mvskoke people. This archive informs Mvskoke people about what is most valuable and most important, our responsibilities to our ancestors, stories, and epistemologies, which are embodied. Mvskokvlke are not tethered to the bounds of MCN but have emplaced themselves in the city and in online communities—anywhere there are Mvskoke people, there is Mvskoke place.

Moonshot: The Indigenous Comics Collection contains a narrative written by Mvskoke-Kickapoo author Arigon Starr. Starr's story "Ue-Pucase: Water Master" is Mvskoke science fiction and futurity; it provides a different context and geography for a deeply rooted Mvskoke story, a context and geography that transcend the current fixity of MCN's boundaries. It is an example of emplacement. The story takes place in a Muscogee Nation that exists in cosmic space and features two Mvskoke men who are junkers, people who collect cast-off objects. In this speculative narrative, they continue the contemporary practices of accessing an alterNative economy of foraging. They return to a postapocalyptic Earth to participate in junking, and their grandmother instructs them not to eat anything they might find. However, when they arrive, one of them finds a can of Spam. Remembering his grandmother's stories of how delicious it is, he feels the visceral pull of this felt knowledge. He eats the Spam, and havoc ensues: he is transformed into Water Master, a large water monster. In this futurity, Mvskoke stories continue, shifting to have different uses within different contexts, in the same way that, in the anecdote that opened this book, my grandfather taught me a medicine song meant to help one be heard clearly and reasonably for use in the context of a pawn shop. (Re)purposing, (re)making, and remembering Mvskoke stories and ways of being in the world are practices of futurity that invoke agentive power through local knowledge and ingenuity, relying upon the self-determination of este-cate sovereignty and producing transformative power and geographies.

CHAPTER 6

It Is Your Turn

Tools of Futurity

This book has been structured to introduce and explain a set of concepts—estecate sovereignty, the decolonization of knowledge, transformational power, and transformational geographies—that are the constituent elements of mapping a path to the next world. This final chapter provides tools that communities, whether big, small, informal, or formal, can use together with their members to provide a platform for producing local knowledge, sorting through and reflecting on individual and collective wants, desires, and issues, moving information through the community, and devising concrete actions. However, these tools are meant to provide a safe space for folks who do not feel comfortable sharing their knowledge at large public meetings. Several of the approaches contained in this chapter are methods I use in my courses, in particular the courses Indigenous Space, Place, and Mapping; Community Participatory Methods; #MMIW (Missing and Murdered Indigenous Women): A Transnational Context; and Indigenous Town Planning Studio. The activities in this chapter provide community-based and individually based exercises that move theories from the previous chapters into practice. However, it is not necessary to proceed in a prescribed order. Further, this chapter is meant to provide a resource for former students going to work in their community and for others who wish to shift knowledge and power to their community's residents. The thinking behind these tools is that they can be carried out one weekend at a time, providing time to engage with community, analyze findings as a group, and reflect on how these results bear on a community's aspirations. For example, one scenario might involve a community arriving at the conclusion that not only do they want to grow their food, but this should be traditional foods such as those grown from heirloom seeds. Or maybe there are not enough people who know how to make women's turtle shell shakers (colloquially known as "turtle shells") or woven belts for stompdance, and the community would like to start educating its members in both traditional agriculture and dance art practices.

Community Exercises

Tools of Este-Cate Sovereignty (Chapter 1)

"WHERE I AM FROM" POEM

Overview

If one dimension of este-cate sovereignty is about understanding one's network of connections to human and more-than-human kin, then the "Where I Am From" poem brings the daily routines and experiences of one's kinship network into sharp relief. After a participant writes the poem, its content provides insight into daily routines and how they are concrete and creative improvisations that make community right now and in the future. Whether you are hearing the rustle of tree leaves that tamp down pressures of urban life or watching your grandmother's hands make your favorite meal of pork and hominy, the trees are just as much kin as your grandmother: they sustain you and sustain community in myriad ways. The poem helps us to make connections between things we take for granted. After one writes and reflects on the poem, the content alerts its author to dimensions of the community that matter: memory, family, home, and place. Prior to chapter 1, I provide a "Where I Am From" poem I wrote, which situates the reader with a better idea of who I am and the vernacular language of my place and my family. This poem is derived from a community exercise that I learned from colleague and friend Professor Levi Romero, New Mexico Centennial Poet Laureate. The poem grounds the reader in the author's worldview. This act of writing concretizes the author's source of power and enables the author to recognize the everyday landscape and kinship connections that do not always get attention and are overlooked. *Epistemology* is related to your belief system and way of knowing the world. This exercise helps participants to see how their way of knowing the world is reflected in the everyday world and places, and to bring out the significance, richness, and importance to storytelling of elements that might otherwise seem banal and ordinary.

Objectives
- Understand what shapes your way of knowing the world (epistemology)
- Understand what shapes your worldview
- Understand the way you feel about place and home (felt knowledge)
- Understand important memories and histories of place

Materials
- Paper
- "Where I Am From" poem template
- Pens or pencils

Activity
Explain to the participants that they will populate the poem template with their information. Provide them with the template handout to fill out. You may also provide them with a blank piece of paper if they wish to rewrite the poem.

There are a few scalable options with this:

Approach 1
Objective: Understand your worldview and that of your community members.
In one two-hour block, provide participants with a blank template. They can spend time on-site writing their "Where I Am From" poem, and, depending on the size of the group, everybody can read their poem.

Approach 2
Objective: Understand your worldview and that of your community members, and identify commonalities—these are the building blocks of futurity. Plan three hours for this approach.
In one two-hour block, provide participants with a blank template. They can spend time on-site writing their "Where I Am From" poem, and, depending on the size of the group, everybody can read their poem.
Devote another hour to discussing what their poems have in common and having a "what is to be done" conversation. How do we continue these experiences now and into the future? If we care about dances, water, fish, human relatives, or landscape, how do we keep them going? How do we prioritize

practices from the poem and elements of the community that make the
practices possible in what we do?

Approach 3

Objective: Publish community poems and take account of the work.

After performing the activity as in the first two approaches, publish poems
in a chapbook (this is one title) or zine (this is another title for a publication with a series of issues) for the community to use in further analyzing
and devising solutions. (For the construction of a chapbook, see the "Zine
Making" activity below in the section "Tools for Decolonizing Knowledge
[chapter 2].") Engage with the poems and content for a sustained amount
of time to understand what the community cares about. Self-publishing
the information provides a future archive for the community, so that their
relatives can understand what they cared about.

The WHERE I AM FROM Template

I am from _____ (specific ordinary item), from _____ (product or place
   name) and _____.

I am from the _____ (home description . . . adjective, adjective, sensory
   detail).

I am from the _____ (plant, flower, natural item), the _____ (plant, flower,
   natural detail).

I am from _____ (family tradition) and _____ (family trait), from _____
   (name of family member) and _____ (another family name) and _____
   (family name).

I am from the _____ (description of family tendency) and _____ (another
   one).

From _____ (something you were told as a child) and _____ (another).

I am from _____ (representation of spirituality or religion, or lack of it).
   (Further description.)

I am from _____ (place of birth and family ancestry), _____ (two food
   items representing your family).

From the _____ (specific family story about a specific person and detail), the
   _____ (another detail), and the _____ (another detail about another
   family member).

I am from _____ (location of family pictures, mementos, archives, and several
   more lines indicating their worth).

Adapted by Levi Romero from the original poem "Where I'm From," by
George Ella Lyon.

If possible, incorporate bilingual references used in your family (Muscogee,
Diné, Tewa, Tiwa, Spanish, German, Italian, etc.). Use words, quotes, common sayings, objects, and images that represent your family's traditions.

Example by Angelina Grey:

Where I Am From / Na'sha'déi' / De donde yo soy

I am from Spider Woman's spinning tools

From the Snow Cap Lard and da'diniilyaa'zh (frybread)

I am from the place of Łlazh'łizhiin (black soil)

K'iinol tsdisii (dust devils), the smell of rain and beauty

I am from the ts'á (sagebrush), the ch'á'oł (juniper trees)

The old lady goat named Daisy, my childhood riding companion

the tarantula I carried home in my two small hands

whose long lost gone limbs I remember

as if they were my own.

I'm from Kit Carson's Scorched Earth Campaign and Hwéeldi' (Bosque Redondo)

from the 1868 Treaty and the Carlisle Experience

I'm from the stubbornness and tough love of Habah

from the half-hearted "love" and abandonment of the Black Sheep Clan.

I am from Asdzaa' Na'dłee'hí' (Changing Woman) and the animals

and the insect people of the previous four worlds.

I'm from na'daał tsó' (yellow corn) and na'daał ghái' (white corn)

I'm from the place of natural springs and da'aké (cornfields)

go'whe' (coffee) and the yaa'teeł (sheepskin mattress)

From the threadbare Levi jeans of Luke Sr.

the soft laughter of shí masani' (my maternal grandmother)

the Lucky Strikes of my great-grandmother

Asdzaa' A'di'ka'i' (the Gambling Woman)

Whose long gone limbs I remember

As if they were my own

The dła'kaał (Navajo dress) that waved behind

Habah as my little feet tried to keep up with her haste,

The long forgotten feel of shí naali's (paternal grandmother) hands,

The commodity cheese and bilaaghana bikós' (canned beef),

And the sign of age and wisdom capsulated in the wrinkles of the skin.

CONNECTING WITH KIN AND FELT KNOWLEDGE

Overview

Our community members, relatives, and friends carry a deep well of experiences that can be understood through oral history and storytelling practices. Sometimes we are not sure how to delve deeper with a neighbor, grandparent, or parent. Connecting with and learning from a relative or community member can provide a deeper sense of how they live, what matters most to them, and what they wish to see continue in the community into the future. The prompts here can generate highly personal narratives that bind our kinship connection to the teller. Where there might be very little written in the contemporary moment, this exercise enables community and family members' stories to be told.

Objectives

- Capture community oral history
- Understand community and individual values
- Build and strengthen connections with kin

Materials

- Audio recorder, with permission from kin whom you are interviewing
- Notepad and pen

Activity

1. Decide on prompts to use. The following prompts are derived from the book *Ties That Bind.*[1] You can test them on a friend or relative for the best wording for your community. You can also create your own prompts. After you have a set of prompts, ask the person you are going to interview which questions they feel comfortable being asked.

   What was the happiest moment of your life? The saddest?

   Who was the most important person in your life? Can you tell me about them?

   What are the most important lessons you have learned in your life?

   Is there any wisdom you wish to share with me?

   What does your future hold?

   What does the future of the community hold?

2. Explain the importance of the individual's stories and ask permission to record.

3. After recording them, you can transcribe or type up the audio recording into a document for the person to review. You can provide the recording and the typed document to the person you interviewed and ask the individual to make choices about what they wish to include or say differently. This gives the individual a chance to edit their story further.

4. If the storyteller does not wish to be recorded or to have their story disseminated, they still shared their life and knowledge with you. It is just as important to simply hear people's stories and make a connection with them.

Options for sharing (with the storyteller's permission):

5. Make a zine or written document to share with the individual and their family. Give the individual a chance to edit their story further, if they wish, before releasing it.

6. Documentation of the person's narrative can be shared with the broader community in a number of ways: using a zine, the local community newsletter, or the tribal newspaper.

7. Create a collection of community oral histories and self-publish. Support from the tribe might be helpful here, to provide production expertise and help with costs.

Tools for Decolonizing Knowledge (Chapter 2)

COMMUNITY TIMELINE

Overview

Often in Indigenous communities the record of the community is either undocumented in written form or has been authored by someone outside of the community. This exercise is meant to develop a community-produced history. For example, one of my students produced a timeline for a women of color hip-hop crew. You can also choose to do this activity with a group of elders to understand pivotal moments in their community, or construct timelines with intersectional groups such as female elders, female youth, and trans adults. The important aspect is the co-construction of the timeline and the required negotiation among the participants. They are producing, analyzing, and presenting their collective knowledge about important community moments, pivot points, and shifts.

Objectives
- Develop a community-generated history in the form of a timeline
- Create a timeline that captures pivot points, crisis points, or important moments in your community, household, or personal life
- Conceive of and construct a linear, chronological version
- Conceive of and construct a nonsequential version

Materials
- Post-it notes or index cards
- Tape
- A surface to post the cards on
- Pens
- Pencils

Activity

Construct a timeline. The timeline does not have to be linear but can be fashioned in whatever shape the participants choose—for example, it could be a spiral or an undulating wave. A nonlinear version might be based around important community moments that branch off into related stories, or around relationships: this could look like a pumpkin vine that branches off into other directions with blossoms and pumpkins. You can choose to use index cards and arrange them on a table, or you can tape them to a surface such as poster board or a long piece of butcher paper. Also, you can use Post-it notes, which makes it easier to rearrange the timeline as the group renegotiates their community's story.

Next, gather a group of individuals and provide Post-its. Ask them to write the most important moments in their community.

Ask them to place each Post-it note with an important moment on the timeline and then to tell the group about the moment.

Prompts:

What are the most important moments in the history of the community?

Think about changes that you've seen in the community over time. When did these various changes begin and end? For example, everybody used to collect firewood up until the 1960s, then after that they shifted to gas heaters. Or, we used to grow our corn for ceremony until the 1990s, but then everyone got too busy commuting to work and driving to buy groceries, and now we buy our corn for ceremony at Walmart.

Participants should collectively discuss the moments that they are mapping on the timeline. There could be agreements or disagreements about the timeline, and in some cases creating these types of timelines sparks memories in the participants that would not necessarily have been invoked on their own. After the group has decided which events stay and where they belong, the timeline can be drawn in a more permanent form, on paper. If there are artists in the group, perhaps this could be turned into a canvas or a community mural.

ZINE MAKING: LOCAL KNOWLEDGE PRODUCTION
Overview

Zines are a form of self-publishing to get out a message. This can be an individual venture or a collective venture. Because we are working with community participatory methods, we want to approach zine making here as a collaborative venture in which several individuals can create input. It becomes a collection of unique submissions by several individuals. Zines can consist of tribal language, collage art, illustrations, photography, community sayings or wisdom, creative writing such as poetry and short stories, community stories and histories, biographies of community members, a list of favorite songs, and instructions on cultural practices. These are only a few examples. Zines can be an opportunity to have agency and authorship of a collective story about a particular community. Some have used a prompt, such as the People of Color Zine Project, which has used themes such as taking up space, letters to younger selves, and words of healing for people of color.

Objectives
- Self-publish community information
- Produce and maintain community knowledge
- Raise awareness about something important
- Understand a community's position on a topic

Materials
- ***Possible materials for hands-on session can include:*** Ephemera (magazines, newspapers, catalogs, postcards, greeting cards); tools (scissors, stapler); writing and art supplies (pens, pencils, markers, watercolor paint, rubber stamps, ink pads); adhesive (glue sticks, double-sided tape); personal content (printed pictures, photocopies of drawings, a favorite poem, an original

poem). These materials can produce pages for analog and digital production. With digital production you will scan the pages you create.

- *Production materials (analog):* Photocopier, or you can make duplicates of your zine by hand, which is labor-intensive.

- *Production materials (digital):* Scanner; scanned images; stock images or clip art; computer with software programs such as InDesign or Word for creating a layout for printing, Illustrator for creating artwork, and Photoshop for editing images or creating a collage (if you search for digital graphic editing tools, you might be able to find some free or low-cost tools for creating and editing digital artwork).

- *Budget:* Consider how much you can spend. Printing in black and white will be the lowest cost. You might be able to access the community's copier to reproduce the zine. If you print on a personal or desktop printer, you will have to consider the cost of ink. Printing in color will cost more, as will heavier-weight paper, which is thicker. The weight of standard copy paper is twenty pounds, while you might use a heavier-weight paper for the cover. You will also need to consider if you want to print it yourself or send it to a printing business. They will be equipped to print front and back as well as to organize the print job to reflect the page order from a master copy that you provide to them. Doing it yourself might involve trial and error in getting the pages ordered correctly. Finally, you can create a pdf file of your zine, post it online, and let others download and print their own copy of the zine.

Activity

1. Create a prompt that participants can structure their ideas around. For example, an Indigenous futurity zine could include some of the following prompts:

    What letter would you write to your future relatives living 150 years from now? What cultural practice would you provide instructions on how to carry out?

    What aspects of family and community do you want to see thriving?

    What would you want them to know about your experiences right now, and what advice would you give them to uplift them?

    What Mvskoke food recipe do you want your relatives to make seven generations from now?

    Write a letter to your ancestor(s).

An Indigenous language zine could ask participants to focus on an important Indigenous-language word. For example, *vnokeckv*, which means "love" in the Muscogee language, and can more specifically mean love and responsibility to one's community. Another example is *gadugi*, which in the Cherokee language means helping one another. After focusing on this work, imagine the ways the concept of vnokeckv presents itself in the community—a grandmother making a ribbon dress, a parent fixing a meal, a spouse maintaining a family garden, a neighbor repairing a car, or someone bringing food to a grieving family. Maybe it is embodied in a poem or in a ceremonial dance.

2. Participants can write, draw, cut pictures, words, and letters from printed material, and use a glue stick to create a small collage. They can write a poem or rewrite a favorite poem that responds to the prompts. Each participant can work on one page. You will provide participants with a sheet of paper that corresponds with the type of zine: thus, for magazine size, provide an 8½" × 11" piece of paper; for digest size, a 5½" × 8½" piece of paper; and for a one-page zine, 2¾" × 4¼" pieces of paper. More information about types of zines and their corresponding page sizes is covered below. Ask participants to put their contents only on the front of the pieces of blank paper: this makes zine construction easier.

    (a) **Magazine size**: a standard piece of copy paper is 8½" × 11", and this is standard magazine size. Each participant's work will cover an 8½" × 11" area, or they can extend to a two-page spread with a total content area of 17" × 11". Hand out pieces of copy paper that participants can glue their work onto or create directly on, such as by writing a poem or letter.

    (b) **Digest size**: a piece of standard copy paper folded in half will cover a 5½" × 8½" area. Participants can extend to a two-page spread with a content area of 8½" × 11".

    (c) **One-page zine**: the whole zine uses a standard piece of copy paper that is folded to create an eight-page zine, with pages that are 2¾" × 4¼".

3. After the participants have completed their work, the pages are assembled into a collection that looks like a booklet—this is a zine. Figure 24 provides a broad overview of zine construction, including the three sizes—magazine, digest, and one-page zine—and ways to assemble them. After collecting all of the participants' contents, sequence them into the desired page order. A

MAGAZINE SIZE: FLAT CONSTRUCTION

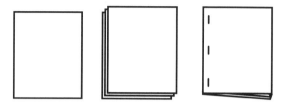

DIGEST SIZE: 1/2 FOLD CONSTRUCTION

ONE PAGE SIZE: 8-PAGE CONSTRUCTION

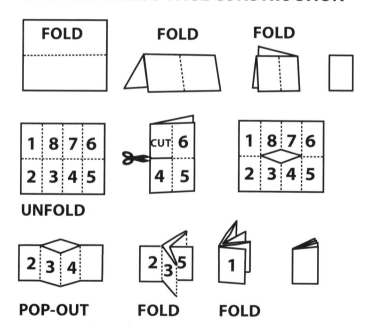

FIGURE 24 Zine construction and folding examples. Illustration by Laura Harjo.

high-tech option for the zine construction is to scan each of your pages as an image file, such as a .jpg or .pdf, and create a digital template to place all of your scanned pages into, using software programs such as Word, InDesign, and Adobe Acrobat.

(a) **Magazine size**: This size has a flat construction. You will take your one-sided pages and arrange them into double-sided pages. You can temporarily paper clip the one-sided pages with their blank sides back to back to create a double-sided page. This enables you arrange and flip through your pages to review, reorder, and decide on how you wish to organize your page order prior to creating the master copy of the zine. Once you have your final arrangement of pages, create a master copy; you will copy your one-sided originals as a double-sided copy.

    Binding option: the simplest approach is to use a standard stapler and staple the stack in three places. Other options include using a hole punch and tying with yarn, ribbon, or another material that will thread through the holes.

(b) **Digest size**: using paper clips, you can clip the half sheets to a full piece of 8½" × 11" copy paper. If you have sixteen pages of half sheets, you will use four 8½" × 11" pages to create a zine. Arranging the pages can get tricky here. A single piece of copy paper is four pages of a digest-size zine, two on the front and two on the back. The first 8½" × 11" page of the digest-size zine will have the front cover and the back cover on one side of the page, and the inside front cover and the inside back cover on the other side of the page. The easiest way to arrange the pages is to paper clip and fold the pages into a digest-size zine, then flip through the whole thing to check the page organization. Once that looks correct and you are satisfied, unclip the pages and use a glue stick to fix two 5½" × 8½" pages to the front and two 5½" × 8½" pages to the back. This locks the order in place. You will take this to a copier and turn these into double-sided copies, so if you are creating a sixteen-page digest-size zine, you will have four double-sided 8½" × 11" pages that you will fold in half.

    Binding option: You can use a stapler. However, you will need a long-reach stapler or a swing-arm swivel stapler, because the reach of a standard stapler is about three inches, and you need the stapler to reach five and a half inches to the center of the digest-size zine.

(c) **One-page zine**: This involves a series of folds: please see figure 24. The easiest way to construct this is to take 2¾" × 4¼" pages, paper clip them, and then fold them into a booklet. If you look to figure 24, you will see the page numbers. After the pages have been arranged into the desired format, remove the paper clips and lock the arrangement into place using a glue stick. You can then create a master copy. You will make a one-sided copy: these are the easiest to mass-produce. Review figure 24 to see how to fold and cut into a miniature eight-page zine. No binding is necessary for this type of zine.

Tools for Collective Power (Chapter 3)

PROUDS/SORRIES: COMMUNITY VALUES

Overview

This approach creates a safe way for community members to share. It also determines the collective status of the community, which enables the community to determine the mode of futurity to draw upon to accomplish their aspirations. This is created out of necessity; often community members do not feel comfortable speaking to a large group. This approach is created in the spirit of refusing the community hearing–style meeting; instead, every single person submits their take on the community, and the community analyzes the collective answers. This is based on an approach I learned from Dr. Dick Winchell, professor of tribal planning at Eastern Washington University. These activities are carried out together: first people are given five pieces of paper to write on, the prompt is provided, the answers are collected either in a basket or some other kind of container, and they are pulled out one at a time. Please be mindful of different abilities such as literacy levels, writing ability, or anxiety about speaking in a group, and adjust your approach to accommodate a variety of abilities.

Objectives

- Understanding what a community values and cares about (Prouds)
- Understanding what a community's concerns are (Sorries)

Materials
- Pens or pencils
- Index cards or Post-it notes
- A basket, hat, or anything to collect the pieces of paper

Activity

The following instructions will be performed twice: first, ask about Prouds, then discuss them; second, ask about Sorries, then discuss them. Then discuss both Prouds and Sorries together. Prouds represent the strengths a community can build on, and Prouds can also be used to address the Sorries. For example, in Winnipeg, Manitoba, people have concerns about feeling unsafe taking local ground transportation; however, the community builds on their kinship network and their own automobiles to create a rideshare program. This is an example of a Proud being used to address a Sorry.

1. On an index card, have participants write five things they are proud about in their community.
2. Collect everyone's proud answers.
3. Read each card. Ask participants to listen for topics or thoughts that seem to be repeating—these are the commonly shared ideas. However, just because only one person mentions a topic does not mean it is not important.
4. After all the cards are read, ask participants to relay what themes or major topics they heard.
5. If the group is large, over a dozen people, then ask people to break up into smaller groups to discuss themes they heard.
6. Ask each group to report the major topics and write them on a large-format 25" × 30" paper pad, also called a flip chart. You may use the following suggestions for capturing the groups' reported major topics: a bulletin board that the index cards can be pinned to, a chalkboard, or a wall surface with butcher paper.
7. Discuss and brainstorm. Brainstorming means that there are not wrong answers: it is a generative process. Thus, everyone's answers are accepted without judgment at that stage.
8. Repeat steps one through seven, this time asking the group what they are sorry about in their community.

9. Return to the things the group is proud about and discuss how the com-
    munity can continue to build on their Prouds. For example, maybe there
    are people gardening, and they could continue to build on this Proud by
    growing Mvskoke heirloom seeds. Have another discussion about how they
    can use what is strong in our communities to respond to the things they are
    sorry about. This might look like gardening and growing heirloom corn and
    pumpkins to address diabetes.

Tools for Emergence Geographies (Chapter 4)

MAP BIOGRAPHY: MEMORY AND SENSE OF PLACE

Overview

Each community and its members carry unique packages of knowledge that
consist of their lived experiences, and they remember and know places through
their senses. For example, the smell of dirt after it rains might evoke particular
memories of a place, or a hot, humid summer might bring memories of softball
tournaments across several different communities. Each community member
carries a sense of place and the history of a place. In terms of community-
building, discussing a community's sense of place helps a community identify
a range of valuable assets, essential places, and resources. For example, springs
and creeks where water is retrieved; places where community members pray,
reflect, or grieve, such as the Haskell Wetlands at Haskell Indian Nations University; or transportation routes including traditional water and land routes,
herding routes, migration routes, and built roads are all deep geographies that
carry stories that in some cases only elder family members or local Indigenous
communities know. All of these stories shape how place is remembered, known,
and felt. This exercise is not solely for understanding places in rural areas or
reservations—in any place where there are Indigenous folks, a conversation
about sense of place can be had. These types of maps have been used to advocate for community concerns or protect sensitive areas. The purpose here is to
document community oral histories and geographies. This approach centers on
a community member's life and mobility through space and place. The "Land
as Kin" exercise is very closely related, but it focuses on connection to land
and is performed with a group. You can choose whether a conversation about
community geographies should happen as a map created by an individual or a
group, or whether a group conversation will work best.

Objectives

- Understand knowledge that is important to individuals, families, and communities
- Understand valued places in the community
- Understand stories of place

Materials

- Low-cost, using found or improvised elements: String or yarn to create areas and paths, objects to mark sites (this can be whatever is available: coins, rocks, small balls of crumpled paper, etc.)
- Low-cost, using drawing skills: Copy paper and writing instruments such as a pen or pencil
- Medium-cost: Poster board, butcher paper, and writing instruments in different colors for different activities

Activity

1. Meet with a community member to create a map biography of their life. In this case it is a mental map, which is a map that is not tied to cartographic references. This means that a map can be created that is not to scale, and the mapping is not bound to the earth alone—it might include the sky, stars, water, and under the earth, to name a few examples. The community member can map by using objects, like coins, and laying them on a table, or by drawing on paper.

2. Ask the community member where they grew up and ask them to map their home and the activities they did as a young person. Follow-up questions might look like: *Where did you grow up? Where did you play when you were growing up? What kind of chores did you have when you were growing up?*

3. Ask the community member to map the places where they lived their adult life and where they worked. Ask them about where they practice(d) community activities—church, stompdance, visiting kin, sports tournaments, etc. Ask them about the approximate years (for example, 1955 or the 1950s).

4. Because the map you create might be temporary—for example, if you use found objects to map a life story—take pictures of the map or maps. Share the map with the community member; the information belongs to them. A note on knowledge privacy and protection: when you digitally

document Indigenous community knowledge, there is always the risk of it being hacked and transferred to unknown parties without the community's permission. You can decide whether the benefit outweighs the risk—this means that you might not need to worry about a map that has all of the softball tournaments in the region, but you might refrain from digitally documenting medicinal plant locations or harvest areas for foods such as *tafvmpuce* (wild onions), ramps, or piñon nuts.

5. You can ask the community member what stands out most to them on their map biography. You can also ask them what the most important places are to them on the map.

6. Repeat this mapping project with other community members to start to develop a community sense of place based on felt knowledge and memories.

7. These mappings can point to geographies that have been invisible in the past.

LAND AS KIN

Overview

Indigenous peoples often spend an inordinate amount of time thinking about and defending land within a Western legal regime: what we have title to, our land rights, our land deeds, locating on earth where our legal description to our land lies. This exercise re-centers Indigenous use and valuing of land, which is a decolonizing action. In planning, the types of zoning categories do not necessarily fit Indigenous uses of and relationships to land. This exercise enables participants to recognize their unique ways of valuing their land.

Objectives

•   Develop a community-generated theory of land
•   Recognize relationships to and uses of land that do not fit within legal thinking about land
•   Shift thinking about land to disrupt conventional and normative ontologies

Materials

•   Post-it notes or index cards
•   Tape
•   A surface to post the cards on

Activity

Consider the following questions to get started:

> *What are land-based activities that you do?*
>
> *Where are places that hold special meaning or stories?*
>
> *Are there places that feel like they make you stronger, or that you find healing?*
>
> *What and where are tribe-specific place names?*
>
> *Are there places you access during different seasons of the year?*
>
> *Are there places you have felt or currently feel connected to during different cycles of your life—for example, as a child, youth, adult, or elder? In the cycles of life you have lived so far, are there experiences that connect you to particular places?*

The group can reflect on these questions or begin to generate other questions that they think relate to Indigenous land use and valuing the land. Participants can write their answers to the above questions on index cards. Next, collect the cards and lay them on a table or fix them to a large piece of butcher paper or poster board hanging on a wall. Then review the cards as a group: Are there activities that sustain the community, such as nourishment, artisanry, social relations, or culture? If prevailing ways of categorizing land include residential, commercial, industrial, and forest, what would a tribal idea of land look like? Perhaps the group yields activities and categories such as blueberry harvesting, blackberry harvesting, wild onion gathering, Bigfoot habitat—labels that are substantially different from simply "forest." Different elements of the land might be present during different seasons, and thinking about land might be related to seasons. The idea here is to look to the group's answers to the questions and then keep discussing them, in order to understand as a group which major topics bubble up and what they as a group care about with regard to their connection to land. Ultimately, the group might come up with a list of five to six things that they value about their connection to land.

APPENDIX

Creek Community Survey

Muscogee (Creek) Community Survey

University of Southern California
Geography Department

INFORMATION SHEET FOR NON-MEDICAL RESEARCH

Muscogee (Creek) Nation: Seven Generation Planning

You are invited to participate in a research study conducted by Laura Harjo, and Dr. Ruth Wilson Gilmore from the University of Southern California. Your participation is voluntary. Please take as much time as you need to read the information sheet. You may also decide to discuss it with your family or friends. You will be given a copy of this form.

PURPOSE OF THE STUDY
We are asking you to take part in a research study because we are trying to learn more about what is important to Muscogee (Creek) Nation tribal members. The answers will be used to create a planning blueprint for a very long range plan- Seven Generations, for Muscogee (Creek) Nation. The goal of this survey is understand what tribal members think are the most important Tribal planning, policy and development areas.

Completion and return of the questionnaire or response to the interview questions will constitute consent to participate in this research project.

PROCEDURES
You will be asked to fill out a questionnaire that should take about 15 minutes to fill out. You will be asked questions about your views on culture, community, and Muscogee (Creek) Nation. There will be questions about your opinions on the Muscogee (Creek) Nation, the culture, and your community, to name a few areas. For example, you will be asked about what policy areas you would focus on if you were leading Muscogee (Creek) Nation.

POTENTIAL RISKS AND DISCOMFORTS
There are no anticipated risks to your participation; you may experience some discomfort at completing the questionnaire or you may be inconvenienced from taking time out of your day to complete the questionnaire/survey instrument, etc.

POTENTIAL BENEFITS TO SUBJECTS AND/OR TO SOCIETY
You may not directly benefit from your participation in this research study.
There may be benefits to Muscogee (Creek) Nation in terms of understanding specific policy areas that might benefit them sometime in the future.

PAYMENT/COMPENSATION FOR PARTICIPATION
You will not receive any payment for your participation in this research study.

POTENTIAL CONFLICTS OF INTEREST
The investigators of this research do not have any financial interest in the sponsor or in the product being studied.

Muscogee (Creek) Community Survey

CONFIDENTIALITY
There will be no information obtained in connection with this study and that can be identified with you. Your name, address or other information that may identify you will not be collected during this research study.

Only members of the research team will have access to the data associated with this study. The data will be stored in the investigator's office in a locked file cabinet/password protected computer. No personal information will be shared with any parties other than the researcher, Laura Harjo. Any analyzed will be created so as to obscure being able to identify any one person completing a survey.

The data will be stored for three years after the study has been completed and then it will be kept indefinitely. Because, this is a seven generation planning research, it is important that this data be kept as an archive as part of direction setting that can inform the next 150 years.

When the results of the research are published or discussed in conferences, no information will be included that would reveal your identity.

PARTICIPATION AND WITHDRAWAL
You can choose whether to be in this study or not. If you volunteer to be in this study, you may withdraw at any time without consequences of any kind. You may also refuse to answer any questions you don't want to answer and still remain in the study. The investigator may withdraw you from this research if circumstances arise which warrant doing so.

ALTERNATIVES TO PARTICIPATION
Your alternative is to not participate.

RIGHTS OF RESEARCH SUBJECTS
You may withdraw your consent at any time and discontinue participation without penalty. You are not waiving any legal claims, rights or remedies because of your participation in this research study. If you have any questions about your rights as a study subject or you would like to speak with someone independent of the research team to obtain answers to questions about the research, or in the event the research staff can not be reached, please contact the University Park IRB, Office of the Vice Provost for Research Advancement, Stonier Hall, Room 224a, Los Angeles, CA 90089-1146, (213) 821-5272 or upirb@usc.edu

IDENTIFICATION OF INVESTIGATORS
If you have any questions or concerns about the research, please feel free to contact Laura Harjo, 213-743-1675, USC Geography Department, 3620 S. Vermont Avenue, KAP 416, Los Angeles, CA, 90089

CLICKING THE "Next Button", INDICATES:
1. YOU 18 YEARS OF AGE OR OLDER
2. YOU GIVE YOUR CONSENT TO PARTICIPATING IN THIS SURVEY

Muscogee (Creek) Community Survey

1. I identify as

☐ Muscogee (Creek)

☐ Alabama-Quassarte

☐ Thlopthlocco

☐ Kialegee

☐ Yuchi

2. What is the ZIP code where you live?

[   ]

3. What is the ZIP code where you grew up?

[   ]

4. If you know your Muscogee clan, please write it in. For example: Bear clan, Wolf clan, Wind clan etc.

[   ]

5. If you know your tribal town, please write it in.

[   ]

6. Reports say that the United States is currently in an economic recession, to what degree are you feeling the effects?

	Not at all	A little	Neutral	Somewhat	A great deal
On the Job (layoffs etc.)	○	○	○	○	○
Finding Employment	○	○	○	○	○
Housing Costs	○	○	○	○	○
Buying Food	○	○	○	○	○
Buying Gasoline	○	○	○	○	○
Buying Medicine	○	○	○	○	○
Paying utilities	○	○	○	○	○

Other areas you are having a hard time with (please specify)

[   ]

Muscogee (Creek) Community Survey

7. If you were Chief for a day what areas would you focus on?

- [ ] Affordable Housing
- [ ] Business Development
- [ ] Community Development
- [ ] Cultural Preservation
- [ ] Education
- [ ] Health Care
- [ ] Job Development

Other (please specify)

[   ]

8. If you were Chief for a day how would you prioritize the following areas?

	Low Priority	Moderate Priority	High Priority
Affordable Housing	O	O	O
Business Development	O	O	O
Community Development	O	O	O
Cultural Preservation	O	O	O
Education	O	O	O
Health care	O	O	O
Job Development	O	O	O

9. Compared to other tribes how well of a job does Muscogee (Creek) Nation perform.

	Poor	Fair	Not Sure	Good	Excellent
Running it's government	O	O	O	O	O
Creating profitable businesses	O	O	O	O	O
Preserving the Creek language and culture	O	O	O	O	O

Muscogee (Creek) Community Survey

10. How well do you think Muscogee (Creek) Nation does in providing the following services?

	Poor	Fair	Neutral	Good	Excellent
Affordable Housing Options	○	○	○	○	○
Art and Cultural Opportunities	○	○	○	○	○
Community Development	○	○	○	○	○
Elder Services	○	○	○	○	○
Health Care	○	○	○	○	○
Job Development	○	○	○	○	○
Preserve and maintain Creek songs, dances and stories	○	○	○	○	○
Teaching the Creek Language	○	○	○	○	○
Tribal Business Development	○	○	○	○	○
Youth Services	○	○	○	○	○

Other (please specify)

[   ]

11. What condition do you think the following will be in within 20 years?

	Poor	Fair	Neutral	Good	Excellent
Affordable Housing Options	○	○	○	○	○
Art and Cultural Opportunities	○	○	○	○	○
Community Development	○	○	○	○	○
Elder Services	○	○	○	○	○
Health Care	○	○	○	○	○
Job Development	○	○	○	○	○
Preserve and maintain Creek songs, dances and stories	○	○	○	○	○
Teaching the Creek Language	○	○	○	○	○
Tribal Business Development	○	○	○	○	○
Youth Services	○	○	○	○	○

Other (please specify)

[   ]

Muscogee (Creek) Community Survey

12. What condition do you think the following will be in within 7 generations? (The year will be around 2150)

	Poor	Fair	Neutral	Good	Excellent
Affordable Housing Options	○	○	○	○	○
Art and Cultural Opportunities	○	○	○	○	○
Community Development	○	○	○	○	○
Elder Services	○	○	○	○	○
Health Care	○	○	○	○	○
Job Development	○	○	○	○	○
Preserve and maintain Creek songs, dances and stories	○	○	○	○	○
Teaching the Creek Language	○	○	○	○	○
Tribal Business Development	○	○	○	○	○
Youth Services	○	○	○	○	○

Other (please specify)

[   ]

13. In what condition do you see the tribe in Seven Generations?

	Much Worse	Somewhat Worse	About the Same	Somewhat Better	Much Better
Politically: Creek Nation's government	○	○	○	○	○
Economically: Creek Nation's ability to create and maintain tribal businesses	○	○	○	○	○
Culturally: The Creek language and cultural knowledge	○	○	○	○	○

Muscogee (Creek) Community Survey

14. To which Creek community do you feel you most belong?

[   ]

15. Are you an active participant in a Creek community?

◯ Yes

◯ No

16. Describe that community and your involvement in it.

[   ]

17. In what ways is the community succeeding?

☐ Has a casino

☐ Has economic development

☐ Located near job opportunities

☐ Revitalizing language

☐ Revitalizing culture

☐ People attend community events and gatherings

☐ People help one another

☐ Sports Tournaments

☐ Tribal Games -stickball, indian football etc.

18. In what ways is the community failing?

☐ No jobs

☐ No educational opportunities

☐ Drug Abuse

☐ Alcohol Abuse

☐ Fighting among community members

☐ No community activities

☐ No central meeting place

☐ Community members not involved in community

19. If you identify with an stompground (ceremonial ground) which one?

[   ]

20. If you identify with a church, which one?

[   ]

Muscogee (Creek) Community Survey

21. How much Creek language do you know?

	None at all	Know some words	Know words and phrases	Know words, phrases and conversational	Know words, phrases, conversational and could teach it
Read	○	○	○	○	○
Write	○	○	○	○	○
Speak	○	○	○	○	○

22. How important to you is participating in Creek ways of life?

	Not At All	Somewhat	Not Sure	Moderate	A great deal
Creek Worldview (Values)	○	○	○	○	○
Stompdance	○	○	○	○	○
Indian Churches	○	○	○	○	○
Creek Language	○	○	○	○	○
Traditional Medicine/Healing	○	○	○	○	○
Stickball	○	○	○	○	○
Community Gatherings	○	○	○	○	○

Other (please specify)

23. How far from the nearest town center do you live? (Write in)

24. In what direction do you live from the nearest town center?

○ North

○ South

○ East

○ West

○ Northeast

○ Northwest

○ Southeast

○ Southwest

25. What is the name of the nearest town or city? (Write in)

26. What is your gender?

○ Male

○ Female

27. What is your age?

Muscogee (Creek) Community Survey

28. Are there missing questions that you think should be asked?

29. Are you interested in providing more input on the direction of Muscogee (Creek) Nation? If so please provide your information.

Name:

Address:

Address 2:

City/Town:

State:

ZIP/Postal Code:

Country:

Email Address:

Phone Number:

GLOSSARY

Creek: vernacular term with which Mvskoke people refer to themselves

este-cate: "red man," vernacular form for referring to other Mvskoke persons and other Indigenous persons regardless of gender

etvlwa: "his town," used in vernacular to mean "town" (*tvlwa* translates directly to town)

etvlwvlke: town, plural form

hesaketv: life, breath

Hesaketvmese: Maker of Breath, God, the giver or taker away of life

heles-hayv: medicine man

honka: monster, malevolent spirit

hvtke: white

Mvskoke: people from a marshy area

Mvskokvlke: Mvskoke people, plural form

mvto: thank you

sokhv: pig, pork

tenetke: thunder

vce: corn

vnokeckv: love

vloneske: plant that stuns fish, used for fishing

yvhv: wolf

NOTES

Introduction

1.   Throughout the text I use *Mvskoke*, *Muscogee*, and *Creek*, which all have the same meaning. *Creek* is a vernacular term still in use. The plural of *Mvskoke* is written as *Mvskokes* or *Mvskokvlke*.

   I use *Mvskoke* as a formal reference to the people from the "Creek Confederacy" and tribal towns affiliated with that region before and after contact, including any of the tribal towns and bands, as well as the Seminoles—our relatives who migrated to Florida. I also use it in reference to ideologies, epistemologies, and worldviews in academic discussion.

   I use *Muscogee* when referring to the official tribal Muscogee (Creek) Nation, or formal organizations or entities within the tribe—for example, Muscogee National Council, our legislative branch. I also use it when referring to the language. However, the tribe is now beginning to call the language *Mvskoke*—this is a new move, and much of the literature calls it *Muscogee* language, while Creek people have self-referenced as either *Creek* or *Muscogee*.

   I use *Creek* when using a voice that is for the community or kinship networks, or to self-reference. I use it in my community survey to ask about Muscogee language and to discuss the results. I tested the survey before administering it to understand what resonated most with community: the terms *Creek language* and *Muscogee worldview* were what resonated most in 2009 with the survey respondents. I also use it when referencing the formation of town settlements in the Southeast: Upper Creeks and Lower Creeks.

2.   For a discussion of the idea of Indigenous culture being frozen in time, see Troy Johnson, "American Indians, Manifest Destiny."

3.   *Este-cate* translates to "red man," or an "Indian." I use *este-cate* because I grew up hearing it used for kinship recognition. Whether we were at home watching TV and saw an Indigenous person on a television show, or whether we were in the public sphere, such as shopping in Tulsa or at the Tulsa State Fair, we would exclaim, "Hey, este-cate!" If we knew them, we might greet them, "Hey, este-cate!" It's a way of saying, "I see you, I acknowledge you," in the public sphere where Indigenous people are either invisible, as when department store staff don't wish to wait on them, or else hypervisible, as when staff watch an este-cate because they think they might steal.

4.   For more on rhetoric of the field of planning and the future feeling out of reach for communities, see Inch and Crookes, "Making Hope Possible?"

5.   Joy Harjo, *Map to the Next World*, 19.

6.   Marchione, *Brief History of Smyrna*, 13.

7.   Howe and Wilson, "Life in a 21st Century Mound City," 19.

8.   Marchione, *Brief History of Smyrna*, 13.

9.   Payne, "Mississippian Period."

10. Moore, "Mvskoke National Question," 164. Euchees are enrolled citizens of MCN and their language is a linguistic isolate; they are currently seeking federal recognition. For more about Euchee language, see Linn, "Grammar of Euchee (Yuchi)."

11. Isham and Clark, "Creek (Mvskoke)."

12. Isham and Clark, "Creek (Mvskoke)."

13. Hurt, "Shaping of a Creek (Muscogee) Homeland," 57–8.

14. Hurt, "Shaping of a Creek (Muscogee) Homeland," 58–9.

15. Hurt, "Shaping of a Creek (Muscogee) Homeland," 60–61.

16. Etheridge, *Creek Country*, 67.

17. Isham and Clark, "Creek (Mvskoke)."

18. Isham and Clark, "Creek (Mvskoke)."

19. Foley, "General Allotment Act," 817.

20. For more on federal government oversight of selecting tribal leadership, see Harring, "Crazy Snake and the Creek Struggle," 379.

21. Littlefield and Underhill, "Crazy Snake Uprising," 310.

22. Littlefield and Underhill, "Crazy Snake Uprising," 311.

23. For more on white settlement related to the Oklahoma land rush and an example of the myth of American exceptionalism, see Hurley, "Five Minute History."

24. Clark, *Indian Tribes of Oklahoma*, 218.

25. Harring, "Crazy Snake and the Creek Struggle," 379; Isham and Clark, "Creek (Mvskoke)."

26. For more on land jurisdiction issues in Oklahoma, see Laura Harjo, "GIS Support for Empowering."

27. For more on expansive dispossession, see Leanne Betasamosake Simpson, *As We Have Always Done*.

28. For the term and concept "unactivated possibilities," see Nersessian, *Utopia, Limited*, 210.

29. Ellen Harjo, in discussion with the author, July 2008.
30. See "Communities Emetvlhvmkvke," title 11 of the Muscogee (Creek) Nation Code, at http://www.creeksupremecourt.com/wp-content/uploads/title11.pdf.
31. This is the practice at my ceremonial grounds, Kellyville (Polecat Stompgrounds), though I cannot speak to whether it is the practice at other ceremonial grounds.
32. See Deer, "Decolonizing Rape Law"; and Andrea Smith, "Decolonizing Anti-rape Law." Both authors discuss short-term needs and long-term goals with regard to using federal systems of laws to protect Indigenous women, while eventually working toward long-term social change movements that create tribal infrastructures to replace federal systems.
33. Ric Anderson, "Autopsy Reveals Dawes Drowned."
34. Ric Anderson, "Inquest Called."
35. Marilyn Bread, in personal discussion with members of Haskell Indian Junior College Student Senate Executive Board, April 1991. During this time, several of the students involved in leading this action were on the student senate at Haskell Indian Junior College, and Marilyn Bread was our faculty sponsor. She treated all with dignity and never spoke ill of anyone, an exemplar of decolonial love thirty years ago—this is nothing new. Mrs. Bread often mentored and counseled us; we were far from home. However, this particular memory is sharp and I can still feel it. I can still remember her pain was palpable and heavy when she shared the loss of her son, as we talked about the violent conditions and the string of deaths and related violent incidents in Lawrence, Kansas. There are other violent stories that I have chosen to leave out and will pick up in future work.
36. Gruver and Anderson, "T Enough."
37. Caron, "Saving Haskell's Soul."
38. Gough, "Way Out," 44. See also Child, *Boarding School Seasons*.
39. Caron, "Saving Haskell's Soul."
40. Lawrence Journal-World, "Haskell Offering Tours."
41. Lawhorn, "After More than Two Decades."
42. Million, *Therapeutic Nations*; Leanne Betasamosake Simpson, "Land as Pedagogy."
43. Joy Harjo offers the spelling *vnvketkv*, describing it as compassion and likening it to the Hawaiian concept of *aloha*. It is the notion that we were put here to take care of each other with compassion, grace, and dignity. Joy Harjo, *Crazy Brave*, 165.
44. Joy Harjo, *Map to the Next World*, 19; Leanne Betasamosake Simpson, "Land as Pedagogy."
45. For more on knowledge given lovingly by the spirits and the process of coming to know through spirits, dreams, and animals, *gaa-izhi-zhaawendaagoziyaang*, see Leanne Betasamosake Simpson, "Land as Pedagogy," 7. In her discussion of the process of coming to know and the spiritual nature of the process, Simpson cites from Geniusz, *Our Knowledge Is Not Primitive*, 67.
46. Chaudhuri and Chaudhuri, *Sacred Path*.
47. Leanne Betasamosake Simpson, "Land as Pedagogy," 8–9.
48. Leanne Betasamosake Simpson, "Land as Pedagogy," 8–9.

49. For two other works that discuss this dynamic, see Navarro, "Solarize-ing Native Hip-Hop"; and Andrea Smith, "Decolonizing Anti-rape Law."
50. McIntosh, "International Forum."
51. Laura Harjo, "GIS Support for Empowering"; Ortega, "ESRI Mapping."
52. For more on authors who critically examine public participation GIS, see Sieber, "Public Participation Geographic Information Systems"; and Schlossberg and Shuford, "Delineating 'Public' and 'Participation.'"
53. Murphy, "CN to Get $2M."
54. Comm. on Resources, Cherokee, Choctaw, and Chickasaw Nations Claims Settlement Act.
55. Cherokee Nation, "Arkansas Riverbed Authority Commissions Maps."
56. Comm. on Resources, Cherokee, Choctaw, and Chickasaw Nations Claims Settlement Act.
57. Sheppard, "Geographical Political Economy," 320.
58. Tuck, "Suspending Damage."
59. Womack, *Red on Red*, 2.
60. See Womack, *Red on Red*; Womack, *Drowning in Fire*; Gouge, *Totkv Mocvse*; Foerster, *Leaving Tulsa*; Joy Harjo, *Map to the Next World*; Joy Harjo, *How We Became Human*; Joy Harjo, *She Had Some Horses*; and Starr, *Super Indian* (vols. 1 and 2).
61. Womack, *Red on Red*. See also Miranda, *Bad Indians*. Miranda writes about picking up pieces and fragments of Indigenous culture and history to narrate our stories.
62. Hunt, "Ontologies of Indigeneity," 29.
63. Tuck and Gaztambide-Fernández, "Curriculum, Replacement, and Settler Futurity," 84.
64. Tuck and Gaztambide-Fernández, "Curriculum, Replacement, and Settler Futurity," 86.
65. Aikau, "Following the Alaloa Kīpapa"; Goodyear-Kaʻōpua, "Protectors of the Future."
66. Dillon, "Future Imaginary." For more on Indigenous futurisms and Dillon's concepts of Native slipstream, contact, Indigenous science and sustainability, Native apocalypse, and *biskaabiiyang* (returning to ourselves), see Dillon's edited anthology of Indigenous science fiction: Dillon, *Walking the Clouds*.
67. Hudson, "Future Imaginary."
68. Hudson, "Future Imaginary."
69. Barker, "Introduction," 31. Although the term *fan* is already gender-neutral, I offer other possibilities of naming fandom—fangirls, fanboys, fanfolx.
70. LaPensée, "Transformations and Remembrances," 89.
71. Starr, *Super Indian*, vols. 1 and 2.
72. LaPensée, *Deer Woman*; LaPensée and Alvitre, *Deer Woman: An Anthology*. The narrative of Deer Woman was one that I heard growing up in Oklahoma. A storied figure who lived on the west side of Oklahoma, she was a beautiful Indigenous woman with hooves for feet, who would enchant men at Indigenous gatherings like a powwow or 49 (a 49 is a social dance that happens after a powwow, some-

times on dirt roads), luring them off into the woods while they were oblivious to her hooves and subsequently stomping on their genitals.

73. Kimberly Robertson, "Las Aunties."

74. Kimberly Robertson, "Las Aunties"; Nixon, "Visual Cultures."

75. Amin, "Moving On"; Jessop, "Reflections on Globalisation"; Dickason, "Future of Historical Cartography."

76. Amin, "Moving On"; Jessop, "Reflections on Globalisation."

77. Hampton, "Forget 2017."

78. Bang et al., "Muskrat Theories"; Martineau, "Creative Combat"; Raheja, "Future Tense," 239; Kuttner, "Futurism, Futurity, and the Importance"; LaPensée, "Transformations and Remembrances"; Nixon, "Visual Cultures."

79. Kaur, *Sun and Her Flowers*, 201.

80. Luk, "Life of Paper," 23. In this quotation, Luk cites from Spillers, *Black, White, and in Color*, 278.

81. Laura Harjo, "Emancipation from the Cupboard."

82. Laura Harjo, "Emancipation from the Cupboard"; Laura Harjo, "Mapping and Social Media"; Laura Harjo, "Indigenous Scales of Sovereignty."

83. Recollet, "Gesturing Indigenous Futurities."

84. Recollet, "Gesturing Indigenous Futurities"; Laura Harjo, "Indigenous Scales of Sovereignty."

> Geographer Neil Smith (1992) lays out a typology for scale. While there are many metaphorical uses of "space" across the humanities, he argues for a material notion of scale. Its role is to understand "constructed geographies of capitalism" or to offer a "spatial language for decentering previously dominant political concerns" (Smith, 1992). It is not clearly demarcated; rather, scale is produced materially as a response to the capitalist class's need for resolving the tension of cooperation and competition. The scale typology that Smith introduces includes the following order: body, home, community, urban, region, nation, and global. Smith provides an example of the nation-state: as the need for economic accumulation expands, so does the scale—thus supranational scales are needed in addition to the nation state such as the United Nations or the World Bank, to enable the processes of capitalist accumulation to expand.
>
> Settler Colonialism aligns with the colonialism epoch of the grand narrative of capitalism. Settler colonialism extends the reach of capitalism. Capitalist organization of space produces particular territories—such as the nation-state. Similarly, settler colonialism yields particular territories. Both overlap and inform one another, however, settler colonial space yields different geographies. Specifically, for MCN what this has meant is that the capitalist nation-state needed to tinker with MCN's scale for settler colonialism to work.

Settler colonialism's material production of scale yields several scales; in the context of MCN, it yields a racialized domestic nation. I have already examined how the state has worked to build a legal apparatus for the control of land in the Indian Removal era in earlier chapters; I now look at it through a scale lens. During that era, the impetus for removal was the need for the capitalist class, in this case, the planter class, to expand into Muscogee territory to accumulate more wealth. Thus, while previously Muscogee people lived in many autonomous tribal towns, it was easier to remove an entire "faceless" Indian nation as opposed to 50 towns with 50 leaders (Green, 1985). "Jumping scale" here means moving Muscogees from the town scale to a national scale. Another example of this within the Marshall trilogy is how these cases devolved Muscogees' political position from the international legal arena to the domestic legal arena. From this position, MCN's scale was easier to manipulate as capitalist space required. What makes this much more difficult for Muscogee people—a reorganization of their space and displacement—is that many indigenous cultures are tied to their aboriginal homelands. Many times over, sovereignty was and continues to be attacked and jurisdiction and territory (scale) reduced.

Because indigenous nations devolved from an international arena to a domestic arena, based on settler colonial acts, indigenous nations are located in the interstices of the nation-state and the sub-national state. This location in the interstices also translates to invisibility in the American psyche. This location is a result of initial scalar calibrations by the federal government and continued upkeep and recalibrations of indigenous people's scale. If indigenous people do not have control of the territory and the land which is still central to culture, sovereignty is a fraught project. But, we have control of our bodies. We can enact sovereignty within our bodies.

A capitalist space economy demands the organization of people and space in a way that resolves cooperation/competition; however, in contrast, Indigenous ways of organizing for development do not always follow dominant development discourse that privileges private land ownership, or exploitation of local land and labor (Good, 1976).

The above is quoted from Laura Harjo, "Muscogee (Creek) Nation," 165–68. Citations from Neil Smith, "Contours of a Spatialized Politics"; Green, *Politics of Indian Removal*; and Good, "Settler Colonialism."

85. Womack, *Red on Red*, 12.
86. Wilson, *Research Is Ceremony*, 137.
87. Linda Tuhiwai Smith, *Decolonizing Methodologies*.
88. Linda Tuhiwai Smith, *Decolonizing Methodologies*, 152, 158.
89. Linda Tuhiwai Smith, *Decolonizing Methodologies*, 158–59.
90. Walter and Andersen, *Indigenous Statistics*, 76.

91. Jolivétte, "Radical Love as a Strategy," 7.
92. Jacob, "When a Native 'Goes Researcher,'" 460. In this quotation, Jacob cites Veroff and DiStefano, "Introduction," 1196.
93. Jacob, *Yakama Rising*, 15.
94. Leanne Betasamosake Simpson defines generative refusal as refusing the logics of settler colonialism and instead opting for Indigenous-grounded actions. Further, she argues that to actively replicate the logics of settler colonialism is to actively self-dispossess from kinship and "relationships that make us Indigenous in the first place." Leanne Betasamosake Simpson, *As We Have Always Done*, 35.
95. Leanne Betasamosake Simpson, *As We Have Always Done*, 48.
96. Laura Harjo, "Indigenous Scales of Sovereignty."
97. Woods, *Development Arrested*.
98. For more on scales as context and product, see Hoffmann, "Geography Should Never Be Why," 5.
99. Jolivétte, "Radical Love as a Strategy," 7.

Chapter 1

1. *Mvskoke* is the name the people call themselves by, meaning "people from a marshy area." It is still commonplace for Mvskoke people to refer to themselves as *Creek*, a name derived from settlers' observation of the proximity of Mvskoke tribal towns to waterways such as rivers, streams, and creeks. Further, there are other federally recognized Mvskoke tribes as well—Alabama-Quassarte Tribal Town, Kialegee Tribal Town, Thlopthlocco Tribal Town, and Poarch Band of Creek Indians.
2. Lyons, "Rhetorical Sovereignty," 449.
3. Joy Harjo, *Map to the Next World*, 19.
4. Massey, *Place, Space, Gender*, 5.
5. Leanne Betasamosake Simpson, *Islands of Decolonial Love*.
6. Wolfe, "Settler Colonialism"; Womack, *Red on Red*.
7. Womack, *Red on Red*, 12.
8. Deer, *Beginning and End of Rape*, xiv.
9. For more on Mvskoke travel to the Milky Way, see Foerster, *Leaving Tulsa*.
10. Andrea Smith, an ethnic studies scholar, articulated an insightful point at the 2011 Critical Ethnic Studies Conference at University of California, Riverside. I interpret her words to mean that people do not need their beliefs and practices to be state-sanctioned in order to enact them. In her plenary presentation she problematized the United States as a state based on genocide and slavery. This makes the power dynamic between the government and marginalized peoples even more problematic. Andrea Smith, "Forum on Social Movements and Activism." See also Million, *Therapeutic Nations*; and Andrea Smith, *Conquest*.
11. Fixico, *American Indian Mind*, 9.
12. Chaudhuri and Chaudhuri, *Sacred Path*.
13. Fixico, *American Indian Mind*.

14. Supernaw, *Muscogee Daughter*.

15. Million, *Therapeutic Nations*.

16. For more on Audra Simpson's logic of refusal, see Audra Simpson, *Mohawk Interruptus*.

17. Cornell and Kalt, "Where Does Economic Development"; Cornell and Kalt, "Sovereignty and Nation-Building."

18. Transformative power and transformative planning are explained in Lane and Hibbard's article "Doing It for Themselves: Transformative Planning by Indigenous Peoples": "Most important is the emancipatory role of planning, its potential to transform the structural dimensions of oppression—what Friedmann (1987) calls a transformative theory of planning." They argue that this transformation happens in sites and institutions that are not immediately visible but almost surely felt deeply by communities. Lane and Hibbard, "Doing It for Themselves," 172. See also Friedmann, *Planning in the Public Domain*. Teaching critical Indigenous or Mvskoke studies or creating an informal system of mutual economic aid within the local community are examples of informal acts of transformative power. See McKnight and Plummer, *Community Organizing*.

19. Alfred and Corntassel, "Being Indigenous," 610.

20. Indian Health Service, "Indian Health Disparities."

21. Warne and Lajimodiere, "American Indian Health Disparities."

22. Warne and Lajimodiere, "American Indian Health Disparities."

23. Warne and Lajimodiere, "American Indian Health Disparities."

24. For more on Indigenous epistemologies driving theory and action, see Alfred, *Peace, Power, Righteousness*; Ladner, "Up the Creek"; and Audra Simpson, *Mohawk Interruptus*. For more on Kaupapa Māori theoretical frameworks, see Pihama, Cram, and Walker, "Creating Methodological Space."

25. Andrea Smith, "Heteropatriarchy and the Three Pillars," 404; Coulthard, "Subjects of Empire"; Corntassel and Witmer, *Forced Federalism*; Lyons, *X-Marks*.

26. The split in attitudes toward organizing for action is similar to the differences in African American organizing. The National Association for the Advancement of Colored People comes from an integrationist standpoint, as opposed to the separatist standpoint represented by groups such as Marcus Garvey's Universal Negro Improvement Association. See Freer, "L.A. Race Woman."

27. Ladner, "When Buffalo Speaks"; Deer, "Toward an Indigenous Jurisprudence of Rape"; Deer, "Decolonizing Rape Law."

28. Byrd, *Transit of Empire*, xxx. For examples of such grounding, see Womack, *Red on Red*; Alfred, *Peace, Power, Righteousness*; Linda Tuhiwai Smith, *Decolonizing Methodologies*; and Alfred, *Wasáse*.

29. Alfred, *Peace, Power, Righteousness*. Taiaiake Alfred and Gerald R. Alfred are the same person; in some of his earlier work he uses the name Gerald Alfred.

30. Joy Harjo, *Map to the Next World*, 19.

31. Alfred, *Wasáse*; Alfred, *Peace, Power, Righteousness*.

32. Alfred, *Wasáse*, 268.

33. Alfred, *Wasáse*, 269.

34. Massey, *Place, Space, Gender*, 5.

35. Woods, *Development Arrested*.

36. Dixon, Iron, and American Public Health Association, *Strategies for Cultural Competency*.

37. Raheja, "Visual Sovereignty."

38. Eagle Woman, "Philosophy of Colonization."

39. On global organization, see Niezen, "Recognizing Indigenism." On decolonization, see Alfred, *Peace, Power, Righteousness*; Alfred, *Wasáse*; and Coulthard, "Subjects of Empire." On understanding tribal relationships to the state, see Corntassel and Witmer, *Forced Federalism*; and Coulthard, "Subjects of Empire."

40. Lyons, *X-Marks*.

41. Coulthard, "Subjects of Empire."

42. Andrea Smith, "American Studies Without America."

43. Andrea Smith, "Forum on Social Movements and Activism."

44. Lebsock, "Listserv Communications."

45. Lebsock, "Listserv Communications."

46. Corntassel and Witmer, *Forced Federalism*.

47. Hall, "Problem of Ideology"; Alexander, "Not Just (Any) Body"; Robert W. Cox, "Gramsci, Hegemony and International Relations"; Wolfe, "Settler Colonialism."

48. Veracini, *Settler Colonialism*.

49. For more on Andrew Jackson's process of Indian removal, see Foreman, *Indian Removal*; and Wallace and Foner, *Long, Bitter Trail*.

50. Doran, "Population Statistics"; Thornton, "Cherokee Population Losses."

51. For more on the settler influence on the forced removal of the five Southeastern tribes, also called the "Five Civilized Tribes" by settlers, see Gilbert, *Trail of Tears Across Missouri*.

52. Other authors describe the violence of forcing Indigenous people out of their homes for Jackson's Indian removal policy: "After the Worchester decision, sixteen thousand Cherokees were driven at gunpoint from their homeland in Georgia over the Trail of Tears.'" Rennard Strickland and William M. Strickland, "Tale of Two Marshalls," 111. "There were many stories of families being interrupted as they sat down to dinner and forced from their homes. They were given little or no time to round up belongings. Protest was sometimes met with a gun butt to the head." Stewart, *Indian Removal Act*, 74.

53. For more on Indian removal, see William M. Strickland, "Rhetoric of Removal"; Rennard Strickland and William M. Strickland, "Tale of Two Marshalls"; and Stewart, *Indian Removal Act*.

54. Wolfe, "Settler Colonialism"; Veracini, *Settler Colonialism*.

55. Rennard Strickland, "Things Not Spoken"; Torpy, "Native American Women and Coerced Sterilization"; DeFine, "History of Governmentally Coerced Sterilization"; Laura Harjo, "GIS Support for Empowering"; Andrea Smith, "Heteropatriarchy and the Three Pillars"; Andrea Smith, *Conquest*.

56. For more on the three Supreme Court cases that comprise the Marshall trilogy that is the basis for contemporary federal Indian law, see Johnson and Graham's Lessee v. McIntosh, 21 U.S. 543 (1823); The Cherokee Nation v. The State of Georgia, 30 U.S. 5 Pet. 1 (1831); Worcester v. Georgia, 31 U.S. 515 (1832). For more on how the Marshall trilogy plays out in a contemporary context, see Ranat, "Tribal-State Compacts."

57. Hart and Lowther, "Honoring Sovereignty," 200.

58. The Cherokee Nation v. The State of Georgia, 30 U.S. 5 Pet. 1 (1831), at 17.

59. For more on Jackson and southern states' role in Indian removal, see Yoo, "Andrew Jackson and Presidential Power"; and Cave, "Abuse of Power."

60. Burleson, "Tribal, State, and Federal Cooperation," 209.

61. Ranat, "Tribal-State Compacts."

62. Fletcher, "Iron Cold of the Marshall Trilogy."

63. Oliphant v. Suquamish, 435 U.S. 191 (1978); Montana v. United States, 450 U.S. 544 (1981).

64. Clinton, "Criminal Jurisdiction"; Wright, "Tribes v. States"; Pevar, *Rights of Indians*; Canby, *American Indian Law*; Leisy, "Inherent Tribal Sovereignty"; Goodman, "Protecting Habitat." For more on rights-of-way through tribal land and civil jurisdiction over non–tribal members, see Strate v. A-1 Contractors, No. 95-1872, 520 U.S. 438 (1997).

65. For more on open and closed areas and tribal authority to zone nonmember land, see Montana v. United States, 450 U.S. 544 (1981). For more on federal Indian law, see Clinton, "Criminal Jurisdiction"; Cohen, *Handbook of Federal Indian Law*; Wright, "Tribes v. States"; Pevar, *Rights of Indians*; Canby, *American Indian Law*; Leisy, "Inherent Tribal Sovereignty"; and Goodman, "Protecting Habitat."

66. Biolsi, "Imagined Geographies."

67. Swyngedouw, *Excluding the Other. Nestedness* is a spatial geography term used among geographers and critical Indigenous theorists to denote the array of geographies within which a spatial unit such as a city, community, or tribal nation might find itself situated, akin to a matryoshka doll, or Russian nesting doll— these nested geographies might be, for example, nation-state, state or province, county, city, community. For more on geographers who oppose the use of nested scales as a neat frozen index of scales, see Jessop, "Reflections on Globalisation"; Jessop, "Crisis of the National Spatio-temporal Fix"; and Kevin R. Cox, "Spaces of Dependence."

68. Canby, *American Indian Law*, 68.

69. For a brief overview of the political power of tribes, see LaFrance, "Culturally Competent Evaluation," 39–40.

70. For more on the ways in which special treatment rhetoric is used to attack treaty rights, see Goldberg, "American Indians and Preferential Treatment."

71. Cornell and Kalt, *Public Choice*; Crawford, "Security Regime Among Democracies."

72. Martone, "American Indian Tribal Self-Government."

73. Goldberg-Ambrose, "Public Law 280."

74. This is related to the pending Supreme Court case *Carpenter v. Murphy*, which relates to the jurisdiction of a Mvskoke man's murder conviction and his prosecution in state court instead of federal court. The linchpin of this case is whether the murder occurred on land that is still reservation land per the 1866 treaty and therefore constitutes Indian country under 18 U.S.C. § 1151(a). For more on this case and MCN's claim that its reservation boundary was never disestablished, see Brief for the MCN as Amicus Curiae, pp. 4–20, Carpenter v. Murphy, No.17-1107 (Supreme Court).

75. Casey, "Sovereignty by Sufferance," 405.

76. Casey, "Sovereignty by Sufferance," 404–5.

77. Cane poles have been used throughout time for fishing, and I am not suggesting that they are unfit or too primitive for fishing. However, I am suggesting that the tools have been subjected to continued injury. Indigenous intelligence and ingenuity provide for ways to improvise new tools out of injured tools.

78. This is communicated in Andrea Smith, "Forum on Social Movements and Activism."

79. Devil's shoestring (*Tephrosia virginiana*), *vloneske* in Muscogee, is a root that is used to stun fish and was a method of Mvskoke fishing. This practice was prohibited by the federal government. For more on devil's shoestring and Mvskoke and Southeastern Indigenous peoples' fishing methods, see Perdue, *Nations Remembered*, 57.

80. Leanne Betasamosake Simpson, *As We Have Always Done*, 35.

81. For more on the icons used for the futurity block prints, see Fundaburk and Foreman, *Sun Circles and Human Hands*.

82. For more on gendered community politics specific to particular tribal and Indigenous nations, see Goeman and Denetdale, "Native Feminisms"; Barker, *Critically Sovereign*; and Audra Simpson, *Mohawk Interruptus*.

Chapter 2

1. Brown and Strega, "Transgressive Possibilities," 10.

2. In pre-removal times, Mvskoke towns were planned and organized in relation to fields. Mvskoke settlements were situated within master-planned field sites; thus, emerging from "the killing fields" can be read as meaning emerging from the town sites that were the site of our removal and from the genocide whereby our kin were killed or died en route to Indian Territory. Etheridge, *Creek Country*.

3. Wilson, "What Is an Indigenous Research Methodology?," 175. For more on Indigenous methodologies, see Kovach, *Indigenous Methodologies*, 21.

4. On knowledge regimes, see Foucault, *Power/Knowledge*; Hall, "Foucault," 81; and Brown and Strega, "Transgressive Possibilities."

5. Burt and Code, *Changing Methods*; Fawcett and Featherstone, "Setting the Scene"; Hill Collins, *Black Feminist Thought*; Brown and Strega, "Transgressive Possibilities."

6.   Brown and Strega, "Transgressive Possibilities"; Linda Tuhiwai Smith, *Decolonizing Methodologies*; Wilson, "What Is an Indigenous Research Methodology?"; Kovach, "Emerging from the Margins."

7.   For more on Indigenous intervention in state-driven planning practices, see Lane, "Indigenous Land and Community Security."

8.   Walter and Andersen, *Indigenous Statistics*.

9.   Linda Tuhiwai Smith, *Decolonizing Methodologies*; Linda Tuhiwai Smith, "Decolonizing Knowledge"; Kovach, "Emerging from the Margins"; Oparah et al., "By Us, Not for Us."

10. Potts and Brown, "Becoming an Anti-oppressive Researcher."

11. Kimpson, "Stepping Off the Road," 89.

12. Kovach, "Emerging from the Margins."

13. Brown and Strega, "Transgressive Possibilities"; Kimpson, "Stepping Off the Road."

14. Hirokawa, "Effects of Music Listening"; Trost et al., "Mapping Aesthetic Musical Emotions."

15. Diaz, "Stepping In It."

16. Armstrong, "Malatchi of Coweta," 5; Martin, "Rebalancing the World," 87.

17. Womack, *Drowning in Fire*; Gouge, *Totkv Mocvse*; Starr, "Ue-Pucase."

18. For more on earthdiver, see Gamber, "Born out of the Creek Landscape," 111.

19. Fixico, *American Indian Mind*, 13.

20. Supernaw, *Muscogee Daughter*.

21. Berezkin, "Seven Brothers and the Cosmic Hunt," 45.

22. Joy Harjo, *Remember*, 35.

23. Milbauer, "Geography of Food," 209.

24. Garret et al., "Laughing It Up."

25. Joy Harjo, *Map to the Next World*, 19–21.

26. For more on connections between time and work, see Linda Tuhiwai Smith, *Decolonizing Methodologies*, 56–59.

27. Linda Tuhiwai Smith, *Decolonizing Methodologies*, 56.

28. Linda Tuhiwai Smith, *Decolonizing Methodologies*, 56.

29. Louis, "Can You Hear Us Now?"

30. Bomberry, "Blood, Rebellion, and Motherhood," 36.

31. Joy Harjo, *She Had Some Horses*, x.

32. Joy Harjo, *She Had Some Horses*, ix.

33. For more on praxis, see Doherty, "Towards Self-Reflection in Librarianship"; and Freire, *Pedagogy of the Oppressed*.

34. Brown and Strega, "Transgressive Possibilities," 9.

35. Jacob, *Yakama Rising*, 107.

36. Fixico, *American Indian Mind*.

37. Abatemarco, "MoCNA—Daniel McCoy Jr."

38. In 2006, while I observed an Eastern Band of Cherokee Indians Tribal Council meeting, a university researcher sought permission to georeference the locations of

the plant bloodroot on Qualla Boundary. The tribal council questioned her, and she stated that she was not going to map the locations—meaning a graphic map—but would "only" GPS the locations for their x- and y-coordinates. The x- and y-coordinates consist of the longitude and latitude coordinates, which actually reveal and compromise locations with a high degree of precision, allowing an individual in possession of them enough information to navigate directly to any identified bloodroot growth areas.

39. Arnstein, "Ladder of Citizen Participation," 216, 219.

40. Arnstein, "Ladder of Citizen Participation," 217.

41. Arnstein, "Ladder of Citizen Participation," 217–20.

42. Belcourt, "MM Interview."

43. Belcourt, "MM Interview."

44. Belcourt, "MM Interview."

45. Belcourt, "MM Interview."

46. MacDonnell, "Families Concerned About Future."

47. Enote and McLerran, *A:shiwi A:wan Ulohnanne.*

48. For a deeper analysis of moving decolonization beyond metaphor and into an active practice, see Tuck and Yang, "Decolonization Is Not a Metaphor."

49. For more on Mvskoke ideas of energy embodied in humans and more-than-humans, see Chaudhuri and Chaudhuri, *Sacred Path*; and Fixico, *American Indian Mind.*

50. Joy Harjo, *She Had Some Horses*, ix.

51. Tuck and Yang, "Decolonization Is Not a Metaphor."

52. The American Legislative Exchange Council (ALEC) is one of many examples of how the politics of recognition works to divide communities and distract their attention toward litigious practices. I learned about ALEC while working as a research fellow for Advancement Project, a civil rights organization. The victories were rewarding, and my first civil rights victory happened with Donita Judge, Southwest Workers Union, and Professor Ray Block. The victory was in a Texas community where there was a mismatch between those in leadership and the racial makeup of the community. The county commissioners, a white male board, gerrymandered voting district maps that would dilute the Latino vote in voting districts that were consistently majority-minority. We collectively thwarted these illegal efforts. I dreamed about seeing these kinds of victories in my hometown. However, I learned about all the ways that the vote of people of color is suppressed, informed by my colleague at Advancement Project, Carolyn Thompson, a dogged voting rights activist and community organizer based in Miami, Florida. The minority vote is foreclosed, for example, by sending out mailers telling people to vote at the wrong place or date; going through the line of people asking them if their house has been foreclosed; having the police posted in close proximity to a voting precinct; and passing voting laws that impact when and where to vote and what form of ID you must have on you to vote. Some of these tactics are carried out by vote suppressors through print media, some are carried out by precinct

watchers, and some are carried out by legislators who make laws related to voter ID and ratify gerrymandered redistricting maps. In this case, the politics of recognition operates to influence laws, policies, and practices that result in strengthening and legitimizing the power of the state over the interests and needs of the community.

53. Coulthard, "Subjects of Empire."
54. Ray, "Preservation over Profits," 611.
55. Ray, "Preservation over Profits," 617; Poarch Band of Creek Indians, "History of the Poarch Band."
56. Ray, "Preservation over Profits," 617; Poarch Band of Creek Indians, "History of the Poarch Band."
57. Ray, "Preservation over Profits," 621.
58. Ray, "Preservation over Profits," 622.
59. Suzan Shown Harjo, "Poarch Creeks Worked Against."
60. The case is *Muscogee Creek Nation, et al v. Poarch Band of Creek Indians, et al*, and the plaintiffs are Muscogee Creek Nation, Hickory Ground Tribal Town, and George Thompson, while the defendants are Poarch Band of Creek Indians, Stephanie Bryan, Robert McGhee, David Gehman, Arthur Mothershed, Keith Martin, Sandy Hollinger, Eddie Tullis, Robert Thrower, PCI Gaming Authority, Bridget Wasdin, Matthew Martin, Billy Smith, Tim Manning, Flintco, LLC, Martin Construction, Inc., Ken Salazar, Jonathan Jarvis, Kevin Washburn, U.S. Department of Interior, Auburn University, D. H. Griffin Wrecking Company, Inc., Buford Rolin, and Garvin Sells.
61. Tsosie, "Challenges to Sacred Site Protection"; Miholland, "In the Eyes of the Beholder."
62. Salsman, "MCN, PBCI File Joint Request."
63. A Law of the Muscogee (Creek) Nation Reaffirming Support for the Protection of the Muscogee Sacred Site of Hickory Ground near Wetumpka, Alabama and Authorizing a Special Appropriation for the Cost of Necessary Measures Related Thereto, Muscogee (Creek) National Council, NCA 18-077 (2018).
64. Conveyed by Cris Stainbrook to the Indian Land Tenure Foundation Board of Directors, February 2017.
65. Martone, "American Indian Tribal Self-Government."
66. Linda Tuhiwai Smith, *Decolonizing Methodologies*.
67. Linda Tuhiwai Smith, *Decolonizing Methodologies*, 2; Said, *Orientalism*, 3.
68. For deeper information about Smith's notion of time, see Linda Tuhiwai Smith, *Decolonizing Methodologies*, 54; for more on Smith's notion of worldviews, see Linda Tuhiwai Smith, *Decolonizing Methodologies*, 61.
69. For more on research with disabled groups, see Kitchin and Tate, *Conducting Research in Human Geography*, 36–41.
70. Said, *Orientalism*; Pain and Francis, "Reflections on Participatory Research."
71. Arnstein, "Ladder of Citizen Participation."
72. This was relayed to me by Dr. Renee Louis in a personal conversation, 2005.

73.   Mr. McCue was a commentator for the session "Oceanic Cartographies: Traditional Seafaring and the Mapping of Indigenous Politics and Poetics," Indigenous Cartography and Representational Politics Conference, March 4, 2006, Cornell University.

74.   Salomón J., "Telling to Reclaim," 189. For more on Western impact on community epistemologies, see Lorde, *Sister Outsider*; and Wilson, *Research Is Ceremony*.

75.   Abatemarco, "MoCNA—Daniel McCoy Jr."

76.   Abatemarco, "MoCNA—Daniel McCoy Jr."

77.   Chambers, "Origins and Practice"; Chambers, "Methods for Analysis."

78.   Kesby, "Participatory Diagramming: Deploying."

79.   Dr. Dick Winchell taught tribal community planning methodologies in his Tribal Planning course at Eastern Washington University, Cheney, Wash.

80.   Linda Tuhiwai Smith, *Decolonizing Methodologies*, 145.

81.   Kesby, "Participatory Diagramming: Deploying."

82.   For more on tending and attending to one's membership in and ethical obligation to one's natal community, see Spillers, *Black, White, and in Color*, 6.

83.   Louis, "Can You Hear Us Now?," 134.

84.   Clan is tied to Mvskoke origin stories. In these stories, there was a great fog and the Mvskokvlke were lost; as they emerged from the fog, they coalesced into groups. One of these groups is the Wolf Clan, which is also called the Grandfather Clan: it is their ethical obligation to take care of the people. One's clan is a form of traditional knowledge passed on through matrilineal lines.

85.   In one example, the Mvskoke burial tradition is to never the leave the deceased alone, but instead to stay with him or her for four days and nights, after which the individual is interred. This results in the extended family and community rotating a watch during that time, keeping one another company and telling stories.

Chapter 3

1.   Leanne Betasamosake Simpson, "Indigenous Resurgence and Co-resistance."

2.   Personal conversation about Mvskoke symbology with Mvskoke/Seminole silversmith Kenneth Johnson, August 2015.

3.   Million, *Therapeutic Nations*.

4.   For more on settler futurity, see Tuck and Gaztambide-Fernández, "Curriculum, Replacement, and Settler Futurity."

5.   Zaferatos, "Developing an Effective Approach"; Hibbard and Lane, "By the Seat of Your Pants."

6.   Goss, "Debate over Indian Removal."

7.   Goss, "Debate over Indian Removal," 50–51.

8.   La Vere, *Contrary Neighbors*.

9.   Carlson, "Federal Policy and Indian Land"; Terry L. Anderson and Lueck, "Agricultural Development and Land Tenure"; McCulley, "American Indian Probate Reform Act."

10. Shoemaker, "Like Snow in the Spring Time"; Cheever, "Confronting Our Shared Legacy," 1039.

11. Carlson, "Federal Policy and Indian Land."

12. Carlson, "Federal Policy and Indian Land"; Terry L. Anderson and Lueck, "Agricultural Development and Land Tenure."

13. Sturm, "Blood Politics."

14. For more on the federal government's management of trust land, see Wood, "Indian Land and the Promise."

15. Oakes and Young, "Reconciling Conflict."

16. Gonzales, "Gaming and Displacement."

17. For more information about criminal jurisdiction in Indian country, see Million, "Policing the Rez"; and 18 U.S.C. § 1153(a). For more on the legal definition of Indian country, see 18 U.S.C. § 1151. For deeper information and discussion about Congress never disestablishing Creek Nation or its reservation, see Carpenter v. Murphy, No.17-1107 (Supreme Court; case pending).

18. For more on the ways in which tribal governmental power devolves, see Corntassel and Witmer, *Forced Federalism*.

19. Gonzales, "Gaming and Displacement."

20. Michael D. Cox, "Indian Gaming Regulatory Act," 774–75; McCulloch, "Politics of Indian Gaming," 102; Mason, *Indian Gaming*.

21. Michael D. Cox, "Indian Gaming Regulatory Act," 775; McCulloch, "Politics of Indian Gaming," 102; Mason, *Indian Gaming*.

22. Veracini, *Settler Colonialism*.

23. Wodak, *Language, Power, and Ideology*; Van Dijk, "Critical Discourse Analysis."

24. Valencia-Weber, "Shrinking Indian Country."

25. Barrow, *Critical Theories of the State*, 101.

26. Swyngedouw, "Marxian Alternative."

27. Lassek, "Council Stands Against Trust Status"; Adcock, "Creeks Buy Jenks Bridge Land."

28. Barber, "Councilors Resist Land Action."

29. Corntassel and Witmer, *Forced Federalism*. See also Flaherty, "American Indian Land Rights."

30. Barrow, *Critical Theories of the State*.

31. Barreiro and Johnson, *America Is Indian Country*; Mike Miller, "Cherokee Nation Long-Range Communication Plan."

32. For an example of such an argument, see Barber, "Council to Vote."

33. Slowey, *Navigating Neoliberalism*.

34. Vizenor, *Survivance*.

35. Corntassel and Witmer, *Forced Federalism*, 34–37.

36. For examples of this trope in action, see Barber, "Council to Vote"; Lassek, "Council Stands Against Trust Status."

37. Fair, "Becoming the White Man's Indian"; Berkhofer, *White Man's Indian*.

38. Fair, "Becoming the White Man's Indian"; Berkhofer, *White Man's Indian*.

39. Fair, "Becoming the White Man's Indian"; Berkhofer, *White Man's Indian*.

40. Corntassel, "Toward Sustainable Self-Determination."

41. Slowey, *Navigating Neoliberalism*.

42. For more on the dynamic of mutual work, see Faiman-Silva, *Choctaws at the Cross-roads*; and McKnight and Plummer, *Community Organizing*.

43. Jacob, *Yakama Rising*, 12.

44. It seemed strange to me when I later found out that in non-Indigenous circles, a truck is usually a marker of masculinity: a truck man is more of a man, but a truck woman is less of a woman. Still, in rural communities as well as communities with alterNative economies, the utility and necessity of a truck trumps its marking of masculinity.

45. For more on Mvskoke community beliefs about vnokeckv, see Rutland, "Vnokeckv."

Chapter 4

1. Emergence from the fog is discussed in Womack, *Red on Red*; Gouge, *Totkv Mocvse*; and Joy Harjo, *Map to the Next World*.

2. Bomberry, "Indigenous Memory and Imagination."

3. For these and other details on the rigors and cruelties of Indian removal, see Fore-man, *Indian Removal*.

4. Supernaw, *Muscogee Daughter*.

5. Dunn, *Tulsa's Magic Roots*, 58.

6. "From 1836 to 1896, the Nation conducted business around the tree and had a significant influence on the surrounding area that would later be known as the City of Tulsa, deriving from the Creek word, 'Tallasi' or 'Tvlvhasse,' meaning 'old town.'" Muscogee (Creek) Nation, "Where It All Began."

7. Foreman, *Five Civilized Tribes*, 161.

8. Green, *Politics of Indian Removal*.

9. Hahn, *Invention of the Creek Nation*.

10. For a more nuanced description of Mvskoke tribal towns before and after removal to Oklahoma, see Hurt, "Defining American Homelands." For more on tribal town spatial organization, see Innes, "Medicine-Making Language," 92–93.

11. Emery, "Tribal Government in North America." An arbor is a structure con-structed out of four posts that has a roof made from leafy tree branches. Arbors are located at the perimeter of the dance grounds and used as shaded seating areas for the men participating in the ceremonies.

12. For more on tribe-specific community-based sovereignty, see Gable, "Sovereignty in the Blood"; and Fixico, "Sovereignty Revitalized."

13. Bell, "Separate People"; Jackson and Levine, "Singing for Garfish"; Hester, "On Philosophical Discourse."

14. Martin, "Rebalancing the World." For a fuller description of the Green Corn Cer-emony, see Chaudhuri and Chaudhuri, *Sacred Path*, 52, 55.

15. Englar, *Seminole*.

16. For examples of this school of thought, see Dean Howard Smith, *Modern Tribal Development*; and Cornell and Kalt, "Two Approaches."

17. Vision 2025 is a project that is the result of Tulsa County voters approving a sales tax increase used to fund regional economic development and capital improvement projects. For more, see Tulsa County, "What Is Vision 2025?"

18. Cherokee Nation, *Ga-Du-Gi*; Seminole Nation, *Pumvyetv, Pum Oponvkv*.

19. Hawtin and Percy-Smith, *Community Profiling*; Christakopoulou et al., "Community Well-Being Questionnaire."

20. Various other names are used for the Creek Festival: Muscogee (Creek) Nation Festival, Mvskoke Festival, and in community settings it is referred to as "the festival." All indicate the same annual event that takes place in June. For example, the official website is creekfestival.org, with the title page "Muscogee (Creek) Nation Festival," and a graphic on the same page that reads "Muscogee Creek Festival." Although I use *Mvskoke* throughout this book, I am using the language from the survey, which is more vernacular, in my survey summary.

21. Hicks, "35th Annual Muscogee (Creek) Festival Preview."

22. Hicks, "35th Annual Muscogee (Creek) Festival Preview."

23. The University of Southern California has an Institutional Review Board (IRB) whose function is to protect human participants involved in surveys. The IRB reviewed my research framework and protocols to ensure that I did not harm the study participants or place them at risk.

24. Chaudhuri and Chaudhuri, *Sacred Path*.

25. The use of "well" here is vernacular language. I tested the survey instrument and adjusted language usage based on community feedback.

26. Leanne Betasamosake Simpson, *Islands of Decolonial Love*.

27. Chaudhuri and Chaudhuri, *Sacred Path*.

28. I use the phrase "doing good" here because it was used in the survey, and when the survey was tested with community people there was a preference for vernacular language.

29. "4 Love of the Game is a nonprofit organization (501c3 pending) established in 2005 by four Native American men with a desire to create opportunities and avenues for Native American youth that combat the rash of suicides, depression, juvenile diabetes, school dropouts and drug/alcohol abuse that has become an epidemic among Native American communities throughout the United States." 4 Love of the Game, "About 4 Love of the Game." The Mvskoke Food Sovereignty Initiative's mission statement is, "Mvskoke Food Sovereignty Initiative works to enable the Mvskoke people and their neighbors to provide for their food and health needs now and in the future through sustainable agriculture, economic development, community involvement, cultural and educational programs." First Nations Development Institute, *Conducting Food Sovereignty Assessments*, 16. Puetake Vcake, operated by Mvskoke tribal members, is a Muscogee language immersion school that serves children.

30. Hanson, "Mvskoke Food Sovereignty Initiative."
31. Hanson, "Mvskoke Food Sovereignty Initiative."
32. The idea of geographies that puncture comes from a conversation with Kelly Finley Davis, April 2018.
33. Summers, "Rural Community Development."
34. Lee et al., "Red Day Star," 153; Cobo, *Astronomía Quitu-Caranqui*; Cobo Arizaga, "Catequilla y los Discos Líticos."
35. Recollet, "Glyphing Decolonial Love"; Recollet, "Gesturing Indigenous Futurities."
36. Linda Tuhiwai Smith, *Decolonizing Methodologies*; Hamilton, Lupfer, and Kerne, "LiveDissent"; Uskali and Gynnild, "First Wave of Drone Journalism."
37. This idea of cracks in the sidewalk was conveyed via personal communication with Dr. Fred Moten.
38. For more on the use of symbolic language as a form of knowledge in Indigenous community planning, see Dominguez, "Plan Indigenous."

Chapter 5

1. For more on MCN's current dialogue and debate regarding proper places and reasons to hold stompdances, see DeLaune, "Policy on Stompdances Under Review."
2. Jay Miller, *Ancestral Mounds*, xviii.
3. Dominguez, "Plan Indigenous."
4. For more on beadwork as a medium to reflect Indigenous histories, see Carmen Robertson, "Land and Beaded Identity."
5. For more on beadwork as ceremony and sacred ontology, see Laura Harjo, Robertson, and Navarro, "Leading with Our Hearts."
6. Martineau, "Creative Combat," 6.
7. Pratt, "Indigenous Artists Join."
8. The conference took place in Temecula, which is in the Pala Mission Band of Indians' territory; however, I use *Pala* as a place name here, which was the practice of the conference conveners, Strong Hearted Native Women's Coalition.
9. Indigenous Action Media, "Accomplices Not Allies."
10. GCC published a piece that focused on MMIW, the WWOS beadwork installation, and the network of beaders who have collectively created WWOS. For more on beading as a community action, see Laura Harjo, Robertson, and Navarro, "Leading with Our Hearts."
11. Laura Harjo, "Indigenous Scales of Sovereignty."
12. Kim Anderson, *Recognition of Being*; Alfred and Corntassel, "Being Indigenous."
13. Hassna, "Understanding Intersections and Impact."
14. For more on cultural symbolic language, see Dominguez, "Plan Indigenous."
15. The symbol that Kenneth Johnson refers to as "Star Knot" has also been referred to as a looped square, and I use this symbol to represent the concept of collective power. For more, see Howe, "And Here Too Comes an Echo."

16. For more on loving relationality and seeing another's light, see Leanne Betasamo-sake Simpson, "Land as Pedagogy"; and Leanne Betasamosake Simpson, *As We Have Always Done.*

17. For more on leaving an archive of knowledge as a form of futurity, see Gómez-Barris, *Extractive Zone.*

18. For more on containerized geographies, see Laura Harjo, "Mvskoke Community Development"; Laura Harjo, "Muscogee (Creek) Nation"; Laura Harjo, "Mapping and Social Media"; Laura Harjo, "Indigenous Scales of Sovereignty"; Laura Harjo, "Indigenous Life Force and Ceremony"; Laura Harjo, "Emancipation from the Cupboard"; and Goeman, "Land as Life."

Chapter 6

1. Isay and Jacobs, *Ties That Bind,* 201–2.

BIBLIOGRAPHY

Supreme Court Cases

Brief for the MCN as Amicus Curiae. Carpenter v. Murphy. No. 17-1107 (Supreme Court). Case pending. https://www.supremecourt.gov/DocketPDF/17/17-1107/64965/20180926161001792_17-1107%20Amicus%20Brief%20of%20Muscogee%20Creek%20Nation.pdf.

Carpenter v. Murphy. No. 17-1107 (Supreme Court). Case pending.

The Cherokee Nation v. The State of Georgia. 30 U.S. 5 Pet. 1 (1831).

Johnson and Graham's Lessee v. McIntosh. 21 U.S. 543 (1823).

Oliphant v. Suquamish Indian Tribe. 435 U.S. 191 (1978).

Strate v. A-1 Contractors. 520 U.S. 438 (1997).

Worcester v. Georgia. 31 U.S. 515 (1832).

Tribal and U.S. Legislation

18 U.S.C. § 1151 (2012).

18 U.S.C. § 1153 (2012).

Comm. on Resources. Cherokee, Choctaw, and Chickasaw Nations Claims Settlement Act. H.R. Rep no. 107-632. September 4, 2002. https://www.congress.gov/107/crpt/hrpt632/CRPT-107hrpt632.pdf.

Communities Emetvlhvmkvke. Title 11, Muscogee (Creek) Nation Code Annotated, 2nd ed. 2010. http://www.creeksupremecourt.com/wp-content/uploads/title11.pdf.

A Law of the Muscogee (Creek) Nation Reaffirming Support for the Protection of the Muscogee Sacred Site of Hickory Ground Near Wetumpka, Alabama and Authorizing a Special Appropriation for the Cost of Necessary Measures Related Thereto. Muscogee (Creek) National Council. NCA 18-077 (2018).

Other Sources

4 Love of the Game. "About 4 Love of the Game." 4 Love of the Game (website). Updated August 8, 2016. https://web.archive.org/web/20160329100630/http://4love ofthegame.org/index.php?option=com_content&view=article&id=2&Itemid=4 (original site discontinued).

Abatemarco, Michael. "MoCNA—Daniel McCoy Jr.: 'The Ceaseless Quest for Utopia.'" *Santa Fe New Mexican*, January 17, 2017. Pasatiempo. http://www.santafenew mexican.com/pasatiempo/art/museum_shows/mocna-daniel-mccoy-jr-the-ceaseless -quest-for-utopia/article_68c04802-e429-11e6-bed8-5b9a97225e5b.html.

Adcock, Clifton. "Creeks Buy Jenks Bridge Land." *Tulsa World*, June 3, 2009.

Aikau, Hōkūlani K. "Following the Alaloa Kīpapa of Our Ancestors: A Trans-Indigenous Futurity Without the State (United States or Otherwise)." *American Quarterly* 67, no. 3 (September 2015): 653–61.

Alexander, M. Jacqui. "Not Just (Any) Body Can Be a Citizen: The Politics of Law, Sexuality and Postcoloniality in Trinidad and Tobago and the Bahamas." *Feminist Review* 48, no. 1 (Autumn 1994): 5–23.

Alfred, Taiaiake. *Peace, Power, Righteousness: An Indigenous Manifesto*. Don Mills, Ont.: Oxford University Press, 1999.

Alfred, Taiaiake. *Wasáse: Indigenous Pathways of Action and Freedom*. Peterborough, Ont.: Broadview Press, 2005.

Alfred, Taiaiake, and Jeff Corntassel. "Being Indigenous: Resurgences Against Contemporary Colonialism." *Government and Opposition* 40, no. 4 (2005): 597–614.

Amin, Ash. "Moving On: Institutionalism in Economic Geography." *Environment and Planning A* 33, no. 7 (2001): 1237–41.

Anderson, Kim. *A Recognition of Being: Reconstructing Native Womanhood*. CSPI Series in Indigenous Studies. Toronto: Women's Press, 2016.

Anderson, Ric. "Autopsy Reveals Dawes Drowned." *Lawrence Journal-World*, October 26, 1989. http://www2.ljworld.com/news/1989/oct/26/autopsy_reveals_dawes_drowned /?print.

Anderson, Ric. "Inquest Called in Fatal Shooting." *Lawrence Journal-World*, April 22, 1991. http://www2.ljworld.com/news/1991/apr/22/inquest_called_in_fatal/.

Anderson, Terry L., and Dean Lueck. "Agricultural Development and Land Tenure in Indian Country." In *Property Rights and Indian Economies*, edited by Terry L. Anderson, 147–66. Lanham, Md.: Rowman and Littlefield, 1992.

Armstrong, Robert F. "Malatchi of Coweta: Creek Diplomacy on the Southeastern Frontier, 1715–1756." Senior honors thesis, Duke University, 1989. https://archive.org /details/malatchiofcoweta00arms.

Arnstein, Sherry R. "A Ladder of Citizen Participation." *Journal of the American Institute of Planners* 35, no. 4 (1969): 216–24. https://doi.org/10.1080/01944366908977225.

Baldwin, Andrew. "Whiteness and Futurity: Towards a Research Agenda." *Progress in Human Geography* 36, no. 2 (2012): 172–87.

Bang, Megan, Adam Kessel, Ananda Marin, Eli S. Suzukovich III, and George Strack. "Muskrat Theories, Tobacco in the Streets, and Living Chicago as Indigenous Land." *Environmental Education Research* 20, no. 1 (2014): 37–55.

Barber, Brian. "Councilors Resist Land Action." *Tulsa World*, July 8, 2009.

Barber, Brian. "Council to Vote Next Week on Arkansas River Land Measure." *Tulsa World*, July 21, 2009.

Barker, Joanne, ed. *Critically Sovereign: Indigenous Gender, Sexuality, and Feminist Studies*. Durham, N.C.: Duke University Press, 2017.

Barker, Joanne. "Introduction." In *Critically Sovereign: Indigenous Gender, Sexuality, and Feminist Studies*, edited by Joanne Barker, 1–44. Durham, N.C.: Duke University Press, 2017.

Barreiro, José, and Tim Johnson. *America Is Indian Country: Opinions and Perspectives from Indian Country Today*. Golden, Colo.: Fulcrum Publishing, 2005.

Barrow, Clyde W. *Critical Theories of the State: Marxist, Neo-Marxist, Post-Marxist*. Madison: University of Wisconsin Press, 1993.

Battiste, Marie, and J. Youngblood Henderson. *Protecting Indigenous Knowledge: A Global Challenge*. Saskatoon: Purich Press, 2000.

Belcourt, Christi. "MM Interview with Metis Artist Christi Belcourt on Walking with Our Sisters WWOS." Video interview by *MUSKRAT Magazine*. YouTube, 2014. https://www.youtube.com/watch?v=ehyOa05ecNA.

Bell, Amelia Rector. "Separate People: Speaking of Creek Men and Women." *American Anthropologist* 92, no. 2 (1990): 332–45.

Bellrichard, Chantelle. "A Timeline of Staff Departures from the MMIWG Inquiry." CBC (website). December 1, 2017. http://www.cbc.ca/news/indigenous/a-timeline-of-staff-departures-from-the-mmiwg-inquiry-1.4419003.

Bender, Margaret Clelland, ed. *Linguistic Diversity in the South: Changing Codes, Practices, and Ideology*. Southern Anthropological Society Proceedings, no. 37. Athens: University of Georgia Press, 2004.

Berezkin, Yuri E. "Seven Brothers and the Cosmic Hunt: European Sky in the Past." *Paar sammukest XXVI, Eesti Kirjandusmuuseumi Aastaraamat* 40 (2012): 31–70.

Berkhofer, Robert F. *The White Man's Indian: Images of the American Indian from Columbus to the Present*. New York: Random House, 1979.

Biolsi, Thomas. "Imagined Geographies: Sovereignty, Indigenous Space, and American Indian Struggle." *American Ethnologist* 32, no. 2 (May 2005): 239–59.

Bomberry, Victoria. "Blood, Rebellion, and Motherhood in the Political Imagination of Indigenous People." In *Reading Native American Women: Critical/Creative Representations*, edited by Inés Hernández-Avila, 21–37. Lanham, Md.: AltaMira Press, 2005.

Bomberry, Victoria Jean. "Indigenous Memory and Imagination: Thinking Beyond the Nation." PhD dissertation, Stanford University, 2001.

Brown, Leslie, and Susan Strega. "Transgressive Possibilities." In *Research as Resistance: Critical, Indigenous, and Anti-Oppressive Approaches*, edited by Leslie Brown and Susan Strega, 1–17. Toronto: Canadian Scholars' Press, 2005.

Burleson, E. "Tribal, State, and Federal Cooperation to Achieve Good Governance." *Akron Law Review* 40, no. 2 (2007): 207–54.

Burt, Sandra D., and Lorraine Code. *Changing Methods: Feminists Transforming Practice.* Peterborough, Ont.: Broadview Press, 1995.

Byrd, Jodi A. *The Transit of Empire: Indigenous Critiques of Colonialism.* First Peoples: New Directions in Indigenous Studies, vol. 4. Minneapolis: University of Minnesota Press, 2011.

Canby, William C. *American Indian Law in a Nutshell.* St. Paul, Minn.: West Group, 1998.

Capriccioso, Rob. "Elouise Cobell, 65, Walks On." Indian Country Media Network. October 17, 2011. https://indiancountrymedianetwork.com/news/elouise-cobell-653 -walks-on/.

Carlson, Leonard A. "Federal Policy and Indian Land: Economic Interests and the Sale of Indian Allotments, 1900–1934." *Agricultural History* 57, no. 1 (1983): 33–45.

Caron, Michael. "Saving Haskell's Soul, the Story of a Threatened Wetland Refuge." Indian Country Media Network. November 10, 2003. https://web.archive.org/web/20170922 022410/https://indiancountrymedianetwork.com/news/caron-saving-haskells-soul -the-story-of-a-threatened-wetland-refuge/.

Casey, James A. "Sovereignty by Sufferance: The Illusion of Indian Tribal Sovereignty." *Cornell Law Review* 79, no. 2 (January 1994): 404–51.

Cave, Alfred A. "Abuse of Power: Andrew Jackson and the Indian Removal Act of 1830." *Historian* 65, no. 6 (December 2003): 1330–53. https://doi.org/10.1111/j.0018 -2370.2003.00055.x.

Chambers, Robert. "Methods for Analysis by Farmers: The Professional Challenge." *Journal for Farming Systems Research-Extension* 4, no. 1 (1993): 87–101.

Chambers, Robert. "The Origins and Practice of Participatory Rural Appraisal." *World Development* 22, no. 7 (1994): 953–69. https://doi.org/10.1016/0305-750X(94)90141-4.

Chaudhuri, Jean, and Joyotpaul Chaudhuri. *A Sacred Path: The Way of the Muscogee Creeks.* Los Angeles: UCLA American Indian Studies Center, 2001.

Cheever, Federico. "Confronting Our Shared Legacy of Incongruous Land Ownership: Notes for a Research Agenda." *Denver University Law Review* 83, no. 4 (2006): 1039–56.

Cherokee Nation. "Arkansas Riverbed Authority Commissions Maps." News release. December 14, 2000. http://www.cherokee.org/News/Stories/Archive_2000/22875.

Cherokee Nation. *Ga-Du-Gi: A Vision for Working Together to Preserve the Cherokee Language.* Tahlequah, Okla.: Cherokee Nation, 2003.

Child, Brenda J. *Boarding School Seasons: American Indian Families, 1900–1940.* Lincoln: University of Nebraska Press, 1998.

Christakopoulou, Sophia, Jon Dawson, and Aikaterini Gari. "The Community Well-Being Questionnaire: Theoretical Context and Initial Assessment of Its Reliability and Validity." *Social Indicators Research* 56, no. 3 (2001): 319–49.

Clark, Blue. *Indian Tribes of Oklahoma: A Guide.* Civilization of the American Indian Series, vol. 261. Norman: University of Oklahoma Press, 2009.

Clinton, Robert N. "Criminal Jurisdiction over Indian Lands: A Journey Through a Jurisdictional Maze." *Arizona Law Review* 18, no. 3 (1976): 503–83.

Cobo, Cristóbal. *Astronomía Quitu-Caranqui y los Discos Líticos: Evidencias de la Astronomía Antigua de los Andes Ecuatoriales.* Quito: Quimera Dreams, 2012.

Cobo Arizaga, Cristóbal. "Catequilla y los Discos Líticos, Evidencias de la Astronomía Antigua en los Andes Ecuatoriales." *Revista de Topografía AZIMUT* 8, no. 1 (June 9, 2017): 41–62.

Cohen, Felix S. *Handbook of Federal Indian Law.* Buffalo: William S. Hein, 1988.

Cornell, Stephen, and Joseph P. Kalt. *Public Choice, Culture and American Indian Economic Development.* Harvard Project on American Indian Economic Development, vol. 27. Cambridge, Mass.: Harvard Project on American Indian Economic Development, Malcolm Wiener Center for Social Policy, John F. Kennedy School of Government, Harvard University, 1988.

Cornell, Stephen, and Joseph P. Kalt. "Sovereignty and Nation-Building: The Development Challenge in Indian Country Today." *American Indian Culture & Research Journal* 22, no. 3 (1998): 187–214.

Cornell, Stephen, and Joseph P. Kalt. "Two Approaches to the Development of Native Nations: One Works, the Other Doesn't." In *Rebuilding Native Nations: Strategies for Governance and Development,* edited by Miriam Jorgensen, 3–33. Tucson: University of Arizona Press, 2007.

Cornell, Stephen, and Joseph P. Kalt. "Where Does Economic Development Really Come From?: Constitutional Rule Among the Contemporary Sioux and Apache." *Economic Inquiry* 33, no. 3 (1995): 402–26.

Corntassel, Jeff. "Toward Sustainable Self-Determination: Rethinking the Contemporary Indigenous-Rights Discourse." *Alternatives: Global, Local, Political* 33, no. 1 (2008): 105–32.

Corntassel, Jeff, and Richard C. Witmer. *Forced Federalism: Contemporary Challenges to Indigenous Nationhood.* American Indian Law and Policy Series, vol. 3. Norman: University of Oklahoma Press, 2008.

Coulthard, Glen S. "Subjects of Empire: Indigenous Peoples and the 'Politics of Recognition' in Canada." *Contemporary Political Theory* 6, no. 4 (2007): 437–60.

Cox, Kevin R. "Spaces of Dependence, Spaces of Engagement and the Politics of Scale, or: Looking for Local Politics." *Political Geography* 17 (1998): 1–23.

Cox, Michael D. "Indian Gaming Regulatory Act: An Overview." *St. Thomas Law Review* 7, no. 3 (Summer 1995): 769–90.

Cox, Robert W. "Gramsci, Hegemony and International Relations: An Essay in Method." *Millennium* 12, no. 2 (June 1983): 162–75. https://doi.org/10.1177/03058 298830120020701.

Crawford, Neta C. "A Security Regime Among Democracies: Cooperation Among Iroquois Nations." *International Organization* 48, no. 3 (1994): 345–85. https://doi.org /10.1017/S002081830002823X.

Deer, Sarah. *The Beginning and End of Rape: Confronting Sexual Violence in Native America.* Minneapolis: University of Minnesota Press, 2015.

Deer, Sarah. "Decolonizing Rape Law: A Native Feminist Synthesis of Safety and Sovereignty." *Wíčazo Ša Review* 24, no. 2 (2009): 149–67.

Deer, Sarah. "Toward an Indigenous Jurisprudence of Rape." *Kansas Journal of Law & Public Policy* 14, no. 121 (2004): 137–40.

DeFine, Michael Sullivan. "A History of Governmentally Coerced Sterilization: The Plight of the Native American Woman." In *Moral Issues in Global Perspective*, edited by Christine M. Koggel, 2nd ed., 37–44. Peterborough, Ont.: Broadview Press, 2006.

DeLaune, Darren. "Policy on Stompdances Under Review." Mvskoke Media. April 10, 2017. Accessed January 29, 2018, https://mvskokemedia.com/policy-on-stompdances-under-review/.

Diaz, Vicente M. "Stepping In It: How to Smell the Fullness of Indigenous Histories." In *Sources and Methods in Indigenous Studies*, edited by Chris Andersen and Jean M. O'Brien, 86–92. New York: Routledge, 2016.

Diaz, Vince, and McCue, Hap. "Oceanic Cartographies: Traditional Seafaring and the Mapping of Indigenous Politics and Poetics." Presentation at the Indigenous Cartography and Representational Politics Conference, Cornell University, March 4, 2006.

Dickason, David G. "The Future of Historical Cartography." *FUTURE*, 2011.

Dillon, Grace. "Future Imaginary." Conference presentation at the 2nd Annual Symposium on the Future Imaginary, Kelowna, British Columbia, August 5, 2016. http://abtec.org/iif/wp-content/uploads/2016/06/Future-Imaginary-Symposium-Kelowna-Grace-Dillon-1.pdf.

Dillon, Grace, ed. *Walking the Clouds: An Anthology of Indigenous Science Fiction*. Tucson: University of Arizona Press, 2012.

Dixon, Mim, Pamela E. Iron, and American Public Health Association. *Strategies for Cultural Competency in Indian Health Care*. Washington, D.C.: American Public Health Association, 2006.

Doherty, J. "Towards Self-Reflection in Librarianship: What Is Praxis." *Progressive Librarian* 26, no. 1 (2005): 11–17.

Dominguez, A. Sixtus. "Plan Indigenous: The Power of Indigenous Planning, Design, and Place in an Urban and University Environment and Beyond." Master's thesis, University of New Mexico, Albuquerque, 2017.

Doran, Michael F. "Population Statistics of Nineteenth Century Indian Territory." *Chronicles of Oklahoma* 53, no. 4 (1975): 492–515.

Dunn, Nina Lane. *Tulsa's Magic Roots*. Tulsa: N. L. D. Corporation, 1979.

Eagle Woman, Angelique A. "The Philosophy of Colonization Underlying Taxation Imposed upon Tribal Nations Within the United States." *Tulsa Law Review* 43, no. 1 (2007): 43–72.

Emery, C. M. "Tribal Government in North America: The Evolution of Tradition." *Urban Lawyer* 32, no. 2 (Spring 2000): 315–48.

Englar, Mary. *The Seminole: The First People of Florida*. American Indian Nations. Mankato, Minn.: Bridgestone Books, 2002.

Enote, Jim, and Jennifer McLerran, eds. *A:shiwi A:wan Ulohnanne = The Zuni World*. Zuni: A:shiwi A:wan Museum & Heritage Center; Flagstaff: Museum of Northern Arizona, 2011.

Etheridge, Robbie. *Creek Country: The Creek Indians and Their World*. Chapel Hill: University of North Carolina Press, 2004.

Faiman-Silva, Sandra L. *Choctaws at the Crossroads: The Political Economy of Class and Culture in the Oklahoma Timber Region*. Lincoln: University of Nebraska Press, 2000.

Fair, Rhonda S. "Becoming the White Man's Indian: An Examination of Native American Tribal Web Sites." *Plains Anthropologist* 45, no. 172 (2000): 203–13.

Fawcett, Barbara, and Brid Featherstone. "Setting the Scene: An Appraisal of Postmodernism, Postmodernity, and Postmodern Feminism." In *Practice and Research in Social Work*, edited by B. Fawcett, B. Featherstone, J. Fook, and A. Rossiter, 5–23. London: Routledge, 2000.

First Nations Development Institute. *Conducting Food Sovereignty Assessments in Native Communities: On-the-Ground Perspectives*. Longmont, Colo.: First Nations Development Institute, 2014.

Fisher, Mark. "The Metaphysics of Crackle: Afrofuturism and Hauntology." *Dancecult: Journal of Electronic Dance Music Culture* 5, no. 2 (2013): 42–55.

Fixico, Donald. *The American Indian Mind in a Linear World: American Indian Studies and Traditional Knowledge*. New York: Routledge, 2003.

Fixico, Donald L. "Sovereignty Revitalized." In *Native American Testimony: A Chronicle of Indian-White Relations from Prophecy to the Present, 1492–1992*, edited by Peter Nabokov, 420–23. New York: Penguin, 1991.

Flaherty, Anne. "American Indian Land Rights, Rich Indian Racism, and Newspaper Coverage in New York State, 1988–2008." *American Indian Culture and Research Journal* 4, no. 37 (2013): 58–84.

Fletcher, Matthew L. M. "The Iron Cold of the Marshall Trilogy." *North Dakota Law Review* 82, no. 3 (2006): 627–96.

Flint Ballenger, Robin. "Tribes' Casino Benefits Extend to All Oklahomans." *Tulsa World*, October 8, 2009. Business Viewpoint. http://www.tulsaworld.com/business/tribes-casino-benefits-extend-to-all-oklahomans/article_4a5d4fd4-e90f-5373-9e54-ce15316c8101.html.

Florio, Gwen. "Cobell, Relative Died on Same Day, Neither Seeing Restitution." Indian Trust Settlement (website). October 17, 2011. http://www.indiantrust.com/article/missoulian_relative.

Foerster, Jennifer Elise. *Leaving Tulsa*. Sun Tracks, vol. 75. Tucson: University of Arizona Press, 2013.

Foley, Jr., Hugh W. "General Allotment Act (Dawes Act), 1887." In *Treaties with American Indians: An Encyclopedia of Rights, Conflicts, and Sovereignty*, edited by Donald Lee Fixico, 672–75. Santa Barbara: ABC-CLIO, 2008.

Foreman, Grant. *The Five Civilized Tribes*. Norman: University of Oklahoma Press, 1985.

Foreman, Grant. *Indian Removal: The Emigration of the Five Civilized Tribes of Indians*. New ed. Civilization of the American Indian Series, vol. 2. Norman: University of Oklahoma Press, 1972.

Foucault, Michel. *Power/Knowledge: Selected Interviews and Other Writings, 1972–1977*. New York: Pantheon, 1980.

Fraser, Nancy. *Unruly Practices: Power, Discourse, and Gender in Contemporary Social Theory*. Minneapolis: University of Minnesota Press, 1989.

Freer, Regina. "L.A. Race Woman: Charlotta Bass and the Complexities of Black Political Development in Los Angeles." *American Quarterly* 56, no. 3 (2004): 607–32.

Freire, Paulo. *Pedagogy of the Oppressed*. 30th anniversary ed. New York: Continuum, 2000.

Friedmann, John. *Planning in the Public Domain: From Knowledge to Action*. Princeton, N.J.: Princeton University Press, 1987.

Fugikawa, Laura. "Domestic Containment: Japanese Americans, Native Americans, and the Cultural Politics of Relocation." PhD dissertation, University of Southern California, 2011. University of Southern California Digital Library, http://digitallibrary .usc.edu/cdm/ref/collection/p15799coll127/id/647691.

Fundaburk, Emma Lila, and Mary Douglass Fundaburk Foreman. *Sun Circles and Human Hands: The Southeastern Indians—Art and Industry*. Tuscaloosa: University of Alabama Press, 2001.

Gable, Ron. "Sovereignty in the Blood: Cultural Resistance in the Characters of James Welch." *Wíčazo Ša Review* 9, no. 2 (1993): 37–43.

Gamber, John. "Born out of the Creek Landscape: Reconstructing Community and Continuance in Craig Womack's *Drowning in Fire*." *MELUS* 34, no. 2 (Summer 2009): 103–23. https://doi.org/10.1353/mel.0.0027.

Garret, Michael Tlanusta, J. T. Garret, Edil Torres-River, Michael Wilbur, and Janice Roberts-Wilbur. "Laughing It Up: Native American Humor as Spiritual Tradition." *Journal of Multicultural Counseling and Development* 33, no. 4 (2005): 194–204.

Geniusz, Wendy Makoons. *Our Knowledge Is Not Primitive: Decolonizing Botanical Anishinaabe Teachings*. Syracuse, N.Y.: Syracuse University Press, 2009.

Gilbert, Joan. *The Trail of Tears Across Missouri*. Missouri Heritage Readers. Columbia: University of Missouri Press, 1996.

Gingold, Dennis M., and M. Alexander Pearl. "Tribute to Elouise Cobell." *Public Land & Resources Law Review* 33 (2012): 189–97.

Goeman, Mishuana. "Land as Life: Unsettling the Logics of Containment." In *Native Studies Keywords*, edited by Stephanie N. Teves, Andrea Smith, and Michelle H. Raheja, 71–89. Tucson: University of Arizona Press, 2015.

Goeman, Mishuana. *Mark My Words: Native Women Mapping Our Nations*. First Peoples: New Directions in Indigenous Studies. Minneapolis: University of Minnesota Press, 2013.

Goeman, Mishuana, and Jennifer Nez Denetdale, eds. "Native Feminisms: Legacies, Interventions, and Indigenous Sovereignties." Special issue, *Wíčazo Ša Review* 24, no. 2 (2009).

Goldberg, Carole. "American Indians and Preferential Treatment." *UCLA Law Review* 49, no. 4 (2001): 943–89.

Goldberg-Ambrose, Carole. "Public Law 280 and the Problem of Lawlessness in California Indian Country." *UCLA Law Review* 44, no. 5 (1997): 1405–48.

Gómez-Barris, Macarena. *The Extractive Zone: Social Ecologies and Decolonial Perspectives.* Durham, N.C.: Duke University Press, 2017.

Gonzales, Angela A. "Gaming and Displacement: Winners and Losers in American Indian Casino Development." *International Social Science Journal* 55, no. 1 (2003): 123–33.

Good, Kenneth. "Settler Colonialism: Economic Development and Class Formation." *Journal of Modern African Studies* 14, no. 4 (1976): 597–620.

Goodman, E. "Protecting Habitat for Off-Reservation Tribal Hunting and Fishing Rights: Tribal Comanagement as a Reserved Right." *Environmental Law* 30, no. 2 (2000): 279–362.

Goodyear-Kaʻōpua, Noelani. "Protectors of the Future, Not Protestors of the Past: Indigenous Pacific Activism and Mauna a Wākea." *South Atlantic Quarterly* 116, no. 1 (2017): 184–94.

Goss, George W. "The Debate over Indian Removal in the 1830s." Master's thesis, University of Massachusetts, Boston, 2011. http://scholarworks.umb.edu/masters_theses/44.

Gouge, Earnest. *Totkv Mocvse / New Fire: Creek Folktales.* Norman: University of Oklahoma Press, 2004.

Gough, Alexandria L. "A Way Out: The History of the Outing Program from the Haskell Institute to the Phoenix Indian School." Master's thesis, University of Arkansas, Fayetteville, 2012. http://scholarworks.uark.edu/etd/545/.

Green, Michael D. *The Politics of Indian Removal: Creek Government and Society in Crisis.* Lincoln: University of Nebraska Press, 1985.

Gruver, Deb, and Ric Anderson. "T Enough." *Lawrence Journal-World*, March 5, 1991. http://www2.ljworld.com/news/1991/mar/05/t_enough/.

Hahn, Steven C. *The Invention of the Creek Nation, 1670–1763.* Lincoln: University of Nebraska Press, 2004.

Hall, Stuart. "Foucault: Power, Knowledge and Discourse." In *Discourse Theory and Practice: A Reader*, edited by Margaret Wetherell, Simeon Yates, and Stephanie Taylor, 72–81. Thousand Oaks, Calif.: SAGE Publications Ltd, 2001.

Hall, Stuart. "The Problem of Ideology." In *Stuart Hall: Critical Dialogues in Cultural Studies*, edited by David Morley and Kuan-Hsing Chen. London: Routledge, 1996.

Hamilton, William A., Nic Lupfer, and Andruid Kerne. "LiveDissent: A Media Platform for Remote Participation in Activist Demonstrations." Paper presented at GROUP 2018: ACM Conference on Supporting Groupwork, Sanibel Island, Fla., January 10, 2018. https://doi.org/10.1145/3148330.3149406.

Hampton, Chris. "Forget 2017—These Indigenous VR Artists Are Imagining Canada's Future 150 Years from Now." CBC (website). June 19, 2017. http://www.cbc.ca/arts/forget-2017-these-indigenous-vr-artists-are-imagining-canada-s-future-150-years-from-now-1.4167856.

Hanson, David. "Mvskoke Food Sovereignty Initiative: Okmulgee, OK." David Hanson (blog). Accessed June 5, 2018. https://web.archive.org/web/20190221063633/https://www.davidhanson3.com/food-stories/2017/11/17/1qak8cdhaglgl8g761ggau61ra8rbx.

Harjo, Joy. *Conflict Resolution for Holy Beings: Poems.* New York: W. W. Norton, 2015.

Harjo, Joy. *Crazy Brave: A Memoir.* New York: W. W. Norton, 2013.

Harjo, Joy. *How We Became Human: New and Selected Poems 1975–2002.* New York: W. W. Norton, 2004.

Harjo, Joy. *A Map to the Next World: Poetry and Tales.* New York: W. W. Norton, 2000.

Harjo, Joy. *Remember.* New York: Strawberry Press, 1981.

Harjo, Joy. *She Had Some Horses.* New York: W. W. Norton, 2008.

Harjo, Laura. "Emancipation from the Cupboard: Rethinking Containerized Geography." Presentation at the Critical Ethnic Studies Conference, University of Illinois at Chicago, Chicago, Ill., September 21, 2013.

Harjo, Laura. "GIS Support for Empowering Marginalized Communities: The Cherokee Nation Case Study." In *GIS for Sustainable Development*, edited by Michele Campagna, 433–50. Boca Raton: CRC Press, 2006.

Harjo, Laura. "Indigenous Life Force and Ceremony: Decolonizing and Mobilizing Community in the Violence Against Indigenous Women and Girls Movement." Presentation at the He Manawa Whenua Indigenous Research Conference, Hamilton, New Zealand, March 8, 2017.

Harjo, Laura. "Indigenous Scales of Sovereignty: Transcending Settler Geographies." Conference presentation at the Native American and Indigenous Studies Association, Austin, Tex., May 29, 2014.

Harjo, Laura. "Mapping and Social Media: Community Organizing and Base Building in the Indigenous Peoples' Movement." Presentation at the Association of American Geographers Conference, Los Angeles, Calif., April 13, 2013.

Harjo, Laura. "Muscogee (Creek) Nation: Blueprint for a Seven Generation Plan." PhD dissertation, University of Southern California, 2012. http://digitallibrary.usc.edu/cdm/compoundobject/collection/p15799coll127/id/675321/rec/4.

Harjo, Laura. "Mvskoke Community Development—Reclaiming and Activating the Etvlwa." Presentation at the Native American and Indigenous Studies Association Conference, Washington, D.C., June 5, 2015.

Harjo, Laura, Kimberly Robertson, and Jenell Navarro. "Leading with Our Hearts: Antiviolence Action and Beadwork Circles as Colonial Resistance." In *Keetsahnak, Our Sisters*, edited by Maria Campbell, Kim Anderson, and Christi Belcourt. Edmonton: University of Alberta Press, 2018.

Harjo, Suzan Shown. "Poarch Creeks Worked Against Native People." Indianz.com. June 5, 2006. https://web.archive.org/web/20181228171136/https://www.indianz.com/News/2006/014305.asp.

Harring, Sidney L. "Crazy Snake and the Creek Struggle for Sovereignty: The Native American Legal Culture and American Law." *American Journal of Legal History* 34, no. 4 (1990): 365–80.

Hart, Rebecca A., and M. Alexander Lowther. "Honoring Sovereignty: Aiding Tribal Efforts to Protect Native American Women from Domestic Violence." *California Law Review* 96, no. 1 (February 2008): 185–234. https://doi.org/10.15779/z38gt51.

Harvey, David, and Mark Davidson. *Social Justice and the City.* London: Edward Arnold, 1973.

Hassna, Rachel. "Understanding Intersections and Impact: Planning, Police Violence, and Reform." Master's thesis, University of New Mexico, 2017.

Hawtin, Murray, and Janie Percy-Smith. *Community Profiling: A Practical Guide; Auditing Social Needs.* Maidenhead, U.K.: McGraw-Hill Education, 2007.

Hernández-Avila, Inés. *Reading Native American Women: Critical/Creative Representations.* Contemporary Native American Communities. Lanham, Md.: Altamira Press, 2005.

Hester, Thurman Lee. "On Philosophical Discourse: Some Intercultural Musings." In *American Indian Thought*, edited by Anne Waters, 263–67. Malden, Mass.: Blackwell, 2004.

Hibbard, Michael, and Marcus Lane. "By the Seat of Your Pants: Indigenous Action and State Response." *Planning Theory & Practice* 5, no. 1 (2004): 97–104.

Hicks, Cherokee. "35th Annual Muscogee (Creek) Festival Preview." *Muscogee Nation News*, June 2009. https://mvskokemedia.com/archives/muscogee-nation-news-editions/.

Hill Collins, Patricia. *Black Feminist Thought: Knowledge, Consciousness, and the Politics of Empowerment.* New York: Routledge, 2002.

Hirokawa, Eri. "Effects of Music Listening and Relaxation Instructions on Arousal Changes and the Working Memory Task in Older Adults." *Journal of Music Therapy* 41, no. 2 (2004): 107–27.

Hoffmann, April Ruth. "'Geography Should Never Be Why a Child Dies': Spatial Narratives and the Pediatric Medical Clinic of the Americas." PhD dissertation, University of Southern California, 2013. http://digitallibrary.usc.edu/cdm/search/field/identi/searchterm/uscthesesreloadpub_Volume8%252Fetd-HoffmannAp-2225.pdf.

Howe, LeAnne. "Comment: 'And Here Too Comes an Echo of Our People at Play' in 'Anompa Sipokni,' *Old Talking Places.*" *Journal of the Illinois State Historical Society* 100, no. 3 (2007): 207–14. http://www.jstor.org/stable/40204686.

Howe, LeAnne, and Wilson, Jim. "Life in a 21st Century Mound City." In *The World of Indigenous North America*, edited by Robert Allen Warrior, 3–26. Routledge Worlds. New York: Routledge / Taylor & Francis Group, 2015.

Hudson, Brian. "Future Imaginary." Presentation at the 2nd Annual Symposium on the Future Imaginary, Kelowna, British Columbia, 2016. http://abtec.org/iif/wp-content/uploads/2016/06/Future-Imaginary-Symposium-Kelowna-Brian-Hudson.pdf.

Hunt, Sarah. "Ontologies of Indigeneity: The Politics of Embodying a Concept." *Cultural Geographies* 21, no. 1 (2014): 27–32.

Hurley, Patrick J. "A Five Minute History of Oklahoma." *Chronicles of Oklahoma* 13, no. 4 (December 1935): 373–75. Accessed September 5, 2018, https://cdm17279.contentdm.oclc.org/digital/collection/p17279coll4/id/2846/rec/19.

Hurt, Douglas A. "Defining American Homelands: A Creek Nation Example, 1828–1907." *Journal of Cultural Geography* 21, no. 1 (2003): 19–43.

Hurt, Douglas A. "The Shaping of a Creek (Muscogee) Homeland in Indian Territory, 1828–1907." PhD dissertation, University of Oklahoma, 2000.

Inch, Andy, and Lee Crookes. "Making Hope Possible?: The Challenges of Playing with Planning's Future Orientation." Presentation at Planning: Practice, Pedagogy, and Place Conference, American Collegiate Schools of Planning, Portland, Ore., 2016.

Indian Health Service. "Indian Health Disparities." Indian Health Service, U.S. Department of Health and Human Services (website). April 2018. https://www.ihs.gov /newsroom/includes/themes/responsive2017/display_objects/documents/factsheets /Disparities.pdf.

Indigenous Action Media. "Accomplices Not Allies: Abolishing the Ally Industrial Complex, an Indigenous Perspective." Indigenous Action Media (website). May 4, 2014. https://web.archive.org/web/20190119052428/http://www.indigenousaction .org/accomplices-not-allies-abolishing-the-ally-industrial-complex/.

Innes, Pamela. "Medicine-Making Language Among the Muskogee: The Effects of Changing Attitudes." In *Linguistic Diversity in the South: Changing Codes, Practices, and Ideology*, edited by Margaret Bender, 90–103. Athens: University of Georgia Press, 2004.

Isay, David, and Lizzie Jacobs. *Ties That Bind: Stories of Love and Gratitude from the First Ten Years of StoryCorps*. New York: Penguin Books, 2014.

Isham, Ted, and Blue Clark. "Creek (Mvskoke)." *The Encyclopedia of Oklahoma History and Culture*. Accessed September 5, 2018, http://www.okhistory.org/publications/enc /entry.php?entry=CR006.

Jackson, Jason Baird, and Victoria Lindsay Levine. "Singing for Garfish: Music and Woodland Communities in Eastern Oklahoma." *Ethnomusicology: Journal of the Society for Ethnomusicology* 46, no. 2 (2002): 284–306.

Jacob, Michelle M. "When a Native 'Goes Researcher': Notes from the North American Indigenous Games." *American Behavioral Scientist* 50, no. 4 (2006): 450–61.

Jacob, Michelle M. *Yakama Rising: Indigenous Cultural Revitalization, Activism, and Healing*. Tucson: University of Arizona Press, 2013.

Jessop, Bob. "The Crisis of the National Spatio-temporal Fix and the Tendential Ecological Dominance of Globalizing Capitalism." *International Journal of Urban and Regional Research* 24, no. 2 (2000): 323–60.

Jessop, Bob. "Reflections on Globalisation and Its (Il)logic(s)." In *Globalisation and the Asia-Pacific*, edited by Peter Dicken, Philip F. Kelly, Lily Kong, Kris Olds, and Henry Wai-chung Yeung, 32–51. London: Routledge, 2005.

Johnson, Jay, Renee Louis, and Albertus Pramono. "Facing the Future: Encouraging Critical Cartographic Literacies in Indigenous Communities." *ACME: An International Journal for Critical Geographies* 4, no. 1 (2015): 80–98.

Johnson, Troy. "American Indians, Manifest Destiny, and Indian Activism: A Cosmology of Sense of Place." In *Place and Native American Indian History and Culture*, edited by Joy Porter, 71–91. Bern: Peter Lang, 2007.

Jolivétte, Andrew. "Radical Love as a Strategy for Social Transformation." In *Research Justice: Methodologies for Social Change*, edited by Andrew Jolivétte, 5–12. Bristol: Policy Press, 2015.

Kaur, Rupi. *The Sun and Her Flowers*. Kansas City, Mo.: Andrews McMeel, 2017.

Kesby, Mike. "Participatory Diagramming: Deploying Qualitative Methods Through an Action Research Epistemology." *Area* 32, no. 4 (2000): 423–35.

Kesby, Mike. "Participatory Diagramming as a Means to Improve Communication About Sex in Rural Zimbabwe: A Pilot Study." *Social Science & Medicine* 50 (2000): 1723–41.

Kimpson, Sally Agnes. "Stepping Off the Road: A Narrative (of) Inquiry." In *Research as Resistance: Critical, Indigenous, and Anti-oppressive Approaches*, edited by Leslie Brown and Susan Strega, 73–96. Toronto: Canadian Scholars' Press, 2005.

Kitchin, Rob, and Nicholas J. Tate. *Conducting Research in Human Geography: Theory, Methodology and Practice*. Harlow: Prentice Hall, 2000.

Kovach, Margaret. "Emerging from the Margins: Indigenous Methodologies." In *Research as Resistance: Critical, Indigenous, and Anti-oppressive Approaches*, edited by Leslie Brown and Susan Strega, 19–36. Toronto: Canadian Scholars' Press, 2005.

Kovach, Margaret. *Indigenous Methodologies: Characteristics, Conversations, and Contexts*. Toronto: University of Toronto Press, 2009.

Kuttner, Paul. "Futurism, Futurity, and the Importance of the Existential Imagination." Cultural Organizing (blog). May 17, 2017. http://culturalorganizing.org/futurism -futurity/.

Ladner, Kiera. "Up the Creek: Fishing for a New Constitutional Order." *Canadian Journal of Political Science / Revue Canadienne de Science Politique* 38, no. 4 (2005): 923–53.

Ladner, Kiera. "When Buffalo Speaks: Creating an AlterNative Understanding of Traditional Blackfoot Governance." PhD dissertation, Carleton University, 2001. ProQuest (NQ67033).

Ladner, Kiera, and Myra Tait. *Surviving Canada: Indigenous Peoples Celebrate 150 Years of Betrayal*. Winnipeg: ARP Books, 2017.

LaFrance, Joan. "Culturally Competent Evaluation in Indian Country." *New Directions for Evaluation* 102 (2004): 40–50.

Lane, Marcus. "Indigenous Land and Community Security: A (Radical) Planning Agenda." Working Paper No. 45, Land Tenure Center, University of Wisconsin-Madison, June 2001.

Lane, Marcus B., and Michael Hibbard. "Doing It for Themselves: Transformative Planning by Indigenous Peoples." *Journal of Planning Education and Research* 25, no. 2 (2005): 172–84.

LaPensée, Elizabeth. *Deer Woman: A Vignette*. Albuquerque: Native Realities, 2015.

LaPensée, Elizabeth. "Transformations and Remembrances in the Digital Game We Sing for Healing." *Transmotion* 3, no. 1 (2017): 89–108.

LaPensée, Elizabeth, and Weshoyot Alvitre, eds. *Deer Woman: An Anthology*. Albuquerque: Native Realities, 2018.

Lassek, P. J. "Council Stands Against Trust Status for Acreage." *Tulsa World*, July 31, 2009.

La Vere, David, *Contrary Neighbors: Southern Plains and Removed Indians in Indian Territory*. Civilization of the American Indian Series, vol. 237. Norman: University of Oklahoma Press, 2001.

Lawhorn, Chad. "After More Than Two Decades of Argument, SLT to Open: Reflections on the Fight That Enveloped the Community." *Lawrence Journal-World*, November 3, 2016. http://www2.ljworld.com/news/2016/nov/03/after-more-two -decades-argument-slt-open-reflectio/.

Lawhorn, Chad. "Leaders Laud Completion of SLT at Ribbon-Cutting; Road to Open to Traffic on Wednesday." *Lawrence Journal-World*, November 4, 2016. http://www2 .ljworld.com/news/2016/nov/04/leaders-laud-completion-slt-ribbon-cutting-road-op/.

Lawrence Journal-World. "Haskell Offering Tours of Large Medicine Wheel Created by Stan Herd." *Lawrence Journal-World*, September 9, 2011. http://www2.ljworld.com /news/2011/sep/09/haskell-offering-tours-large-medicine-wheel-create/.

Lebsock, Kent. "Listserv Communications to North American Indigenous Peoples Caucus." Response at meeting of the North American Indigenous Peoples Caucus (NAIPC) in preparation of the tenth session of the UN Permanent Forum on Indigenous Issues (UNPFII), March 19–20, 2011, in Blue Lake, Calif.

Lee, Annette S., Jim Rock, William Wilson, and Carl Gawboy. "The Red Day Star, the Women's Star and Venus: D(L/N)akota, Ojibwe and Other Indigenous Star Knowledge." *Science in Society* 4, no. 3 (2013): 153–64.

Leisy, Andrea K. "Inherent Tribal Sovereignty and the Clean Water Act: The Effect of Tribal Water Quality Standards on Non-Indian Lands Located Both Within and Outside Reservation Boundaries." *Golden Gate University Law Review* 29 (1999): 139.

Linn, Mary Sarah. "A Grammar of Euchee (Yuchi)." PhD dissertation, University of Kansas, 2001. ProQuest (AAT 3018513).

Littlefield, Jr., Daniel F., and Lonnie E. Underhill. "The 'Crazy Snake Uprising' of 1909: A Red, Black, or White Affair?" *Arizona and the West* 20, no. 4 (1978): 307–24.

Lorde, Audre. *Sister Outsider: Essays and Speeches*. Berkeley: Crossing Press, 2007.

Louis, Renee Pualani. "Can You Hear Us Now? Voices from the Margin: Using Indigenous Methodologies in Geographic Research." *Geographical Research* 45, no. 2 (2007): 130–39.

Luk, Sharon. "The Life of Paper: A Poetics." PhD dissertation, University of Southern California, 2012. http://digitallibrary.usc.edu/cdm/compoundobject/collection /p15799coll3/id/1520/rec/18.

Lyons, Scott Richard. "Rhetorical Sovereignty: What Do American Indians Want from Writing?" *College Composition and Communication* 51, no. 3 (February 2000): 447–68.

Lyons, Scott Richard. *X-Marks: Native Signatures of Assent*. Indigenous Americas. Minneapolis: University of Minnesota Press, 2010.

MacDonnell, Beth. "Families Concerned About Future of Indigenous Women Inquiry." *CTV News Winnipeg*, May 14, 2017. https://winnipeg.ctvnews.ca/families-concerned -about-future-of-indigenous-women-inquiry-1.3412444.

Marchione, William P. *A Brief History of Smyrna, Georgia*. Charleston: The History Press, 2013.

Martin, Joel W. "Rebalancing the World in the Contradictions of History: Creek/Muskogee." In *Native Religions and Cultures of North America: Anthropology of the Sacred*, edited by Lawrence Sullivan, 85–103. New York: Continuum, 2000.

Martineau, Jarrett. "Creative Combat: Indigenous Art, Resurgence, and Decolonization." PhD dissertation, University of Victoria, 2015.

Martone, F. J. "American Indian Tribal Self-Government in the Federal System: Inherent Right or Congressional License." *Notre Dame Law Review* 51, no. 4 (1976): 600–635.

Mason, W. Dale. *Indian Gaming: Tribal Sovereignty and American Politics.* Norman: University of Oklahoma Press, 2000.

Massey, Doreen. *Place, Space, Gender.* Minneapolis: University of Minnesota Press, 1994.

McCulley, Kristina L. "The American Indian Probate Reform Act of 2004: The Death of Fractionation or Individual Native American Property Interests and Tribal Customs?" *American Indian Law Review* 30, no. 2 (2005): 401–22.

McCulloch, Anne Merline. "The Politics of Indian Gaming: Tribe/State Relations and American Federalism." *Publius* 24, no. 3 (1994): 99–112.

McIntosh, Ian. "The International Forum on Indigenous Mapping, Vancouver." Cultural Survival (website). Accessed January 17, 2018, https://www.culturalsurvival.org/news/international-forum-indigenous-mapping-vancouver.

McKnight, Joyce, and Joanna McKnight Plummer. *Community Organizing: Theory and Practice.* 1st ed. Boston: Pearson, 2014.

Miholland, Sharon. "In the Eyes of the Beholder: Understanding and Resolving Incompatible Ideologies and Languages in US Environmental and Cultural Laws in Relationship to Navajo Sacred Lands." *American Indian Culture and Research Journal* 34, no. 2 (2010): 103–24.

Milbauer, John A. "The Geography of Food in Eastern Oklahoma: A Small Restaurant Study." In *The Taste of American Place: A Reader on Regional and Ethnic Foods*, edited by Barbara G. Shortridge and James R. Shortridge, 201–13. Lanham: Rowman & Littlefield, 1998.

Miller, Jay. *Ancestral Mounds: Vitality and Volatility of Native America.* Lincoln: University of Nebraska Press, 2015.

Miller, Mike. "Cherokee Nation Long-Range Communication Plan." Master's thesis, University of Nevada, Las Vegas, 2007. http://digitalscholarship.unlv.edu/theses dissertations/555.

Million, Dian. "Policing the Rez: Keeping No Peace in Indian Country." *Social Justice* 27, no. 3 (2000): 101–19.

Million, Dian. *Therapeutic Nations: Healing in an Age of Indigenous Human Rights.* Critical Issues in Indigenous Studies. Tucson: University of Arizona Press, 2013.

Miranda, Deborah A. *Bad Indians: A Tribal Memoir.* Berkeley: Heyday, 2013.

Moffat, David. "First Nations Community Planning Model." *Places* 16, no. 1 (2004): 20–23.

Moore, John H. "The Mvskoke National Question in Oklahoma." *Science & Society* 52, no. 2 (1988): 163–90.

Murphy, Jami. "CN to Get $2M from Arkansas Riverbed Lawsuit Dismissal." *Cherokee Phoenix*, January 12, 2015. http://www.cherokeephoenix.org/Article/index/8831.

Muscogee (Creek) Nation. "Where It All Began: Muscogee (Creek) Nation Reflects Arrival to Indian Territory, History of Council Oak Tree." News release. Octo-

ber 24, 2018. https://www.mcn-nsn.gov/reflects-arrival-to-indian-territory-history
-of-council-oak-tree/.

Navarro, Jenell. "Solarize-ing Native Hip-Hop: Native Feminist Land Ethics and Cultural Resistance." *Decolonization: Indigeneity, Education & Society* 3, no. 1 (2014):
101–18.

Nersessian, Anahid. *Utopia, Limited: Romanticism and Adjustment.* Cambridge, Mass.:
Harvard University Press, 2015.

Niezen, Ronald. "Recognizing Indigenism: Canadian Unity and the International
Movement of Indigenous Peoples." *Comparative Studies in Society and History* 42,
no. 1 (2000): 119–48.

Nixon, Lindsay. "Visual Cultures of Indigenous Futurisms." *Guts*, January 27, 2018.
http://gutsmagazine.ca/visual-cultures/.

Oakes, Leslie S., and Joni J. Young. "Reconciling Conflict: The Role of Accounting in
the American Indian Trust Fund Debacle." *Critical Perspectives on Accounting* 21,
no. 1 (2010): 63–75.

Oparah, Julia Chinyere, Fatimah Salahuddin, Ronnesha Cato, Linda Jones, Talita Oseg-
uera, and Shanelle Matthews. "By Us, Not for Us: Black Women Researching Preg-
nancy and Childbirth." In *Research Justice: Methodologies for Social Change*, edited by
Andrew Jolivétte, 117–37. Chicago: Policy Press, 2015.

Ortega, F. M. "ESRI Mapping for the Traditional Management Plan for the Sargento
Estuary, Desemboque, Sonora, Mexico." Talk presented at the International Forum
on Indigenous Mapping, Vancouver, British Columbia, March 11, 2004.

Owen, Patricia. "Who Is an Indian?: Duro v. Reina's Examination of Tribal Sovereignty
and Criminal Jurisdiction over Nonmember Indians." *BYU Law Review* 1988, no. 1
(1988): 161–82.

Pain, Rachel, and Peter Francis. "Reflections on Participatory Research." *Area* 35, no. 1
(2003): 46–54.

Payne, Claudine. "Mississippian Period." The Encyclopedia of Arkansas History and
Culture (website). Updated May 24, 2018. Accessed June 16, 2018, http://www
.encyclopediaofarkansas.net/encyclopedia/entry-detail.aspx?entryID=544.

Perdue, Theda. *Nations Remembered: An Oral History of the Five Civilized Tribes, 1865–
1907.* Norman: University of Oklahoma Press, 1980.

Pevar, Stephen L. *The Rights of Indians and Tribes.* 4th ed. Oxford: Oxford University
Press, 2012.

Pihama, Leonie, Fiona Cram, and Sheila Walker. "Creating Methodological Space: A
Literature Review of Kaupapa Maori Research." *Canadian Journal of Native Education* 26, no. 1 (2002): 30–43.

Poarch Band of Creek Indians. "History of the Poarch Band of Creek Indians." Poarch
Band of Creek Indians (website). Accessed June 12, 2018, https://web.archive.org/web
/20190121221506/http://www.poarchcreekindians.org/westminster/tribal_history.html.

Potts, Karen, and Leslie Brown. "Becoming an Anti-oppressive Researcher." In *Research
as Resistance: Critical, Indigenous, and Anti-oppressive Approaches*, edited by Leslie Allison Brown and Susan Strega, 1–17. Toronto: Canadian Scholars' Press, 2005.

Pratt, Stacy. "Indigenous Artists Join in Los Angeles' #JailBedDrop." *First American Art Magazine*, January 12, 2018.

Raheja, Michelle. "Future Tense: Indigenous Film, Pedagogy, and Promise." In *Sources and Methods in Indigenous Studies*, edited by Chris Andersen and Jean M. O'Brien, 239–46. New York: Routledge, 2016.

Raheja, Michelle H. "Visual Sovereignty." In *Native Studies Keywords*, edited by Stephanie Nohelani Teves, Andrea Smith, and Michelle H. Raheja, 25–34. Tucson: University of Arizona Press, 2015.

Ramirez, Renya K. *Native Hubs: Culture, Community, and Belonging in Silicon Valley and Beyond*. Durham, N.C.: Duke University Press, 2007.

Ranat, R. "Tribal-State Compacts: Legitimate or Illegal Taxation of Indian Gaming in California?" *Whittier Law Review* 26, no. 3 (2005): 954–80.

Ray, Ashley. "Preservation over Profits: The Conflicting Interest of Hickory Ground and Exploring Options for Preserving the Sacred Parcel." *American Indian Law Journal* 2, no. 2 (2017): 611.

Recollet, Karyn. "Gesturing Indigenous Futurities Through the Remix." *Dance Research Journal* 48, no. 1 (May 10, 2016): 91–105.

Recollet, Karyn. "Glyphing Decolonial Love Through Urban Flash Mobbing and *Walking with Our Sisters*." *Curriculum Inquiry* 45, no. 1 (2015): 129–45.

Robertson, Carmen. "Land and Beaded Identity: Shaping Art Histories of Indigenous Women of the Flatland." *RACAR: Revue d'art canadienne / Canadian Art Review* 42, no. 2 (2017): 13–29.

Robertson, Kimberly. "Activating Recuperation: How Community Mobilization Is Decolonizing Violence Against Indigenous Women and Girls." Roundtable presented at the Native American & Indigenous Studies Association, Honolulu, Hawai'i, May 20, 2016.

Robertson, Kimberly. "Las Aunties." In *Deer Woman: An Anthology*, edited by Elizabeth LaPensée and Weshoyot Alvitre. Albuquerque: Native Realities, 2018.

Rutland, Amanda. "Vnokeckv: The Language of Love." Mvskoke Media. February 4, 2016. https://web.archive.org/web/20181230203716/https://mvskokemedia.com/vnokeckv-the-language-of-love/.

Sack, Robert David. *Conceptions of Space in Social Thought: A Geographic Perspective*. London: Macmillan, 1980.

Said, Edward W. *Orientalism*. New York: Pantheon Books, 1978.

Salomón J., Amrah. "Telling to Reclaim, Not to Sell: Social Movement and Resistance Narratives and the Question of Justice." In *Research Justice: Methodologies for Social Change*, edited by Andrew Jolivétte, 185–98. Chicago: Policy Press, 2015.

Salsman, Jason. "MCN, PBCI File Joint Request for Stay in Hickory Ground Case." Mvskoke Media. December 8, 2017. https://web.archive.org/web/20181228173155/https://mvskokemedia.com/mcn-pbci-file-joint-request-for-stay-in-hickory-ground-case/.

Schlossberg, Marc, and Elliot Shuford. "Delineating 'Public' and 'Participation' in PPGIS." *URISA Journal* 16, no. 2 (2005): 15–26.

Seminole Nation. *Pumvyetv, Pum Oponvkv: Seminole Nation ANA Language Assessment Project Final Report*. Seminole, Okla.: Seminole Nation, 2009.

Shahjahan, Riyad A. "Being 'Lazy' and Slowing Down: Toward Decolonizing Time, Our Body, and Pedagogy." *Educational Philosophy and Theory* 47, no. 5 (2015): 488–501.

Sheppard, Eric. "Geographical Political Economy." *Journal of Economic Geography* 11, no. 2 (2011): 319–31.

Shoemaker, J. A. "Like Snow in the Spring Time: Allotment, Fractionation, and the Indian Land Tenure Problem." *Wisconsin Law Review* 2003, no. 4 (2003): 729–88.

Sieber, Renee. "Public Participation Geographic Information Systems: A Literature Review and Framework." *Annals of the Association of American Geographers* 96, no. 3 (2006): 491–507.

Simpson, Audra. *Mohawk Interruptus: Political Life Across the Borders of Settler States*. Native Studies Anthropology. Durham, N.C.: Duke University Press, 2014.

Simpson, Audra. "Paths Toward a Mohawk Nation: Narratives of Citizenship and Nationhood in Kahnawake." In *Political Theory and the Rights of Indigenous Peoples*, edited by Duncan Ivison, Paul Patton, and Will Sanders, 113–36. London: Cambridge University Press, 2000.

Simpson, Leanne Betasamosake. *As We Have Always Done: Indigenous Freedom Through Radical Resistance*. Indigenous Americas. Minneapolis: University of Minnesota Press, 2017.

Simpson, Leanne Betasamosake. *Dancing on Our Turtle's Back: Stories of Nishnaabeg Recreation, Resurgence and a New Emergence*. Winnipeg: Arbeiter Ring Publishing, 2011.

Simpson, Leanne Betasamosake. "Indigenous Resurgence and Co-resistance." *Critical Ethnic Studies* 2, no. 2 (2016): 19–34.

Simpson, Leanne Betasamosake. *Islands of Decolonial Love: Stories & Songs*. Winnipeg: ARP Books, 2013.

Simpson, Leanne Betasamosake. "Land as Pedagogy: Nishnaabeg Intelligence and Rebellious Transformation." *Decolonization: Indigeneity, Education & Society* 3, no. 3 (2014).

Slowey, Gabrielle. *Navigating Neoliberalism: Self-Determination and the Mikisew Cree First Nation*. Vancouver: UBC Press, 2008.

Smith, Andrea. "American Studies Without America: Native Feminisms and the Nation-State." *American Quarterly* 60, no. 2 (2008): 309–15.

Smith, Andrea. *Conquest: Sexual Violence and American Indian Genocide*. Cambridge, Mass.: South End Press, 2005.

Smith, Andrea. "Decolonizing Anti-rape Law and Strategizing Accountability in Native American Communities." *Social Justice* 37, no. 4 (2011): 36–43.

Smith, Andrea. "Forum on Social Movements and Activism." Plenary presentation at the Critical Ethnic Studies and the Future of Genocide: Settler Colonialism / Heteropatriarchy / White Supremacy Conference, University of California, Riverside, March 12, 2011.

Smith, Andrea. "Heteropatriarchy and the Three Pillars of White Supremacy: Rethinking Women of Color Organizing." In *Women in Culture: An Intersectional Anthology for Gender and Women's Studies*, edited by Bonnie Kime Scott, Susan E. Cayleff, Anne Donadey, and Irene Lara, 2nd ed., 404–12. West Sussex: Blackwell, 2017.

Smith, Andrea. "Unsettling the Privilege of Self-Reflexivity." In *Geographies of Privilege*, edited by France Winddance Twine and Bradley Gardener, 263–79. New York: Routledge, 2013.

Smith, Dean Howard. *Modern Tribal Development: Paths to Self-Sufficiency and Cultural Integrity in Indian Country.* Contemporary Native American Communities, vol. 4. Walnut Creek, Calif.: AltaMira Press, 2000.

Smith, Linda Tuhiwai. "Decolonizing Knowledge: Toward a Critical Indigenous Research Justice Praxis." In *Research Justice: Methodologies for Social Change*, edited by Andrew Jolivétte, 205–10. Chicago: Policy Press, 2015.

Smith, Linda Tuhiwai. *Decolonizing Methodologies: Research and Indigenous Peoples.* 2nd ed. London: Zed Books, 2012.

Smith, Neil. "Contours of a Spatialized Politics: Homeless Vehicles and the Production of Geographical Scale." *Social Text* 33 (1992): 55–81.

Spillers, Hortense J. *Black, White, and in Color: Essays on American Literature and Culture.* Chicago: University of Chicago Press, 2003.

Starr, Arigon. *Super Indian, Vol. One.* Edited by Janet Miner. West Hollywood, Calif.: Wacky Productions Unlimited, 2012.

Starr, Arigon. *Super Indian, Vol. Two.* Edited by Janet Miner. West Hollywood, Calif.: Wacky Productions Unlimited, 2015.

Starr, Arigon. "Ue-Pucase: Water Master." In *Moonshot: The Indigenous Comics Collection, Volume 1*, edited by Hope Nicholson, 66–72. Toronto: Alternate History Comics, 2015.

Stewart, Mark. *The Indian Removal Act: Forced Relocation.* Snapshots in History. Minneapolis: Compass Point Books, 2007.

Strickland, Rennard. "Things Not Spoken: The Burial of Native American History, Law and Culture." *St. Thomas Law Review* 13, no. 1 (Fall 2000): 11–18.

Strickland, Rennard, and William M. Strickland. "A Tale of Two Marshalls: Reflections on Indian Law and Policy, the Cherokee Cases, and the Cruel Irony of Supreme Court Victories." *Oklahoma Law Review* 47 (1994): 111–26.

Strickland, William M. "The Rhetoric of Removal and the Trail of Tears: Cherokee Speaking Against Jackson's Indian Removal Policy, 1828–1832." *Southern Journal of Communication* 47, no. 3 (1982): 292–309.

Sturm, Circe. "Blood Politics, Racial Classification, and Cherokee National Identity: The Trials and Tribulations of the Cherokee Freedmen." *American Indian Quarterly* 22, no. 1/2 (1998): 230–58.

Summers, Gene F. "Rural Community Development." *Annual Review of Sociology* 12, no. 1 (1986): 347–71. https://doi.org/10.1146/annurev.so.12.080186.002023.

Supernaw, Susan. *Muscogee Daughter: My Sojourn to the Miss America Pageant.* Lincoln: University of Nebraska Press, 2010.

Swyngedouw, Erik. *Excluding the Other: The Production of Scale and Scaled Politics.* London: Arnold, 1997.

Swyngedouw, Erik. "The Marxian Alternative: Historical-Geographical Materialism and the Political Economy." In *A Companion to Economic Geography*, edited by Trevor J. Barnes and Eric Sheppard, 41–59. Oxford: Blackwell, 2000.

Thornton, Russell. "Cherokee Population Losses During the Trail of Tears: A New Perspective and a New Estimate." *Ethnohistory* 31, no. 4 (1984): 289–300. https://doi .org/10.2307/482714.

Torpy, Sally J. "Native American Women and Coerced Sterilization: On the Trail of Tears in the 1970s." *American Indian Culture & Research Journal* 24, no. 2 (2000): 1–22.

Trost, Wiebke, Thomas Ethofer, Marcel Zentner, and Patrik Vuilleumier. "Mapping Aesthetic Musical Emotions in the Brain." *Cerebral Cortex* 22, no. 12 (2011): 2769–83.

Tsosie, Rebecca. "Challenges to Sacred Site Protection." *Denver University Law Review* 83, no. 4 (2005): 963–80.

Tuck, Eve. "Suspending Damage: A Letter to Communities." *Harvard Educational Review* 79, no. 3 (2009): 409–27.

Tuck, Eve, and Rubén A. Gaztambide-Fernández. "Curriculum, Replacement, and Settler Futurity." *JCT (Online)* 29, no. 1 (2013): 72–89.

Tuck, Eve, and K. Wayne Yang. "Decolonization Is Not a Metaphor." *Decolonization: Indigeneity, Education & Society* 1, no. 1 (2012): 1–40.

Tuck, Eve, and K. Wayne Yang, eds. *Youth Resistance Research and Theories of Change*. New York: Routledge, 2013.

Tulsa County. "What is Vision 2025?" Vision 2025 (website). February 22, 2019. https:// vision2025.info/.

Uskali, Turo, and Astrid Gynnild. "The First Wave of Drone Journalism: From Activist Tool to Global Game Changer." In *Responsible Drone Journalism*, edited by Turo Uskali and Astrid Gynnild, 23–43. New York: Routledge, 2018.

Valencia-Weber, G. "Shrinking Indian Country: A State Offensive to Divest Tribal Sovereignty." *Connecticut Law Review* 27, no. 4 (1995): 1281–1322.

Van Dijk, Teun A. "Critical Discourse Analysis." In *The Handbook of Discourse Analysis*, edited by Deborah Schiffrin, Deborah Tannen, and Heidi E. Hamilton, 466–85. Malden, Mass.: Blackwell Publishers, 2001.

Veracini, Lorenzo. *Settler Colonialism: A Theoretical Overview*. Houndmills, Basingstoke: Palgrave Macmillan, 2010.

Veroff, Jody, and Anna DiStefano. "Introduction." *American Behavioral Scientist* 45, no. 8 (April 1, 2002): 1196. https://doi.org/10.1177/0002764202045008002.

Vizenor, Gerald Robert, ed. *Survivance: Narratives of Native Presence*. Lincoln: University of Nebraska Press, 2008.

Wallace, Anthony F. C., and Eric Foner. *The Long, Bitter Trail: Andrew Jackson and the Indians*. Hill & Wang Critical Issues. New York: Hill & Wang, 1993.

Walter, Maggie, and Chris Andersen. *Indigenous Statistics: A Quantitative Research Methodology*. Walnut Creek, Calif.: Left Coast Press, 2013.

Warne, Donald, and Denise Lajimodiere. "American Indian Health Disparities: Psychosocial Influences." *Social and Personality Psychology Compass* 9, no. 10 (2015): 567–79.

Wilson, Shawn. *Research Is Ceremony: Indigenous Research Methods*. Halifax: Fernwood Publishing, 2008.

Wilson, Shawn. "What Is an Indigenous Research Methodology?" *Canadian Journal of Native Education* 25, no. 2 (2001): 175–79.

Wodak, Ruth. *Language, Power, and Ideology: Studies in Political Discourse*. Amsterdam: John Benjamins, 1989.

Wolfe, Patrick. "Settler Colonialism and the Elimination of the Native." *Journal of Genocide Research* 8, no. 4 (2006): 387–409. https://doi.org/10.1080/14623520601056240.

Womack, Craig S. *Drowning in Fire*. Sun Tracks, vol. 48. Tucson: University of Arizona Press, 2001.

Womack, Craig S. *Red on Red: Native American Literary Separatism*. Minneapolis: University of Minnesota Press, 1999.

Wood, Mary Christina. "Indian Land and the Promise of Native Sovereignty: The Trust Doctrine Revisited." *Utah Law Review* 1994, no. 4 (1994): 1471–1613.

Woods, Clyde Adrian. *Development Arrested: The Blues and Plantation Power in the Mississippi Delta*. Haymarket Series. London: Verso, 1998.

Wright, J. Bart. "Tribes v. States: Zoning Indian Reservations." *Natural Resources Journal* 32, no. 1 (1992): 195–206.

Yoo, John. "Andrew Jackson and Presidential Power." *Charleston Law Review* 2 (January 2007): 521–83.

Zaferatos, Nicholas Christos. "Developing an Effective Approach to Strategic Planning for Native American Indian Reservations." *Space and Polity* 8, no. 1 (2004): 87–104.

INDEX

Page numbers in *italics* represent illustrations.

ABOUT THE AUTHOR

Laura Harjo is a Mvskoke scholar, geographer, planner, and Indigenous methodologist. She is an assistant professor of community and regional planning at the University of New Mexico.